An English Wife in Berlin; a Private Memoir
of Events, Politics, and Daily Life in
Germany Throughout the war and the Social
Revolution of 1918

AN ENGLISH WIFE IN BERLIN

Evelyn Blücher

AN ENGLISH WIFE
IN BERLIN

A PRIVATE MEMOIR OF EVENTS, POLITICS, AND
DAILY LIFE IN GERMANY THROUGHOUT THE
WAR AND THE SOCIAL REVOLUTION OF 1918

BY

EVELYN, PRINCESS BLÜCHER

NEW YORK
E. P. DUTTON & COMPANY
681 FIFTH AVENUE

Printed in the United States of America

INTRODUCTION

EVELYN, Princess Blücher, the writer of these memoirs, is a daughter of the late Mr. Frederick A. Stapleton-Bretherton, of Rainhill Hall, Lancashire. Her mother was a daughter of the twelfth Lord Petre. She was married in 1907 to Prince (then Count) Blücher, great-great-grandson of the famous Marshal "Vorwarts," who turned the tide of Waterloo in favour of the sorely harassed British army. The old Prince, his father, whom he succeeded in the title and estates in July 1916 (*vide* page 144), had quarrelled for many years with the Prussian and Austrian Governments, and lived in retirement on the island of Herm, which he leased from Great Britain, and where he was famous for rearing kangaroos. Shortly after the outbreak of war the French Government raised a complaint against his domicile so near their coast, and after considerable pressure the British felt bound to summon him to leave the island and come to London. Further unpleasantness here during the alien scare led to his deportation and return to the ancestral estate of Krieblowitz, in Silesia, which was presented to the old Marshal by the nation in recognition of his services, just as Strathfieldsaye and Apsley House were to the Duke of Wellington. Here he died from the effects of a fall from his horse on July 12, 1916, after many years' estrangement from his two elder sons.

Count and Countess Blücher, apart from the latter's
large influential family circle, were well known in English
society, and lived in this country continuously up to the
outbreak of war, when the Count's nationality forced them
to go to Germany and join the not inconsiderable colony
of "internationals" who made their home at the Esplanade Hotel in Berlin.   Here, in spite of the supervision
which existed, they lived in a state of freedom which
compared favourably with the treatment of aliens here.
They met everybody of note; and were in a position to
see and hear everything that went on in the military and
political world.   From the very day of their dramatic departure with the German Embassy from London, down
to the end of the 1918 revolution, Princess Blücher made
a point of jotting down in the form of a private journal,
intended for her mother, all the varied events and experiences which passed before her eyes during these
critical years, and very few things of any importance
seem to have escaped her acute and penetrating observation.   As a detailed record of the war from the German
side, seen through English or neutral eyes, these jottings
constitute the most interesting document which we are
likely ever to possess on the subject; the personal
memoirs by generals or statesmen which have appeared
so far being more concerned with the defence of their
own conduct than with the accurate representation of
events.   Facts new to English readers, or at any rate
not generally known, and unexpected side-lights on
the characters of many public men (to say nothing of
the much-abused German nation) come out in these
shrewd and absolutely honest records, written without ·
any ulterior view of publication, and yet with a literary
grace and fluency which many historians might envy.
In parts, both the nature of the subject and the style

remind one irresistibly of Pepys, as he fluttered about collecting news and opinions from every one of note, and jotted them down with his own crisp comments. We see here, for the first time nakedly revealed, the longing for peace and readiness to make great sacrifices which permeated all classes in Germany from the highest civilian circles of the Government downwards, months before the world outside was aware of or believed in it. We see the bitterness of the struggle between the military and civil elements over the submarine question; the ambiguous position of the Kaiser between the two parties, and his futile efforts to exert a restraining influence over the Frankenstein monster he had created; the true feeling of the people towards the war and the Government; the growing causes of the social revolution; and last but not least, the extent of the organisation which existed for relieving the hardships of the prisoners of war, and the time and trouble given to this end by many even of the most influential and powerful men in Germany.

The care of British prisoners and wounded was the special task to which Princess Blücher, in conjunction with two other ladies in a similar position, Princess Pless and Princess Münster, devoted herself from the very first days of her exile. It would require, as she says, a separate volume to record all the efforts and correspondence of these three English women, hampered as they were by restrictions and prejudice, in their endeavour to trace the whereabouts of wounded and missing soldiers, to send comforts and necessaries to those who lacked them, to uproot the barbarities existing in certain camps, and in many other ways to bring hope and solace to those other English women at home whose sorrows lay heavy on their hearts. A little only, but enough, has been published of these memoirs to show the method on which they worked and the wide range of their activities. Tales of individual brutality which came to their notice and were reported to Headquarters for inquiry, as well as letters from escaped or exchanged prisoners, have mostly been omitted in view of the abundant evidence on the subject which already exists in this country.

Of the Kaiser's personal responsibility for the war and its conduct the view taken in the memoir is probably a reasonable one, especially when it is remembered that the Kautsky revelations were unknown at the time and were only dimly surmised. His direct influence on events appears to have been much smaller than his bravado.

A very interesting detail to which attention may be called is the full and curious information about Sir Roger Casement's mission to Germany and its tragic ending Casement, in his better days, when he was a popular member of the British consular service, and before his mind had become unhinged by the Putumayo atrocities, was an old friend of the Blüchers, and the account of his terrified interview with the Princess in Berlin, just before his fatal journey to Ireland, is of great if mournful interest. It need hardly be said that the Blüchers, whatever pity they may have felt for the wretched man, lent no assistance to his mission, but did their utmost to discountenance and thwart it.

The moderate tone of these memoirs, neither violently pro-English nor markedly anti-German, should do something towards a restoration of good feeling between the two nations after peace has cleared the air. The writer's difficult position, between natural love for her own people and loyalty to her husband's country, in which she was forced to live, had at least this advantage, that it enabled her to see both sides of the question, and to view with more impartiality incidents which to partisan eyes appeared all black or all white. On both fronts she had

friends and relations. Of her own family, four brothers
were fighting on our side. One of them fell at Ypres in
November 1914, another is lamed for life. Of her four
brothers-in-law, Admiral Sir Edward Charlton was Commander-in-Chief at the Cape and Admiral of the mine-
sweepers; Colonel Rowland Feilding had command of a
battalion of Connaught Rangers, and was through much
of the hardest fighting; Commander Throckmorton was
a mine-sweeping patrolling assistant (K.H.M.) at Rosyth
and Scapa Flow; and Commander Kenneth Dewer was
on active service in H.M.S. *Prince of Wales,* as well as at
the Admiralty. Her unmarried sister, Monica, nursed for
three years at a London hospital, and with another sister,
Mrs. Feilding, was mainly responsible for the vast amount
of correspondence on this side relating to missing and
wounded prisoners. Unlike most of the German nobility,
her husband, Prince Blucher, owing to his long residence
in England, held no military commission, but devoted
himself with great zeal to Red Cross work in his honorary
capacity of a Knight of Malta. His Foreign Office connections in both countries enabled him on more than one
occasion to be of service in reducing or mitigating the
friction arising out of incidents connected with the war.

H. C. M.

AN ENGLISH WIFE IN
BERLIN

August 1914.—Shall I ever forget those last three days in England? We were in the country staying with my family, and had to hurry back to London at the first rumours of war. My husband went straight to the Embassies, and negotiations were at that moment going on between the Ambassadors and Sir Edward Grey. All had great hopes of an arrangement.

Then Sir Edward Grey appealed to the House, and for twenty-four hours nothing definite came out, whilst the crowds outside and the "man in the street" were growing more and more impatient. The Press, issuing "Specials" every hour, was helping to work up popular feeling; and then suddenly the dreadful news came.

We had been told that immediately war was declared the Ambassador and party would leave at once, and that we must be in readiness The Banks were closed for four days in succession to prevent a panic, which made everything more difficult for us. Late on Tuesday afternoon, the 4th of August, we got notice to be ready to leave quite early on Thursday morning I was so stunned by the suddenness of it all, that I cannot recall clearly what took place after that, but I remember how my family came up at once to be with me to the last, Rowland and Edith Feilding arranging everything for us, packing up our house, dispersing the household, in fact doing everything to save us trouble, they themselves being just as worried by what it meant in the future to them; and then

1

my brother Vincent, my sister Freda and her husband and my sister-in-law Bertha, all came to bid us farewell. Luckily when I had parted from my parents three days before, none of us realized the seriousness of the situation.

All the time friends kept coming in to say good-bye, and tried to cheer us, one way or another. One friend, wishing to warn us, frightened me terribly; he said: "Mind that your passports are absolutely in order, as some people returning to England were held up, and the men of the party were taken out and shot before the women's eyes." The thought of the risks we might be going to face made me ill with terror, as although we were going with the Embassy, we were not members of it, and they could not promise to take entire responsibility; and I knew that our passports were not in order.

I could not bear the thought that my husband should be in such danger for a single moment. I went straight to the Foreign Office and saw Sir William Tyrrell, whom I knew very well, and told him my fears. He was not very reassuring. He laughed it off, however, and said · "The Dutch frontier is said to have been invaded by the Germans, and one cannot answer for the safety of any German travelling through Holland in consequence." He told me they were at that moment cabling through to The Hague to ascertain whether it would be safe or not.

That evening a telephone message came to say: "Be prepared to leave at 7.30 to-morrow morning," and so it had to be done. Our passports were not put in order properly until we were absolutely on the voyage *en route* for the Hook.

The last evening passed quickly. My brothers and sisters came in, and my brother Vincent had been to the Foreign Office to inquire about the safety of our voyage. He brought back the most consoling news I had had that day, having heard it said that the English vessel conveying the German Ambassador would be the safest spot in Europe throughout the following day. This ship, however, was not to prove so entirely safe as one was led to suppose.

We rose at four o'clock in the morning, and at six o'clock we left the house, Baron Kühlmann, who lived close by, sending for our luggage and servants to go with his. I could not help being amused when I remembered the disappointment of little Pat, the page-boy, at my husband not departing in full-dress uniform, the only proper way of making an exit according to him. "I know he has a German uniform, for I unpacked it myself on July 1st," he insisted to the maid. I am afraid, however, that his wishes were impracticable anyhow, as my husband, not having served in the German army, possessed no military uniform.

My sister-in-law accompanied us to the station. Whilst driving to Liverpool Street, even at that early hour, we saw placards and papers everywhere announcing German disasters and 3500 Germans killed. The scene at the station I shall never forget, with 250 Germans and their luggage congregated on the platform, and the special train in readiness. The Austrian Ambassador and many of the Embassy members came to see us off, and we all had our various friends with us.

The Ambassador and Ambassadress (Prince and Princess Lichnowsky) arrived at the last minute and got straight into the train, the Ambassadress quite heart-broken, and making no attempt to hide her grief. The train steamed out of the station amidst a hushed silence, people on the platform weeping, and the men with hats off standing solemnly silent. It was as if a dead monarch was being borne away.

The journey from London to Harwich was uneventful, but our arrival there was even more impressive than the scene at the London station. Soldiers and sailors were drawn up at attention, and the Admiral came to meet the train and escorted us to the boat through the lines of men all saluting as we passed. And we met with such civility from the Admiral and every one that it was difficult to realize we were going out of this country to become its bitterest enemy.

I could not face the departure of the ship, and went down to hide myself in the cabin. I could not look upon the shores of my beautiful England fading from sight, not knowing when I should see it again, nor what would happen, or who would be missing from there, before I returned. The Ambassador and Ambassadress stood on deck, receiving salutes, until there was no more to be seen, and then all went down to luncheon.

It was a beautiful day, with the sea like glass, and under other circumstances we should have enjoyed the voyage. We had one adventure which might have led to disastrous results. About four or five miles away from the mouth of the Thames we sighted a flotilla of British torpedo boats. From the distance it was one of the most impressive and threatening sights I have ever seen. "How vicious it looks!" said the Ambassador, and that just describes it.

And now for our adventure. Three shots were fired at us, one coming within thirty yards of our bow. Most of us did not realize what was going on until afterwards, or we should have been terrified. But we heard a whizzing in the air, and ran to the side to see what had happened, and then the boat was stopped. The Captain explained afterwards that the whole thing was due to carelessness. The Foreign Office had wired that morning to the English Fleet to say that a vessel would be conveying the Ambassador to the Hook, and that it would fly the German flag on the main-mast and the Union Jack at the stern. The Union Jack, it was said, was too small, and had not been seen by the flotilla, and so they stopped us. Speaking to us about it afterwards, the Captain said: "I soon hauled down the German flag. Another little mistake like that could send all on board to Kingdom Come." He then proceeded to tell us of the sinking of a German mine-layer on that very spot the night before, hence the caution of the British flotilla.

We made great friends with the Captain, and when he

found that I was English, and a sister-in-law to one of the Admirals whom he knew well, he became most friendly and sat in our cabin for a long time, giving us his views on the war, etc. He also promised to take some letters back to England for me, and to send a wireless message to my family to say we had arrived safely as far as the Hook.

We reached the Hook about 5 o'clock, and found a special train waiting for us, which conveyed us eventually straight to Berlin without a single change, which was one of the greatest distinctions and luxuries that we could possibly have had. For I heard from our friends afterwards of the discomforts of their journeys. The very highest in the land were subject to delays and irregularities when not attached to the Embassy. Some of them, it seemed, were turned out every hour to make place for troops, and had to show their passports, sometimes ten or twenty times a day, and were crowded into third-class carriages without any regard for their first-class tickets and their passports. All had to give way to the troops which were hastening to the front

An officer of our party was to have been married that day to an English girl, who is going to wait for him, he says.

We had many interesting conversations during the journey. The sadness and bitterness of all these Germans leaving England struck me intensely. Here we are, they say, being dragged away from the country that has been our home for years, to fight against our best friends. They all blamed the officials in Berlin, who had, they said, grossly mismanaged the negotiations. It had been an obsession in some of the German officials' minds for years past, that Russia meant to attack them. "Well then," said someone of the party, "why not wait until they do it? Why commit suicide to avoid being killed?"

"What chance have we," said someone else, "attacked practically on every side?"

"Is no one friendly to Germany?" asked another.

"Siam is friendly, I am told," was the bitter reply.

As we crossed the frontier, the people began to recognize our train, and we got quite a reception from the village girls along the route. They came and stood outside our windows and sang national war songs and patriotic hymns, and at one or two stations they presented a bouquet to the Ambassadress.

Passing us in an almost continuous stream on the other way were the trains full of troops, shouting, laughing, singing, and waving their hands, intense joy and excitement depicted on their faces. The Germans are indeed a warlike race. I have, at last, seen them stirred out of their morose dulness, and what I used to think their everlasting heaviness. The thing that impressed us most was the absolute order and expeditiousness of everything and everybody *en route,* especially as soon as we had crossed the border.

Our train journey was slow, but absolutely comfortable, and we reached Berlin safely on the evening of the 8th. It was impossible not to be impressed with the immense enthusiasm prevailing all along the line. No less than 66 troop trains had passed the day before, yet there was no disorder, we were not kept waiting longer than half an hour at one station, and refreshments were handed out to soldiers and civilians everywhere gratis.

BERLIN, *August* 9, 1914.—Dazed and stunned as I am by the awful events of the last week, I will try and keep some diary of our experiences, jotting them down more or less consecutively as they happen   The thunderstorm which has broken so suddenly over England and Europe has altered the whole tenour of our lives, and whirled us away into an exile which I hope will be but a short one. Everything has come so unexpectedly that I wake up in the morning saying to myself that it was only a bad dream; but the hard reality soon forces itself on my outer view again, and I have to grapple with the situation as well as I can.

.   .   .   .   .   .

Sitting in my pretty shaded room in the Esplanade Hotel, right in the middle of Berlin, I can see the Esplanade terrace looking gay and festive with summer guests in the hotel garden, flanked by beautiful old trees in the background, and although I cannot hear the words I know what every one down below is speaking of. Across my brain floats a confused vision of swiftly moving scenes, like an imperfect cinema film; white cliffs and blue waters, anxious-eyed travellers, yellow corn-fields and groups of sunburnt peasants, women pausing in their work and staring with hand-shaded eyes, as again and again we were forced to stop to let the never-ending procession of troop-filled trains hurry by on their way to the West; shouts of enthusiasm, fluttering of handker-chiefs, bursts of song, flushed eager faces of soldiers, field-grey uniforms, white-robed girls and women with the Red Cross on their arms, offering food and drink to the thirsty men. And all this, which might seem to be some great national festival, means but the entry of death and foul disaster.

There is a great coming and going in the hotel. Already I have met several acquaintances all breathless and feverish to hear the latest bit of intelligence from the War Office.

Amongst the faces I saw were those of Prince and Princess Victor Wied, old acquaintances. He is lame, and is therefore only doing night-watch at the Castle; his wife is a pretty woman of 23. They are full of anxiety as to his brother's fate, the King of Albania, who has been deserted by all foreign Powers, and must be abso-lutely stranded. People here don't seem to have much pity for him; they look upon him as an adventurer forced into the rôle of a would-be king by his wife's ambition

On my arrival last night I was so worn-out that I went straight to bed; but my husband, who went at once to see his cousins, Count and Countess F. Larisch, and de-liver some documents, had long talks with them as well as with Prince Münster. He came back with papers and

a whole bunch of news.   The Germans have already
forced events, and advanced so quickly that one can
hardly grasp the facts as one hears them.   I almost felt
a physical blow when I heard of the fall of Liége.   The
German point of view is that if they don't get their
troops into Belgium, the English and French armies will
be there before them, so that it is a toss-up who is first.
People are contemplating the first encounters on the
French borders with horror.   The modern untried weapons
of war, they say, exceed the conjectures of the most san-
guinary imagination.   Two hundred aeroplanes have been
dispatched from here yesterday.   I hear a whole Russian
brigade has been already captured by the Germans, and
seventy deserters came over to the German lines, complaining bitterly of the hardships and ill-treatment they
had to endure during the mobilization.   I wonder if it
is true that Paris is in a wild state of panic and demoralization?   I try to grasp what all this means, my chief feeling being one of intense sorrow and pain that England
has entered the lists and against Germany.   I dare not
think of all the complications which may arise in this case
for me, my nearest and dearest there fighting face to
face with friends and relations here.

.   .   .   .   .   .

Horrible particulars keep coming in of the taking of
Liége.   The Germans had reverses at first, it seems.   The
losses on both sides are enormous.   Four thousand Belgians have been taken prisoner, and a quarter of the Belgian army, they say, has been annihilated.   The Germans
have lost 1500 dead or wounded, and already officers
known to us have fallen   General Bülow was shot by
mistake by his own sentry.   Young Count Arnim-Boit-
zenburg has been killed in a patrol.

.   .   .   .   .   .

Countess Larisch spent the whole morning with us.
Our conversation was very sad, but it was good to have
an old friend to talk to.   The excitement and enthusiasm
all over the city are enormous.   The Kaiser is the most

adored man of the moment, and during a great speech he delivered the other day on the balcony of the castle, in spite of the people standing densely thronged together, the silence was so great that one might have heard a pin fall. Certainly the whole nation are backing him this time, and if he has been criticized for his actions in the past, this war-cry is making him the most popular man in Germany. His six sons have already left for the front Prince Eitel-Fritz is to command the first Life-Guards, whose privilege it is always to be first at the front and to lead the whole Army. It means certain death, they say, and yet he went off smiling, and gave a dinner the night before, when he and his guests were in the most boisterous spirits.

Countess Larisch's two younger brothers are leaving for the French front to-night. Countess Henckel's husband has already gone, and a lady has just been in to see me who came straight from parting from her only son, a boy of 21. She described how heartrending were his excitement and delight at going off with the rest, and how she could hardly hide her grief when beaming with pride he showed her the little metal disc with his name on it, which every soldier wears for identification in case of being killed.[1] Seeing all this anxiety around me, I felt my own fears to be selfish, and ask myself, how could I bear the separation from husband and sons in the same proud spirit of heroism? In fact this seemingly unfeeling heroism often puzzles me. There is hardly any thought of life and love and relations in the young men going away, but a sort of reckless joy in the certainty of the near death awaiting them.

At dinner I sat between Prince Wied and Major Langhorne, the Military Attaché to the American Embassy. The latter advised me to wear an American badge in the street, and not talk English there. Notices forbidding the language are being posted up. From him I learnt

[1] This boy was killed within a month

of the extraordinary spy-fever prevailing here as everywhere. People are being arrested all over the country, and the most harmless individuals are accused of being spies if they look the least different from their neighbours. Continual mistakes are being made, which often lead to fatal results for the victims.

The English Embassy were treated very badly, and I was told that an Englishman had been lynched by the crowd for having called out "Down with Germany." The hotel proprietor, however, assured me that Berlin is safer than it ever was before, as all the Russian spies had been seized and taken away to the country to be shot. What a carnage, if it were true! He says numbers of them disguised as German officers go about carrying bombs. Personally I disbelieve such stories.

I have heard that poor young Count Arnim was one of the first to fall at an outpost skirmish at Liége; he was only 21, an eldest son, who would have succeeded to enormous wealth and estates.

.   .   .   .   .

One of the chief things that strike me so far is the bitter resentment which the whole nation seems to feel at England's entering the war. It is a feeling that increases hourly. I cannot understand this absolute revulsion, when I think of the almost exaggerated expressions of admiration and affection which were so widely spread formerly. It seems to have changed in a night, and although a few individuals try to be moderate, they cannot; and to be "English" is synonymous with "blackguard" in the eyes of most people. There still seems to be a flickering spark of hope in some of the papers here that England may be only pretending to come in. They emphasize the wish of the English nation to remain neutral, and maintain that it was a few ministers who have done all the mischief, and that the English Socialists could still prevent further intervention, if they really wanted to, even at the stage things have already reached.

Exactly what was the real cause of the war no one seems to know, although it is discussed night and day. One thing grows clearer to me every day: neither the people here nor there wished for war, but here they are now being carried off their legs with patriotism, at seeing so many enemies on every side. It is said in England that Germany provoked the war, and here they emphatically deny it   To me it seems that Europe was thirsting for war, and that the armies and navies were no longer to be restrained. Certainly here, the militarists grew weary of the long lazy peace as they called it, and if the Kaiser had not proclaimed war, he would have been in a precarious position. There are two men at the head of affairs: one is called stupid and the other dangerous. The dangerous one has won the day, and brought the war to a head. Lord Northcliffe seems to be responsible on the other side.

.   .   .   .   .   .

I have just been reading the story of the German mine-layer. It is not one to be proud of, it seems to me. The mines were laid absolutely in the roadstead outside the Thames. This is not considered fair play, and will cause much bitterness on the other side. It has already sunk the English destroyer *Amphion,* and God only knows how many mines she was able to lay before she was sunk herself.

.   .   .   .   .   .

Sunday, August 9, 1914.—To-day we went to Mass at 11 o'clock in the Hedwig Kirche, which is a fashionable meeting-place for smart Berlin, where it is accustomed to congregate on the steps every Sunday to gossip over the news. I could not help comparing it with my last remembrances in February just six months ago. Then every one had a laugh or joke on his lips. We were all dressed in our best, discussing the last Court Ball, or the latest scandal, criticizing and abusing our neighbours, and bent on enjoying life to the full. Now the women were sad and quiet, with none of the vivacious sparkle of other days; they only welcomed us with a pressure of the hand, tears often pouring down their faces. There were the Hohenlohes, the Reischachs, the Ratibors, the Sierstorpffs, and poor little Princess Ratibor, who, the last time we met her, was the leading spirit in a gay romping set at a large shooting party, had all one side of her face plastered up, having been shot by mistake by their own Polish peasants when motoring to the station. Their car had been suspected of being one of the many hostile automobiles which are said to be driving all over Germany filled with gold and spies. Another of the dangerous myths current amongst the people.

.   .   .   .   .   .

This afternoon Count Oppersdorff came in to see Gebhard and talk things over. He was pretty optimistic, and thinks that things cannot last ten weeks. Afterwards Gebhard went to see Baron Jagow, whom he found terribly harassed and anxious, and was able to enlighten him, and through him many others, as to the difficult position England had been in Prince Münster then came, and together they went over the situation thoroughly, and were both agreed that it is almost impossible to make the officials and military authorities here regard the situation from an impartial point of view, or realize that England could not "with honour" leave France in the lurch. People here maintain the contrary. "England could have remained neutral. Her guarantees to France were of a strictly defensive character, and the French action was clearly offensive, as they commenced bombing at the frontiers even while negotiations were in progress, whilst Russia hurried on mobilization before they had been finished" In any case they maintained that England could have assumed an armed neutrality, ready to intervene should there be any danger of France being crushed.

I have to keep my opinions to myself, but I long to say to them that perhaps England did not come in until Belgium's neutrality had been violated.

If one hears what the Austrians and Bohemians have to say, one might think that the German Government was throwing dust in the world's eyes. They maintain that Austria was inclined to word the ultimatum to Serbia leniently, not for the sake of Serbia, but because they were wide awake enough to see that the grievance must be localized, if Europe was to be saved an appalling war; but the German Government (if not the Emperor himself) worded it in such a way that there was no loop-hole for escape. On the inevitable becoming known, people here got into a panic, and they felt they must make terms with England at any price; so the "feelers," the bribes, were put into play, and Baron Kuhlmann's proposal to England took place, that if England kept out of the war Germany would promise to leave the French coast alone. Could England choose any other course than the one she pursued? Good, they say; but could we do otherwise than stand by Austria, when Russia insisted on mobilization?

.   .   .   .   .   .

Several English people came in to tea, and one lady gave an account of how she had just seen a spy caught in the street. He had been dressed as a woman, and had been hooted by the mob to the police-station, had made one last desperate struggle to escape, and was shot. I cannot help wondering myself if all these "spies" that are being persecuted in the streets are not often the most innocent people in the world. All the inherent qualities of cruelty and ferocity seem to be aroused in mankind simply by the word war.

.   .   .   .   .   .

Gebhard has had another long and interesting talk with Prince Münster and Prince Pless. The latter is going to headquarters with the Kaiser, near the seat of war, but no one at present seems to know where that is. Prince P. has promised to try and influence the Kaiser and make him comprehend the English side of the question in keeping their word to the French. The Kaiser cannot recognize the necessity of it; his shock and surprise were genuine when he realized what England was doing; he had not thought it possible. To his friends standing near him he said: "To think that Nicholas and Georgie should have played me false! If my grandmother had been alive, she would never have allowed it."

Popular hatred here is centred on the shade of King Edward VII.; he is supposed to have been the moving spirit in forming the encirclement of Germany.

The more I hear things discussed from the German standpoint, the more astonished I am at the fighting character of the Germans They take to war as a duck takes to water, to judge at least by the eager faces of the people in the streets and their talk. One would almost think that this terrible outbreak was a long-hoped-for chance of showing their inherent qualities of bravery and manliness, coupled with a military genius which is unequalled among other nations. No one seems to be enthusiastic about the war in England, to judge by the papers. The English are a peaceful, unsoldierly merchant folk, and money is the standpoint of the average man; and the possibility of the Bank Act being suspended prevents any false glamour of war dazzling his sense of law and order. He does not care about the German, but neither does he hate him; and as his country is not in immediate danger, he will not catch fire so easily. Germany, on the other hand, is persuaded that if she refuses to fight, hordes of French and Russians will be overrunning the land in a few weeks, if not days.

The marvellous military organization is, I must confess, overpowering; everything goes off without a hitch. Within a few days 70 Army Corps were in the field, every train full of troops starting and arriving to the minute. This means, with trebled corps of war-time, some 5,600,000 men already at the frontier. One thing that strikes me in the new German masculine being is the improvement in his looks since the field-grey uniform

has been introduced. The German as a rule has no style;
he usually looks as if he had a bad tailor; but put him
in uniform and he looks smart at once.

We lunched with Count Ballestrem at the Kaiserhof.
He is one of the Knights of Malta, and is arranging for
Gebhard to get some work in connection with the Red
Cross League. He has promised to cash our cheques,
which is a great relief, as no man of business here will
accept an English one.

Blue skies and a burning sun, and involuntarily one
thinks of the happy harvest-time of other years, and now
death is reaping its ghastly red harvest, and already the
newspapers seem printed in blood. The details of the
Russian reverse are too horrible to dwell on. A whole
battalion of 900 men killed in the space of a few moments.
It seems that really the best thing to be hoped for is one
huge decisive battle between the French and the Germans,
which might put an end for ever to the bloodshed.

As for England, I hardly dare imagine what may
happen It is a constant dread to me to think of all
those I love being in danger and anxiety. One can do
nothing as a woman but remain passive and look on, although on a perfect rack of torment. The German navy
won't be able to do much harm, as it is shut up in
the Baltic, so that we shall have no huge naval disasters. I suppose, however, one great sea battle will
have to take place, although the German navy own
they won't have a chance against the English on the
open sea.

BERLIN, *August* 10, 1914.—I feel I must take up some
work, for this passive waiting is too much for my nerves.
So I have been to see Princess Pless about Red Cross
work. I met Countess Sierstorpff, Princess Jane Lynar,
and Count Hochberg there. We all went to a Klinik, to
hear Dr. Hiss lecture on first aid. Princess Pless is

already fully trained, and is bent on going to the front, as soon as the wounded begin to arrive. Princess Lynar and I have decided to get attached to some Lazarett in Berlin, where the lighter cases will be brought later on.

On parting with the Pless party, Count Hochberg said: "Good-bye; the war will be over in two months, and you and I will be meeting again in England." I smiled at this cheerful prophecy; it is the thing I am praying for night and day.

BERLIN, *August* 11, 1914.—To-day I went to the police station to get my passport, as until now it has been impossible for me to be out in the streets alone without an American badge. It is now forbidden to speak English through the telephone or in any public place.

Gebhard met Baron Kühlmann downstairs (the late Secretary of the Germany Embassy in England). He travelled over with us. He was very much upset, for he had just changed a lot of money for travelling to head-quarters at the front, when a telegram arrived ordering him to go to Stockholm this evening, as the German minister has utterly broken down, owing to the great strain on his health of the last few weeks.

.   .   .   .   .   .

News has just arrived of a German victory in Alsace; the losses are said to be heavy.

The fall of Liége is an accomplished fact, and people have ceased being astonished at it. They are hurying on with the victorious troops which are already in Namur. This seems to have been an act of unprecedented strategy and valour, only field-guns being used. In three days the town capitulated. People say that the Belgians fight badly, and that the army is utterly demoralized Already ghastly rumours are being spread of cruelty to Belgian civilians, and their ill-treatment of the wounded German soldiers. The Austrian and German Armies have united on the Eastern frontier, and the Russian Army is being driven into Bessarabia.

This afternoon we went to a big American meeting at the Rathaus, where the American Ambassador and the Mayor of Berlin addressed them, and tried to impress them with the intense friendship existing between the two countries   The Ambassador omitted mentioning the subject of a ship which was to be chartered to take Americans home, and for news of which most of them had attended the meeting, being chiefly business people over on the Continent for a holiday.   There are, I hear, 75,000 Americans in Germany, and 25,000 alone in Berlin.   Amongst those at the meeting was Baroness Sternburg, the pretty little American widow of the late German Ambassador in Washington.   She is a friend of mine of former happier days.

.   .   .   .   .   .

Countess Sierstorpff brought me an introduction for attending one of the first-aid courses which are to commence to-morrow.   I shall be glad to take up some systematic work which will distract my attention from the gruesome details of the newspapers.   One piece of news, however, did me a good deal of good to-day; it was from some German refugees who have just arrived in Berlin, and who assured me that all England is against the war, and a regular propaganda is being spread against it.

.   .   .   .   .   .

BERLIN, *August* 12, 1914.—This morning I went off to the Bethanien Krankenhaus, where my nursing course is being held.   It took a long time getting there, but it is a magnificent place.   It is so big, it is almost like a town in itself, and perfectly modern and up-to-date in every respect.   We were about thirty ladies attending the course, and Count Hochberg the only man.   I did not hear the names of all the ladies.   I sat next to Princess Ernst Günther, the Emperor's sister-in-law.   The doctor is one of the cleverest and best-known men in Berlin.   He lectured splendidly, demonstrating all his remarks on a small boy.   The nurses told us they are expecting wounded every moment. The German casualties are already 3000 dead and 4000 wounded on the Belgian field alone.

.   .   .   .   .   .

In the evening there is usually a large gathering of friends in the lounge of the Esplanade. We are an international collection of birds of passage, united by a common feeling of suspense and anxiety. There were Prince and Princess Wied, he expecting orders to go off any moment, and Prince and Princess Hohenlohe-Langenburg. Prince H. is leaving for the front to-morrow night. He is a cousin to King George, and looks and is English in every way. Prince Stolberg was also of our party, besides Countess Seherr-Thoss and her parents.

We talked of the size of the different armies, and they said that the German army has refused 1,300,000 volunteers, as not being required at present. The French army up to now is 3,000,000, and the Russians are putting 6,000,000 into the field. The famous escape of the cruiser *Goeben* was freely discussed; her adventures have been really marvellous, and Germany is greatly elated, as anything like getting the best of England in a naval tug-of-war sends their spirits up with a run.

.   .   .   .   .   .

Whilst dining with Count Ballestrem at the "Astoria," to our great amazement Baron Roeder and his wife suddenly walked in. We had heard that they were in Switzerland, unable to get here. They are very old friends of ours. He has been the Master of Ceremonies in Berlin for many years, and is a confidant of the Kaiser. She is English. She has two daughters married, one to a German, and one to an Englishman, and they are fighting on opposite sides.

We were delighted to meet again, so often in the past we had agreed with one another on the difficulties of marrying a man of another nation; how one's patriotism gets trodden upon, and how the thorns prick us in both countries at once. Their journey seems to have been appalling, and lasted eight days instead of twenty-four hours, as they were continually being turned out of the trains they were in, and finally arrived in an empty troop-train which was in the most filthy condition possible.

BERLIN, *August* 14, 1914.—The Austrian Diplomatic Corps from St. Petersburg have arrived at the Esplanade, *en route* for Vienna. They are all very depressed at leaving so many friends behind them. We are expecting the Austrian Embassy also from London in a day or two. They are all friends of mine. I wonder if they will bring me any letters from home.

Three young counts have suddenly turned up here too; they were stopped at Southampton, on their way from Washington, but were allowed to proceed on their way after having satisfied Scotland Yard that they were not spies. Of course I accosted them with eager questions about England, and what they told me has reassured me in some measure. What relieved me most was to hear that the English Expeditionary Force has not yet left, and cannot arrive before to-day or to-morrow. Please God, they will arrive too late for the great battle going on. We have heard nothing certain for the last forty-eight hours, but as no news means bad news nowadays, we believe some great fight is taking place.

BERLIN, *August* 16, 1914.—We have left the Esplanade and have settled down in a smaller hotel near the Klinik, where I am going to nurse.

The Emperor left this morning for headquarters at the seat of war. None knows where it is, not even the Empress. He was attended by a few officials, Baron Jagow amongst them. He was very solemn and pensive and would express no opinion to any one, and refused to see any one a few days before leaving. It is being said that he has gone to Mainz, and that a big battle is being fought at Namur.

News comes trickling in from England. No naval engagement so far, thank God.

August 17, 1914.—Attended my lectures with many others. Am learning a great deal. We practise bandaging and putting splints on one another. Wounded have already arrived, but it must be fearful at the front. Sixty more nurses have been telegraphed for.

BERLIN, *August* 19, 1914.—Poor Baroness L—— got news that her husband was mortally wounded, and went off at once to see him. He had died meanwhile, and the poor woman got shot herself passing through a village on the frontier. They leave two small orphan children.

Every one is admiring the Empress as woman and mother. She has six sons and one son-in-law going into danger, and in the midst of preparations for departure she was the calmest and most cheerful of every one, and helped to pack things with her own hands. Every newspaper sets her up as an ideal for German women, willing to offer everything and without complaint for the weal of the Fatherland. But I think a poor woman who offers her only son is even more to be pitied and praised.

The first French prisoners have arrived, and are being sent to work at the harvest.

BERLIN, *August* 21, 1914.—Great news, the fall of Brussels! Fierce joy reigns everywhere. The bells ring out in the moonlight air, there are shouts and cries of pride and gladness in the streets, and people embrace one another, frantic with delight. The Pope is dead, the poor old man. It is certain that the shock of the fearful outbreak of war hastened his end.

BERLIN, *August* 23, 1914.—I am beginning nursing in earnest, and have taken up work at the Franciscan sanatorium, where the sisters are all nuns. To-day I wore uniform for the first time, and I shall assist at some difficult operations soon.

BERLIN, *August* 24, 1914.—This new work prevents my mind from dwelling too constantly on the sadness of the times. I see so much suffering that I feel my own home-sickness is almost a sin in comparison to the pain there is in the world; and as I hope and believe things cannot go on like this much longer, I must try and fight against it.   There are already many wounded in Berlin; in one hospital Germans and Belgians can be seen peaceably smoking and chatting together at the windows, whilst the people bring them improvised offerings of flowers, cigarettes, etc.   Amongst the Russian wounded, so many have been observed to have slashes over their heads that they were asked the reason, and said their officers had hit them with their swords to make them advance.

BERLIN, *August* 26, 1914.—On returning from my hospital work to-day, I nearly fainted with joy at seeing a letter from my mother lying on my dressing-table.   It is the first news I have received from home, and on the fact becoming known, every one came to congratulate me, as if I had performed some special feat.   No one else had heard from England yet, but I knew my mother would manage to get news through in some way, for in the most difficult situations she has never failed her children yet.   I remember how my brother, who died in Africa, used to tell us that when he was once up country for a year on the Gold Coast, whenever a native runner was seen in the distance his brother officers used to turn laughingly to him, saying: "There's your runner bringing your weekly letter from your mother, lucky fellow."

.   .   .   .   .   .

What a terrible thing the new Krupp 42-inch mortar is. It was kept very secret until now.   It is so powerful, they say, that it can destroy any modern fort with a few shells, and smashed three forts round Liége in half an hour.

There are gloomy reports from the East Front.   The Russians are well into East Prussia, and we hear dreadful stories of their cruelty to the population there.   General v. Pritzelwitz has been recalled for his blunders, and a

General Hindenburg, quite an old man, has taken his place. They say he knows every inch of the ground in East Prussia, and the German troops are again getting the upper hand. A great battle is raging in Poland. The Austrians have the chief work there, and all my best friends and many of my husband's relations are fighting there. Last night, Princess Rosa Hohenlohe brought her son to introduce to me He is such a handsome youth, only seventeen years old, and 6 feet 2 inches tall. He looked so radiant in his new uniform, at the thought of soon going out to the front, that it made me quite sad to see him. I asked his mother why she did not try to keep one so young back for some time. She answered that the temptation was indeed great, but that no mother would be forgiven if she showed weakness at a time like this; so that although her heart was breaking, she must keep up a smiling face.

BERLIN, *August* 31, 1914.—This morning there were details of the naval engagement near Heligoland. Both sides fought gallantly, and the papers here add especial thanks to the English for the way they saved so many of the German crews from drowning. There seems to be much more chivalry shown on sea than on land, where the troops are mowing one another down like dried grass.

BERLIN, *September* 1, 1914.—To my horror, another English defeat has been reported at St. Quentin. I hear they have been driven back at Maubeuge and Mons, and I can hardly think of it without tears. I have made out a list of my relations and friends, and sent them to the doctors in the frontier towns, asking them to let me know if their names are on the lists. I mean to find out some way of getting news, in spite of all regulations to the contrary. The German papers all say the English fought splendidly, but are wanting in training and discipline, and . . . I hold my tongue at this criticism and only say that England has often begun a campaign with reverses, but in the end she is indomitable.

BERLIN, *September 2*, 1914.—To-day I went out to the Grünewald to see the arrival of trains full of wounded, in the hope that I might see some English and help them, but it turned out to be a false report, and they were only transport trains carrying troops from the Western Front to Russia.   There was a tremendous reception, but the troops looked too weary to respond to it, very different from those of a short time ago.   The railway carriages were all decorated with flowers, and to my intense indignation stuffed-out figures of men dressed in the uniforms of English Grenadier Guardsmen were fastened on to some of the trucks.   I am haunted with the thought of who may have worn just one of these uniforms.

From Baroness Roeder's windows we watched some of the victorious regiments with their captured guns march past.   There was music, with captured Russian, French, and English flags, and poor weary Cossack horses dragging the guns.   I heard details of the defeat of the French and English at St. Quentin.   Baron Reischach, who had been there, said that the English cavalry had been caught in a French stampede and had been forced to retire.   The infantry had been overwhelmed in spite of their efforts at resistance.   I heard that at the roll-call after the battle, only three men of one battalion answered the call.

The Zeppelins are said to be creating a panic all over Europe, but even here many people say they are not fair warfare.   A woman may not carry arms, and is shot if she tries to defend herself; yet a bomb from a Zeppelin can kill her and her children any day.

BERLIN, *September 4*, 1914.—Again news of German successes everywhere.   Everything seems to fall at their approach.   They are nearing Paris rapidly.   Nothing is talked of night and day but the expected entry there.   The Russian hordes are being driven like cattle into the lakes and morasses of East Prussia.   Hindenburg is marvellous, they say.

In the midst of all the tragedy of to-day, very funny things too sometimes happen. I called on a Mrs. D , an English lady who is detained here, and who is very nervous and depressed in consequence. When I arrived at the hotel she was in bed, and whispered to me, "Shut and lock the door, and speak very low; I have got something to show you," whereupon she pulled from under her pillow a copy of the *Daily Mail,* already three weeks old. I could not help bursting out laughing, to think we had come to rejoicing over an old copy of the *Daily Mail.*

BERLIN, *September* 6, 1914.—

> Lieb Vaterland magst ruhig sein,
> Fest steht und treu die Wacht am Rhein.

I think I shall hear these words ringing in my ears to my dying day. The whole life in the Germany of to-day seems to move to the rhythm of this tune. Every day troops pass by my window on their way to the station, and as they march along to this refrain, people rush to the windows and doors of the houses and take up the song so that it rings through the streets, almost like a solemn vow sung by these men on their way to death There is no doubt the whole nation is worked up to a frenzy of patriotism which is sometimes very moving, and at other times very aggravating, as they are incapable of comprehending the mentality of any one to whom "Das Vaterland" is not the one country worth living and dying for in the world. They are fighting against a world of devils, they say, and have risen like one man to do it.

We lunched with Herr and Frau Solf. He is the Colonial Minister, and is intensely depressed at the loss of the German colonies, Samoa, etc. I laughingly told him to cheer up, as according to the newspapers here, he would soon have the English ones too, as Germany intended forcing England on to her knees, if only to save the colonies. He assured me he would be satisfied to get back his own alone.

BERLIN, *September* 6, 1914.—Countess Lori Oppers-dorff, one of my best friends, has just arrived from Russia, after a ten days' journey alone with her maid. She had heard endless abuse of Germany, and of the atrocities of the troops. In fact, every country is circulating the most appalling stories of the brutality of the enemy; and here one hears horrible details of the cruelty of the French and Belgian women towards the German troops. Thank God I have not yet heard a single word breathed of this kind about the English soldiers, although the general view is that they are as innocent of military science and strategical tactics as the babe unborn. The only thing they do say about the English is that they are using dum-dum bullets, which inflict most horrible wounds.

I asked a German officer whether the prevailing reports of the cruelty of the German soldiers to the Belgian population were true, and he told me they were much exaggerated, but that in Aix there were thirty officers lying at that moment in hospital, with their eyes put out by women and children in Belgium. The troops who hear these things go mad with rage, and revenge their comrades by burning and killing as they pass through the land. This sounds to me quite incredible.

    .   .   .   .   .   .

BERLIN, *September* 7, 1914.—The last few days I have met so many people and heard so many different reports, that I hardly know what to believe or think. On Sunday last we met the Henckels, Larisches, Hohenlohes, etc , and in the afternoon Countess Doda Oppersdorff (the beautiful Polish wife of Count Oppersdorff) came in and brought Baron Goldsmith Rothschild from the German Embassy in England, with Count Talleyrand, whose relations are all in Paris. Count Talleyrand says that Zeppelins are not really so alarming as people think, and that a bomb from a Zeppelin could not hit a Dreadnought. Zepplins are only of use in bombarding towns, and no single one could get across to London, and that it is quite impossible for the German fleet to do any damage to the English Channel fleet. But on the other hand I have authentic evidence that a Krupp gun is being constructed which can shoot from Calais to Dover. That is why the troops are being hurried up there. One officer even asserted that in a fortnight German troops will be in England. I don't believe that this is as easy as they think.

BERLIN, *September 7*, 1914.—On making further inquiries, I have heard that the Germans cannot bombard London, as it is an unfortified town. Many letters arrive now unopened from home, some very old.

This morning quite early I received a telegram from one of my sisters, asking for news of a young cousin of ours, who is missing from the English Expeditionary Force. I had been inquiring every day to see if any relations' names were on the lists of the wounded, but now I wired to every hospital on the Rhine, entered his name at every centre, and went to the War Office personally. Every one is kind and sympathetic in helping us to trace him, but we have heard nothing as yet. Princess Pless is helping me. She has relations fighting on the other side. I have just had a note from her saying she has been to see some of the English prisoners, and she will take me with her next time if possible.

BERLIN, *September 8*, 1914.—I was sitting working together with Princess Hohenlohe to-day. She was just talking about her son, and saying how relieved she was that he was not going out until October, as the fighting on the Russian Fronts is too horrible for words, when the door opened and he came in, looking so handsome and young in his uniform. Every one asked him how he had managed to get leave so suddenly from Potsdam, and he answered laughing that he had managed to get a half-holiday, and had come to spend it with her. I at once guessed the reason, and retired to leave them alone. My husband and I again met him in the evening and drawing us aside he said, "I am really going straight to the front to-morrow, as the losses amongst the officers in my regiment are fearful. We young ones have to replace them. I have not told my mother; I want to spare her the parting."

BERLIN, *September* 9, 1914.—Maubeuge has been taken, one of the strongest French fortresses. It was a tremendous fight, they say, and for the first time I hear unqualified praise of the English. They are said to have fought magnificently, and only surrendered when everything was in flames. No news yet of my cousin. He is never out of my thoughts, and we spend our days inquiring for him

.   .   .   .   .   .

To-day we heard a piece of news which interested us. Old Prince Blucher, my father-in-law, has been turned out of his island of Herm. It has been seized and confiscated by the English Government, and articles of all sorts are being printed about the Prince in the English papers.

.   .   .   .   .   .

The mothers and wives here seem only to exist in trying to catch a glimpse of their men-relatives who pass to and fro between France and Russia, as troops are secretly being withdrawn from the West Front, things are so bad in Russia. The sidelights I get of the war are often terrible. Numbers of regiments are being sacrificed wholesale; and a General whom every one is naming will, they say, be brought before a court-martial for sending a whole battalion to certain death, only to clear the way for the other troops. Another German battalion has been decimated by its own side, being mistaken for the enemy. Human life seems to be absolutely valueless nowadays, and as all speed-limit has been taken off the military motor cars, they fly along so fast that people are being killed all over the country.

From the many jokes being made at the expense of the Highland kilt, I judge that some Scotch regiments must have been captured, and this will be a help to me in tracing out the whereabouts of my acquaintances   I have heard nothing of my cousin up to now, as it is forbidden to give the names of the wounded at the military hospitals. I can only glean news by making friends with the doctors

BERLIN, *September* 11, 1914.—The chief themes of conversation are the "German atrocities" and the English dum-dum bullets, both of which each country denies. The Germans declare they were never brutal unless in self-defence, but the stories one hears of the brutality of certain German regiments to the Belgian civilians I fear I know are partly true, and then on the other hand Prince A Salm, writing to a relation, says he saw with his own eyes two Belgian girls of 16 and 12 years old mutilating a wounded German in an absolutely indescribable manner.

.   .   .   .   .   .

The first wet day since our arrival; every one depressed in consequence. People are hinting at a serious defeat somewhere, as the flags have been ordered to be taken away from the streets.

At the Adlon Hotel this morning I talked to Count Talleyrand and Baron G. Rothschild. They have relations in all countries, so that their sympathies are very broad. They declare that the English have defeated the Germans on the left flank outside Paris.

BERLIN, *September* 12, 1914.—No news means bad news, and nothing is heard of the operations round Paris. Another panic is being caused by the doubts as to America's neutrality. She is financing France, it seems, and this is a great shock to Germany, although President Wilson has published a letter expressing his readiness to intervene in both countries for peace. The new Pope too has expressed his views in the same way. I hope that this will all tend towards opening up negotiations, but people here talk so much of the Freemasons' war, and of the society being so strong everywhere, that the Pope will be ignored.

BERLIN, *September* 18, 1914 —Strange that we hear so little of the fighting round Paris. We have all been expecting to hear of their triumphant entry every day. The fighting, they say, is very hard, and there are tremendous losses on either side, but I am beginning to think the tide has turned against the Germans, hence this sudden silence.

Most of our friends are very international, so that our conversation often grows doubtful, as our sympathies are very divided. Indeed we feel torn in two sometimes with anxiety and the conflict of our feelings.

Princess Münster, who is English by birth (sister to Lord Kinnoull), writes in the same strain, as her son is fighting here, and her cousin on the other side. She is helping me to make inquiries for my relation. My application to the Empress through Countess Brockdorff to see the English prisoners has been refused, as the regulations have become stricter. We all know why, although it is supposed to be a great secret. Princess Pless is said to have visited some prisoners without permission. As she came away she was heard to say, "Keep up your spirits," which has been interpreted into a hope for the English gaining the war, and has caused much bitterness amongst the Anglophobians here. It seems to me to have been a very harmless remark.

.   .   .   .   .   .

We have at last discovered means of buying the *Times,* and have bought up as many old numbers as we can get. And at last we can see what the English are really doing or thinking. It is as if a thick curtain dividing us from the outside world had suddenly been drawn aside, giving us a glimpse of it.

What curious reports are being circulated in England. Great French and Russian victories are being mentioned; the French are said to be already in possession of the frontier towns; the Russians are said to be quite near Berlin; whilst Berlin is in flames, and in a state of starvation, panic, and revolution.

How shall we ever know the truth in any country? Some people tell me that the German official telegrams are incorrect, but I believe their sins are more of omission than of commission. How I dread the sight of the casualty list in the *Times*. I shudder each time I read it, but it is a tremendous help to me, as in this way I am able to learn the names of all the regiments that have been sent out, and the whereabouts of their engagements, so that I can give every information when inquiring at the Central Office for missing or wounded. Good news from home so far.

BERLIN, *September 20*, 1914.—We lunched with a party of big finance magnates to-day. The conversation turned on the Emperor, and his visions of gaining the supremacy of the world by destroying the British fleet by means of submarines and Zeppelins. I don't believe for a moment that he will ever gain this end, but Germany has more and better submarines than England, and the magnificent English Dreadnoughts could do little against them. Lord Charles Beresford (or Sir Percy Scott) was quite right when some years ago he begged England not to continue spending money on big battleships, but to build more submarines, as therein lay the future safety or danger of the sea.

One of the ladies of the party was the wife of one of the commanders of the camps. She commented on the extraordinary difference in the characters of the military prisoners. According to her, the French and Russians are dirty and never wash themselves, and loaf about grumbling all day. The English are clean and smart, and always cheerful, and, as she added, they can be kept amused and occupied for hours by giving them a ball to knock about. A typical German description of the game of football!

I should like some day to write the praises of the English prisoners, just from what I have heard from Germans who have visited the camps or been in command of them.

"You cannot make an English officer grumble or complain," said one German officer to me. "If he does not like a thing, well, he bears it in a dignified way or else he turns it off into a joke. Nothing makes some of our German officers more mad with rage than when they go and shout out their commands in the highly dictatorial manner some of them have, and find that the command is only received with a chorus of laughter from the English officers."

.   .   .   .   .   .

To-day I took some copies of our precious *Times* to show to Princess Pless. Alone together, we threw off our mask of passive waiting, and confessed to one another our burning interest in England and the English. In society we are always being watched in a so-called friendly suspicious manner, but here we are free to express our innermost thoughts.

BERLIN, *September* 23, 1914.—Nothing definite is known as to the fate of the Germans round Paris; it is a harder fight than people anticipated. I hear that it is the English who have turned the luck of the German army, and are keeping them at bay. Every one has been expecting the entry of the Kaiser at the head of his troops into Paris for ten days past, but it looks as if he would not get there now.

.   .   .   .   .

We lunched with the new Austrian Ambassador and his wife, Prince and Princess G. Hohenlohe. The great topic of interest was the destruction of the three English cruisers by the German submarine. What a terrible thought it is, the picture of those splendid ships with their gallant crews slowly sinking without having been able to defend themselves in any way. Only 700 of 2000 men were saved. Here there is great rejoicing, but I feel sick at heart.

BERLIN, *September* 28, 1914.—Countess C——, an American, has to-day arrived in Berlin from England, where she has been with her children since the outbreak of the war. From her we hear graphic descriptions of England, and gather how little they know of the real state of affairs here. She said that the English papers reported Berlin to be in a state of famine and revolution, so she had brought provisions with her for three weeks and two huge sacks of flour. Of course she was very much laughed at for this. Of the German victories nothing was known, General Hindenburg's campaign in East Prussia never having been mentioned in the English press. She accounted for it by the fact that all the telegrams come from Petrograd, and the Russians let nothing through. On my asking her, "Does no one in England know the truth?" she replied that a few days before she had met a Colonel M. E.—— of the Foreign Office, who had just been ordered abroad to fill up the gap left by some officer, and on her congratulating him and asking him if he were not delighted to be going out, he answered, "No, I belong to the Foreign Office, and therefore unfortunately know the truth and that there is no reason for congratulation." She also said that she had spoken to a well-known newspaper correspondent, who was writing optimistic articles for the *Times*. She remarked that the day's news looked very well for England, and he had replied, "I think it all looks damned bad, but we must never let that be known."

Last week some 800 English women from here went home, and one of them wrote to me shortly afterwards and said (in cipher) that Kitchener had muzzled the Press, and that it is fearfully strictly censored.

BERLIN, *September* 30, 1914.—The Hohenlohes have left Berlin. We shall miss them dreadfully, having been always together for the last six weeks. Their boy has not been in an engagement so far.

I am doing regular hospital work and spend all my mornings in the operating-room, where civilians as well as soldiers are treated. It is heart-rending to see so many fine strong men maimed and crippled. Helping thus, the terrors of war seem to be brought nearer to our eyes. They are such nice men too, with nice manners, and are so grateful for a word of kindness, and so thoughtful for each other's sufferings. As I help to bandage them, I always feel inclined to ask if they have been killing or torturing women and cripples, for they look as if they could hurt nobody. I refrain, however. I am perhaps happiest in my doubts.

BERLIN, *October* 1, 1914.—People are beginning to realize gradually that some great mistakes have been made in the West, and that if France had recognized the position, things might have become very serious for this country. As it was, Germany had time to hurry up re-inforcements from Belgium. General von Kluck went forward too fast, with no reserves behind him, and part of his army was cut off.

BERLIN, *October* 2, 1914.—I had tea at the American Embassy, and met the whole American clan there. They refuse now to send letters or telegrams to England, on the ground that it is not neutral. People who have been staying in England gave me various news, as, for instance, the great precautions that are being taken against Zeppelins. One lady said she was staying at The Hague when Captain Nicholson from one of the three sunk cruisers was brought in. He was unconscious, but recovered afterwards. He described the sinking as a very fine naval feat, the submarine having come two hundred miles from its base, and being in imminent danger the whole time.

BERLIN, *October* 3, 1914.—Count Talleyrand has brought me some illustrated London papers with pictures of the airship patrols for defending the coasts against Zeppelins. Only a few days ago the military officials here asked for a hundred volunteers for an action that would mean certain death. Every one guessed Zeppelins for England They got the hundred men within one day. They intend trying to blow up the London docks and the Woolwich Arsenal, I am told.

The military and naval authorities here are very candid in their criticisms of the relative strengths of the different countries They say the moral effect the British troops have had on the French since their arrival is marvellous, as the French were demoralized; also that the French and English aeroplanes are better than the German.

BERLIN, *October* 4, 1914.—We lunched at the Carlton Hotel with the Roeders, Lori Oppersdorff, and Baron Jagow, the Chief of the Police. Every one is expecting the fall of Antwerp. Prince Münster came in the afternoon with fresh lists of wounded and missing English officers, and told us that he was considered to have pro-English sympathies because he had tried to do an act of kindness to some English officers who are prisoners of war. He had been given leave to visit the English officers, but it had been postponed on account of Major Yate having escaped. This poor officer was recaptured and thereupon committed suicide, but he spoilt the chances of more liberty for the other officers thereby.

BEBLIN, *October* 9, 1914.—Antwerp has fallen! The news came early this morning. Again great public rejuicings. Bells ringing, houses flagged, cannon firing, and the people drunk with exultation. How things will end if the Germans go on piling up successes I don't know.

It is no good noting particulars; every one in the world will know them in a few days; but from what I hear, all hopes of the Allies outflanking the German right wing are dispersed. My own feelings are chiefly of distress and dismay, when I see all the thanksgivings celebrated here.

BERLIN, *October* 12, 1914.—Sometimes one's feelings are hurt beyond description. On the evening of the fall of Antwerp, there was a large dinner party at the Esplanade. We were present It had become an understood thing among us that during this time of anxiety and suspense no one should wear smart décolleté evening dress. However, some of the outside guests did not know our rule, or if they did they ignored it, and one lady arrived in a very transparent low-necked dress, suitable for a grand ball in the height of the season. Some one remarked: "You are very smart to-night, madame" "Yes," she said, with a beam of pleasure. "I put this on to celebrate the fall of Antwerp; but wait until you see the dress I am keeping for the day when England is beaten."

I could have stabbed her, and I think if looks can hurt, my look must have penetrated into the marrow of her bones. Some one afterwards apologized to me, but I did not want any personal apology. The point was that, whoever was the victor, hundreds and thousands of men of all countries were at that moment lying in their death agony in consequence.

. . . . . .

General Moltke, they say, has resigned, owing to ill-health according to public accounts, but in reality it seems that great differences have arisen between him and the Kaiser. Moltke wanted to make straight for Calais. If he had done this, people here affirm that Germany would have won the war already, as if the German army had reached the coast before the English arrived there, the French would have been defeated. It seems, however, that the Kaiser's personal vanity and his weakness for theatrical pomp and show got the upper hand. He countermanded Moltke's orders, and insisted on the troops making for Paris, which he hoped to enter at the head of his victorious army. It is being whispered here that this defeat on the Marne may prove the decisive turning of the war, and the greatest misfortune for Germany, in spite of her successes everywhere else.

BERLIN, *October* 13, 1914.—We had a very animated discussion at dinner last night. A German diplomat was present, and we almost fell out on the everlasting subject of which nation was the chief cause of the war. I, being of English birth, can only see the facts from the English point of view. My husband tried to explain that the mistake had been made years ago, when Germany refused the offer of an alliance with England, and continued enlarging her navy. I believe it was under Prince Bülow's *régime*. However, our German diplomat still maintained that Russia is entirely responsible for the outbreak, egged on by France and England. Of course we ended up by some one saying, "Well, what about Bethmann's 'scrap of paper'?" To which the diplomat was in an ecstasy of delight at being able to retort, "Lord Salisbury must have been of the same opinion when he said in one of his speeches that 'Agreements were made to be broken.' "

We gradually left this dangerous ground, for I suppose the question will never be satisfactorily answered, and discussed the different qualities of the soldiers of the belligerent nations. I was glad to notice that the Germans made a point of praising the behaviour of the English officers and men. They admired their equipment and splendid physique, and their dogged determination in face of odds. Several stories were related of their kindness to the wounded and captured. These remarks did a great deal towards comforting my wounded pride and the pain I have felt at the English reverses at St. Quentin and Maubeuge. I have never yet heard of any tales of cruelty on the part of my countrymen.

.   .   .   .   .   .

Talking to some wounded soldiers the other day, I asked them what had turned the tide of luck in the Marne battle. They said it was the number of fresh English troops that had told. They had arrived in all sorts of vehicles, and he himself had seen London street omnibuses arriving on all sides, still with their gay advertisements painted on them. They looked as if they had come over from Piccadilly without a stop. I thought the man was imagining this, but an officer has corroborated this story, and told me they were so unprepared in all these matters that they took any conveyance ready to hand.

BERLIN, *October* 14, 1914.—The victory of Tannenberg will go down to posterity as one of the most marvellous of modern times. Some of the horrors of it are so ghastly that an eye-witness, an officer, who has just returned from there, says it will live in his dreams to his dying day. The sight of thousands of Russians driven into two huge lakes or swamps to drown was ghastly, and the shrieks and cries of the dying men and horses he will never forget. So fearful was the sight of these thousands of men, with their guns, horses and ammunition, struggling in the water, that, to shorten their agony, they turned the machine-guns on them But even in spite of that, there was movement seen among them for a week after. And the mowing down of the cavalry brigade at the same time, 500 mounted men on white horses, all killed and packed so closely that they remained standing. The officer says that this sight was the ghastliest of the whole war.

DERNEBURG, *October* 16, 1914.—Here I am arrived and settled at Derneburg, Prince Münster's place near Hildesheim, Hanover. I travelled with Princess Münster and her niece, Countess Marie Platen, who is staying here.

We left Berlin at 8 o'clock in the morning, and got here at 2, and the peace of it is indescribable. It is a most beautiful old castle, which was once a monastery. It is surrounded by a park with lovely trees and woods, and a lake in front, and hills in the distance. It is like suddenly being transplanted back to one of the old beautiful homes in England, and the life we lead here is thoroughly English. We go for long walks in the woods, and visit the stables, gardens and farm. The servants are all the old-fashioned sort of deferential loyal country people, and the village consists of the wives and children of the men working on the estate; and we just go round daily, talking to them and asking them news of their relations who are in the war. After the strenuous life of gossiping and society in Berlin this is like reaching a haven of rest, and it is difficult to realize that there is such a fearful thing as war going on in the world.

We are not altogether idle, however. Princess Munster and I get numberless letters and telegrams daily from quite unknown people in England and elsewhere, imploring us to send news of their relations. Directly we get such a wire or letter, we have to begin pulling the strings, which means no end of writing. We have to send the names in to the governors of each prison, and to the head doctor of each hospital at which we think he is likely to be. We are not allowed to be told who *is* in these places, and are only told who is *not* there.

The authorities are most loth to give any information, and so we try to extract it from them by various roundabout routes; but it takes a long time, and we always feel sorry for those anxious relations waiting for the answer. But if we dare to show too much interest and anxiety, we are told we are pro-English at once.

DERNEBURG, *October* 18, 1914.—There are ninety men gone to the war from these two little villages alone, therefore the whole place is in a state of waiting suspense. Yesterday the poor village doctor got a post-card to say his son had been killed in action at the siege of Antwerp Only the day before he had had a letter from him, describing the horrors of the life in the trenches, but saying he was well, and that that part was nearly over.

The gardener has just returned wounded, and we have been having a most interesting conversation with him. He had been out since the beginning, and to outward appearance looks a most effeminate, soft little creature; yet he has been through continual hardships for the last two and a half months, mostly in Belgium. He said he had never experienced any *franc-tireur* trouble, and where he was, the German soldiers behaved in an orderly way, and paid for everything they took in the villages. And in the Belgian hospital where he was, nothing could have been more peaceful or comfortable, and the English, French, Belgians and Germans had all their meals together, and sat and smoked together in a most friendly fashion, and that there was no real hate among them.

The villages through which they passed, where the population was peaceful, they left unmolested; but when the villagers fired on the soldiers, then they were ordered to burn down and to shoot into the middle of the escaping inhabitants if they were still armed. Thus many innocent perished with the guilty.

.   .   .   .   .   .

One hears of such fearful horrors from those returning. One young German wounded officer, who had been spending his convalescence here, said that his regiment had been practically annihilated by their own side, through a mistake of his Colonel's It was in Belgium, and they had arranged to scour a wood in silence, two different regiments from different sides, during the night. The Colonel, forgetting the arrangement that it was to be done in silence, suddenly shouted a word of command, and this was understood to be the signal to fire on the enemy. And then one regiment simply mowed down the other in the pitch dark, and the noise was so fearful that no one could hear the shouting to "cease fire" until it was too late. One regiment practically ceased to exist, except for this young officer and about forty men. He was in such a state of collapse from the horrors of the recollection that he was nearly out of his mind.

Count Freddie Münster, Prince Munster's son, also had a horrible experience of the same sort, but escaped unharmed. He and his regiment were patrolling, and had to ride through a village which, when they entered it, appeared to be deserted. All the blinds were down, every window and door apparently shut, and not a soul to be seen. Suddenly the clock struck three, and at that moment a volley of bullets poured from every window, and the patrol had to gallop away into a wood, where they came under the fire of their own artillery, and suffered much loss before the mistake was discovered.

DERNEBURG, *October* 29, 1914.—The Germans declare that not only are black troops being sent against them, but that the English convicts are being set loose on them, that they recognize them by the "blue convict brand" on their arms   If I tell them the English do not brand their convicts, and these are only tattoo marks, they won't believe me   Also they assert that many of the British soldiers carry knives with a special twist in them, meant to scoop out the eyes of the wounded Germans. When I tell them that these are knives carried by the sappers to cut their way through the forests, etc , they only shrug their shoulders and tell me I am pro-English.

The ever-increasing number of reports of cruelty and bullying towards English prisoners is making me quite desperate. Thank God, Gebhard is joining me to-day, and we will set to work in good earnest to try and get to the roots of the matter. We are sending accounts of brutality to the Foreign Office here, and I intend getting them reported at Headquarters, so that the perpetrators may be run to ground and punished, if not now, after the war.

We have now a complete list of the unwounded English officers, and are able to write to them and send them parcels, and altogether try to do something to brighten their lives a little bit. It is, however, very difficult to reach the wounded prisoners, as communication is almost impossible owing to the disorganization of the trains.

.   .   .   .   .   .

The news becomes daily more and more desperate, and things are not going well for Germany. They have been driven back by the Russians in Poland, and on the West the English have made such a magnificent stand that the German advance along the coast and to Calais has proved a most stupendous undertaking, and they have made very little progress.

The description of the fighting is too horrible to write about, and I cannot think of it. Here the papers say that the English losses are in four figures, and that whole regiments have been mown down by the German big guns, and that the trenches have been stormed and there has been hand-to-hand fighting.

The English naval guns are covering the coast. They are even firing into Ostend, which causes much comment here, as they say Ostend is an unfortified town; and there are hundreds of English inhabitants there whom the German commander had to ask to leave, to protect them against their own guns. That is what is told us here.

DERNEBURG, *November* 1914.—The chief topic at present is the defeat of the Russians at Lodz; it is said to be an enormous victory for Germany.

They are all beginning to be anxious about Italy, which apparently becomes more war-like and unneutral every day. But Germany sounds as confident as ever, though she has changed her tone a little. Now they say that they never had any intention of going to Calais, or that they have given up the idea, but personally I know they find it a more difficult task than they expected. One of my "candid friends" told me that the English have flooded the country, and that was what really turned them back   To use his own expression: "We had provided for twenty contingencies, but this was the twenty-first."

They may get there yet, but whether they deny wanting it or not, my personal opinion is, and it is shared by many, that the possession of Calais is the one great object of the war now from the Emperor's point of view. I think he has set his heart on this more than on anything else in the world.

They have given up the idea of landing in England, and I don't think the highest authorities ever really thought it would be possible. They kept up the idea, as the population enthused more about this than about anything else, and it was the ambition of most of the soldiers fighting in the West. The authorities say candidly that they only contemplated it seriously just after the fall of Antwerp, when everything seemed to be playing into their hands, and they thought they could make an unexpected dash along the coast. They had the transports ready, so it is said. The Zeppelin raids also have been a slight disappointment to Germany They had been waiting for the fogs, and then expected to make a demonstration on the English coast, or near London. But I personally think that the shutting up of civilians in England in concentration camps has something to do in preventing this.

BERLIN, *December* 1914.—On our return to Berlin at the end of November we were startled by the announcement that Sir Roger Casement had arrived there. The wonder was how an Irishman, and an ex-Consul of the English Government, could have found his way here. But we were more interested than most, as we knew him well. He had been in Africa with my husband, and we had also seen a good deal of him in London at various times. We knew his anti-English feelings well, and his rabid Home Rule mania, but we did not expect it to have taken this intense form of becoming pro-German.

However, he had not been here many days before he came to see us. He told us the whole story, which can be read in any newspaper, of how when war broke out he went over to America, and there spent his time working among the Irish-Americans, advising them to go home, not to enlist for England, etc., telling them that England was only sending their countrymen to their death, and that in the future the only reward they would get was a promise of Home Rule which they had no intention of fulfilling.

His efforts were, I suppose, crowned with some success, as eventually he determined to make his way into Germany to try and work up the Irish prisoners against England. His adventures on the journey are well known, and on his arrival in Norway, the British Minister, Mr. Finlay, offered a reward to any one who would bring him into their hands. Sir Roger, however, after a great deal of correspondence with some of his acquaintances in the Foreign Office in Berlin, was eventually allowed to enter Germany, and was then given free access to the prison camps where the Irish prisoners were

My husband went to him shortly after his arrival and tried to show him what a false position he had put himself in, and that he had better leave the country as quickly as possible, but it was no use So after that we refused to see him or have anything more to do with him. When we first saw him, he was most enthusiastic and certain of success, his idea being to try and make the Irishmen promise that if they were free they would not fight for England, and would use their influence to prevent recruiting in Ireland. He was not really successful anywhere. In fact, he soon became offended, because he said the Berlin Foreign Office did not trust him enough. We hinted to him that no one ever really trusted a traitor, at which he was greatly incensed, protesting that he was not that; and he was hardly less so when others, trying to soften down the name, called him an Irish rebel. He did not like that either.

His measure of success with the Irish prisoners may

be summed up in the answer he got from one very raw
Irishman whom he asked whether he did not hate Eng-
land. The Irishman's reply was: "Well, we may hate
England, but that does not make us love Germany."

One bit of good news amidst the prevailing gloom. I
have just been able to send a telegram to Lord Edmund
Talbot through the Red Cross, to say that his son, who
has been missing for some weeks, is now in hospital near
Lille. How I came to obtain this information was as
follows. I was hurrying through the hall of the
Esplanade Hotel when an officer stopped me and said,
"Excuse me, but are you not related to Lord Edmund
Talbot?" On my replying that I was, he said, "I am
Count Welsczek, and a few days ago I was fortunate
enough to be able to render first aid to his son, Captain
Talbot of the 11th Hussars. I and some brother officers
were riding through a lane on the outskirts of Lille, when
we were attracted by something moving in the ditch,
which on nearer inspection we discovered to be a wounded
English officer lying covered in mud and quite unconscious. We administered restoratives, and he soon re-
vived enough to be taken to a hospital. The first remark
he made, in his semi-conscious state, when being picked
out of the ditch, was, 'I should like to have a bath,
I'm so muddy' "; at which they all laughed very much,
saying how like an Englishman it was to prefer having
a bath to food or anything else in the world.

.   .   .   .   .   .

Speaking of this relation reminds me of a great adventure, no less than a visit to my cousin Captain Trafford,
who is a prisoner at Crefeld. I have never written about
it, as I was told to keep it a secret so as to prevent others
asking for the same privilege.

It was indeed a very notable event my being allowed
to see him, as the barrack regulations are extremely
rigid on this point, and ladies are not supposed to be
admitted at all. That an exception was made in my case
was only due to the intervention of General v. Bissing,

who smoothed away all the difficulties and gave me leave to enter. And although I am perfectly conscious of all the rumours of his harshness which are current in the outside world, I shall not easily forget this spontaneous act of kindness to me.

I found my cousin looking very well and in quite good spirits, in spite of the hardships he had gone through during his three weeks at the front, and also in spite of the discomforts I knew he must be experiencing in the camp. But as I was not allowed to speak to him alone, I could not really learn much about the true state of affairs at Crefeld, and it was a great trial to me and my husband to have to get up and go away as the clock struck the appointed hour, without being sure of being allowed to come again and not being able to do more in the way of adding comforts and luxuries for him and other officers, who we knew had arrived there with nothing but what they stood up in; however, the commander and other officers at the camp were most courteous to us, and I have since realized what a great concession it was my being allowed to go there at all. One lives to learn to be thankful for small mercies in these days.

BERLIN, *March* 1915.—My husband is now regularly attached to the hospital train equipped by the Knights of Malta This Order is very ancient, and purely religious in character, almost equivalent to the Knights of St John in England Its present members are still recognized in Austria as possessing sovereign rights in that country. The German branches in Silesia and on the Rhine are recognized as corporations for voluntary "Ambulance Service in War Time." Its organization is autonomous, and distinct from the Red Cross Society under the regulations of the Hague Convention. It is recognized by all the belligerent countries and is under the protection of international law.

The Order possesses great wealth in Austria, and a strict investigation into ancestral quarterings is required, both for honorary knights and knights of justice, the latter being required to take the vow of celibacy. The Austrian Order has equipped no less than seven ambulance trains during the war, whilst the German branches have two trains running, the Silesian and the Rhenish-Westphalian.

I felt very proud as I saw him start off on his first journey, wearing his smart new uniform with the Red Cross band on his arm. It was a comfort too to know what a good work he was undertaking, when he might have been setting off on such a different errand. I feel rather ashamed now of a somewhat bitter remark I made one day to a friend whose husband was at the front, and who came with me to see G. off. "Don't you feel proud of him?" she said, and I answered: "Yes, indeed I do, and thank God he is going out to cure and not to kill." I rather regretted it when I saw the tears come into her eyes as she said: "But think of me, having to see my husband off to the West, to be one of those who are forming the human wall round our country to prevent so many enemies entering, to wipe us off the earth."

BERLIN, *April* 1915.—Glancing back over the last six months—one of the few things that really impressed themselves on my memory was the sinking of the *Blucher* by the English on January 24.

How well I remember the proud moment when, six months after my marriage, the Emperor sent for me in the middle of a Court ball in Berlin and asked me to launch the new cruiser *Blücher.* How well I remember his words as he smilingly said to me: "I expect you will get into trouble with your English relations if you launch my battleships, now won't you?" His well-known charm of manner attracted me so much, as it does all others. And then, four months after that date, we went to Kiel, and in the presence of Prince Henry of Prussia and the Princess, and General von der Goltz and others, I made my first German speech and broke the champagne bottle, and the *Blücher* floated gracefully into the water.

After the ceremony we went up to the castle for luncheon with Prince and Princess Henry of Prussia (she being sister to the Czarina of Russia and an English princess). We talked England, England, England—she telling us every little anecdote she could think of about her happy days at Windsor with old Queen Victoria, and how she and her sister had so intensely enjoyed rummaging in the old curiosity shops in the town of Windsor, saying laughingly: "We enjoyed mostly getting bargains of old bits of furniture, etc., which we had our suspicions had begun life in the castle itself, and had been 'looted' by servants at different periods, and found their way into these shops."

Among this party for the launching was my sister Freda, who had come out from England with us for it, and since then she is married to Admiral Charlton, who is now at the Admiralty; and, who knows? maybe he was the very man who controlled this particular episode in the naval warfare!

The *Blücher* had, from the very beginning, ranked as an antiquated man-of-war, and was the slowest unit in the fleet. So it was arranged that she should be chosen to bear the brunt of battle, and stay behind to be sacrificed if necessary, to give the others time to retreat.

The captain of the *Blücher*, when rescued out of the water, was taken to Edinburgh, and on his way there, got into conversation with the English naval officer in command of the guard over them. The German officer had told him that an Englishwoman had launched the *Blücher*, and that her photograph had gone down in the ship. "Yes," answered the English naval officer, "I happen to know all about it, as the lady is my sister-in-law. My name is Throckmorton." It is curious how small the world is.

BERLIN, *May* 1915.—For many weeks past I seem to

have been leading an existence apart, cut off from all communion with my surroundings. My brother Wilfred's death at Ypres, of which I received news in November, seemed to render all the old familiar intercourse impossible Now I am beginning once more to see people a little.

In Holy Week (the week before Easter) my husband was away on one of his journeys with the Lazarett-Zug, and Count and Countess Larisch (Fritzi and May) asked me to go and stay with them here in Berlin, as I was quite alone.

It was a homelike, peaceful time, and did me much good. May and her three little girls and I used each morning to go to Mass at the little Convent Chapel attached to the hospital at which I used to nurse. There we met Countess Henckel and her daughters, Princess Löwenstein with her children, and Countess Tattenbach, all cousins and connections. We used to meet outside the church-door twice each day, discussing the same news. It was like living in a little peaceful world of our own, in the centre of this big city, and this life of religion had a very soothing effect on my harassed nerves.

I shall always remember one evening service early in the month. I had been kneeling there, trying to pray, when the music broke out into a beautiful hymn to the Mother of God, beseeching for comfort for all, in this time of grief. I was awakened by it, as if from a long dream, and I looked round, and the scene that I saw struck me to the heart. The altar all ablaze with candles and flowers, the Blessed Sacrament exposed there above, the priest and acolytes, the incense, and the congregation, all wrapt in their devotional hymn; Countess Henckel and her daughters, in nurses' dress, having come straight from their work in the hospital; Princess Löwenstein and all her small children kneeling around her; Countess Larisch with her little daughters; the nuns of all ages and sizes; the wounded soldiers, some with their arms in slings, some with faces bandaged up,

some on crutches, having limped straight in from the
wards; and many unwounded soldiers in their tattered
uniforms, home for a few days' leave and spending it
thus. And at the back of the chapel knelt my husband
and Prince Löwenstein; my husband in the uniform of
the Knights of Malta, with the Red Cross badge on his
arm, Prince Löwenstein in the field uniform of the
Bavarian army, leaning on their swords, with their eyes
fixed on the tabernacle. These two officers, and all
these soldiers and the congregation, were singing that
hymn from the very depths of their hearts. They were
absolutely oblivious of the outer world as they knelt
there and poured out their supplication to God in this
hymn to the Blessed Virgin Mary.

I stopped and asked myself. "Can you hate these
people as you think you do, can you not see any good in
them, can you not understand how they suffer too, and
picture their homes being stricken and what they are
enduring as well as your own countrymen?" and as I
listened my resentment gave way, and I prayed for these
people who were suffering as much as myself, if not more.

It is in times of stress like this that the consolations
of religion appeal most strongly to us. How often in
the night, when we lie and think about all the bitter
suffering in the world, might we not seek in spirit to
grope our way through time and space, and by the power
of our will make our presence felt by some lonely dying
soldier, who might close his eyes in peace could he feel
our helpful hands or hear our grateful whisper in his
dying ears, "Thanks, dear brother, sleep well." We
too might gain some comfort in the knowledge that the
last moments of the dead are not spent in anguish and
pain, for death is mostly far kinder than life and infinitely
more merciful than man, and steeps the tired senses in a
dream wherein all else is forgotten but the happy peaceful
memories of childhood.

We Catholics too can find great consolation in the

belief that those hours of pain which may have preceded the end will shorten their passage through Purgatory in the next life, and could they let us know, as they sometimes do in dreams and visions, they would most certainly implore us not to grieve so much for them or doubt as to their well-being now, for our tears and pain are probably for them the one alloy to their perfect peace in heaven.

.   .   .   .   .   .

I had been in correspondence with Prince Löwenstein about my brother, who was first reported missing after the battle of Ypres. He was quartered at Comines, near the fighting line of that district, and the trouble and real sympathy he showed me in my anxiety impressed me in a way that few other things have done for a long time He several times rode out specially to the surrounding district to make inquiries about him, and rode up to the dressing-stations and field-hospitals of the district, and also to the abandoned trenches and graveyards, in the hopes of getting a clue. And sometimes, when passing a wayside cross, he would get down from his horse and copy the name of the fallen officer, and send it to me in the hope it might bring some little consolation to a bereaved relation.

At the beginning of May he came back on leave for a few days, and I went to see his wife and him at their apartment. His real and intense kindness and sympathy touched me very much—the way he tried to give me every detail about the search, and at the same time spare my feelings as to the hopelessness and sadness of the aspect of warfare in that particular part of the country.

BERLIN, *May* 1915.—May 8, 1915, will live vividly in my memory for the shock that we received by the sinking of the *Lusitania*. How can I find words to write about it? And yet I cannot pass over the event that caused more sensation throughout the world than the greatest victory or the greatest defeat. "Sinking of the *Lusitania* by a German submarine" was the headline in our German paper that morning, without any details of importance. A great loss of life had been the just punishment for that liner that was carrying munitions to the enemy of Germany. Neutral America was providing these munitions (a breach of neutrality, said Germany), and what sacrifice could be too great a punishment for that!

The Germans themselves were amazed—oh yes; but proud—proud of what one little submarine could do, of what power a few men in a little nutshell under the water could wield—what a wonderful method of warfare it was, and how soon England must give in if confronted with this power. At last the world would recognize the awfulness of the German navy, and see that Germany must become mistress of the seas, as she could prevent others from crossing the water in safety whenever she pleased. In one respect the Germans were right. The world does recognize the awfulness of that kind of warfare, but not with admiration!

The Americans here in the hotel, and those of the Embassy staff, had always professed to be neutral. They had been cordial and friendly towards the Germans they met, had gone out together, had played tennis, and so forth. But a sudden change now took place. The Americans openly avoided the Germans, almost cutting their friends of the day before. Friendly intercourse was absolutely out of the question. Their rage and horror at the idea that Americans had been killed knew no bounds, and they gave vent to their views in unguarded terms. One German turned to me and said, "You and other English ladies here have self-control, but these American ladies, once they are roused, do not care how or where they express their feelings."

BERLIN, *May* 1915.—I was rung up on the telephone by a Dr. Johansen, who said he would like to come and see me   We made an appointment for the next evening, when he told me he had come to thank me on behalf of some of the English prisoners for all I had been doing for them, and that he was the doctor appointed for the officers at Blankenburg, and so saw them nearly every day.

He had become devoted to Colonel G——, although he said, "I ought to hate him, as his regiment killed my only son at Mons; but I love the man, in fact I love all the British officers."

I asked if there was anything I could do for any of them, and he said no, he did not think so at present, and added: "Don't send Colonel G—— any cigars or cigarettes; the poor man is overpowered by the number that are sent him, as there is no place to keep them and he can't smoke them all." I replied that I purposely had not sent any, and the only thing I could send him that I knew he would appreciate was the only thing he would not be allowed, and that was the English *Times*. "No," he said very decidedly, "that is absolutely against the rules; but," and he looked at a pile of the *Times* lying on my table, "of course, if I happened to have some newspapers in my pocket, I might drop them as I went past his door, by accident," and he gave me a knowing look. I at once rolled them up and he stuffed them into his pocket, and as he went towards the door, he said, "My mother was English, but we don't say too much about that at present, do we?"

A few days later he offered to take my husband to see Colonel G—— and the other officers. We rang up the following morning to fix a day, and the answer to the telephone was, "The doctor died suddenly last night." It was a great shock to us—one more friend gone.

.   .   .   .   .   .

To-day I went to tea with the Duchess of Croy. She is one of the many young American wives of the German nobility, and is the daughter of Mr. Leishman, who was at one time Ambassador in Berlin. She told me of an awful journey she had a short time ago when she

was in their place in the country. She got a telegram
from her husband to say he was being sent from the West
to the East, and would be passing Cologne, and could
she meet him there. Their place was some miles out of
Cologne, and she had not much time to spare. She had
to hire an old village taxi, their own motors having all
been taken, and had to implore the man to drive as hard
as ever he could. Just as they were nearing Cologne a
tyre burst. She was in despair, and had to get out and
kneel down in the middle of the road, and work her
hardest to help the chauffeur to put it right, every minute
thinking she was missing her husband. She was only
twenty, and her baby was only three weeks old, so
altogether she was not very fit for being left in such a
plight. However, they got it mended and dashed on.
Then, on reaching the station, there were more difficulties
in the form of German red tape. They flatly refused to
let her on to the station without a pass. As a brilliant
idea, she said she had an important telegram for her
husband from the War Office, and they then said they
must see the telegram. Her patience nearly gave way
at that, but she realized all would be lost if she did not
carry it through, so she said, "How dare you insult me
by asking me to show you a private communication from
the War Office; I shall report you for this." It acted
like magic, and they fell back and let her through, just
in time to see her husband's train come in.

A young officer, just home on leave for a few days in
Berlin, said to me to-day that he was longing to get back
to the front so as to have a little peace and quiet, where,
as he said, there is not so much venomous hatred and
vindictiveness against the enemy, and no incessant talk
of cruelties, reprisals, etc. He added: "Out there we all
do our duty, the enemy as well as ourselves; we obey
the orders, and do what we are told, and have no time
to think or feel all this horrible hatred and revenge."

Some one just returned from Neuve Chapelle says that the battle there was one of the most ghastly of the whole year. The Germans had hidden a machine-gun in practically every window and every door of the cottages, and when the English marched through they were just mown down. Their losses (Germans) during that fight were appalling—18,000, and the British were 12,000. The English attacked sixty times in three days, throwing all their strength apparently on that one spot for the moment.

Prince Münster said he witnessed a sad sight the other day. A man in the trenches had to watch his son dying by inches a few hundred yards away from him (between the trenches) and was powerless to help or reach him. He was his only son, and he saw him fall wounded and then die slowly, with many other wounded, lying there in the open ground.

And I have just been told of another sad sight from the East Front. The Germans went forward to clear a captured Russian trench, and found in it a fine-looking Russian officer sitting upright, motionless, gazing at a photo of a most beautiful woman and two little children. He was stone dead.

BERLIN, *June* 15, 1915 —It is now a month since the *Lusitania* was torpedoed. We have read all the comments in the English and American papers, and I have studied the attitude of the people here towards that horrible deed. Even those who admire it from the scientific point of view seem in their inmost hearts ashamed of it, and do not care to defend it—but rather on the ground that it was politically a mistake. I believe the Kaiser thoroughly disapproved of it, and I have seen a letter written by one of the royal princesses (not of German birth) in which it was condemned as piratical and barbarous.

I suppose the question whether there really was ammunition on board the *Lusitania* will never be satisfactorily settled, as the secret must remain in the hands of a few men who for very good reasons will certainly keep it to themselves.

BERLIN, *June* 10, 1915.—Amongst the numerous afflictions visited upon us by the war, the "spy-fever" is one of the worst. It has indeed reached such a height that it seems as if every second person at least is on the verge of lunacy, and that this venomous attitude towards your neighbour is a new form of war-pestilence. People are proud of the way in which modern science has coped with infectious ailments, but no science seems able to suppress this newest form of mental disease, to which womankind seems particularly addicted. The seemingly most righteous member of our sex will, without a qualm of conscience, inform on her most innocent neighbour, apparently to satisfy some innate instinct for playing the detective, or for making herself important. I could relate dozens of instances of malicious and misleading informers within my own knowledge. It is impossible that all the people who have been persecuted as such are in reality spies. From what I hear, the "spy" epidemic seems to be international, and weak-minded females in England and France have fallen a prey to the same affliction.

Has the word "spy" lost its ancient disagreeable meaning? It almost seems to be an honourable calling now, or it is at least if you are a member of the secret service, for you not only receive a very high salary in every country, but you are regarded as an upright and honourable gentleman, and a very useful member of society, whilst the private "spy" is looked upon as a criminal only worth shooting.

A conversation with a neutral this afternoon has turned my thoughts this way. We were really discussing the different methods of the German and English secret service, and whilst listening to the details he gave me of the enormous sums which both countries had spent on it, I could not refrain from saying that they had neither of them been very effective, considering the utter ignorance and surprise expressed by both at the outbreak of the war.

He admitted that it was not always easy to distinguish between spies, traitors, and secret service agents. The English officials, he said, were bombarded with anonymous letters from charitable persons who felt bound to lay at least one victim at the feet of justice. This kind of information, which is always offered gratis at the time of any sensational crime, is of little or no value, and is generally the outcome of hysterical imagination. He told me that the much-abused English Intelligence Department had not been quite so fast asleep as the good lady-informers supposed, and that for three years before the war the names of all the German residents in England had been noted. Their correspondence had been systematically opened and censored during that period, and within twenty-four hours of the declaration of war no less than twenty-five out of twenty-six recognized paid spies had been taken into custody. The twenty-sixth, who escaped through the over-zeal of one of the aforesaid females, was eventually captured, and before three months were over they had unearthed a whole nest of suspicious individuals, and interned them for the duration of the war. On questioning him as to the relative merits of the two countries, he judged the English secret service to be better than the German, as more men who had been touring in Germany, financed by the Government, got back to their own country in time. As to the morality of spying in general, I expressed my doubts about the ethics of men who go round accepting the hospitality of friends, all the time trying to elicit information which is meant to harm their country. He, however, took another view of the case, and expressed his admiration for men who risk their lives and stop at nothing to help their native land, without receiving any kudos. As an example he mentioned Baden-Powell, who, in his book published after his visit to Germany in 1910-11, boasts how he accepted hospitality at the Emperor's table, whilst in between he gained as much useful information as he could, from less exalted personages, by means of bribes.

I remember myself a story which Count R—— told me in June 1914. He complained that his whole pleasure in the Kiel regatta week had been spoilt for him by an English friend, whom he was entertaining, trying by every means in his power to gain knowledge of the depths and sounding of the Canal, during casual conversation with him and his friends.

．　　．　　　．　　．　　　．

A few days ago Gebhard and I and Gustav (G.'s brother) went to see the English prisoners working on the road near Lichterfelde. No one was supposed to know they were there, and no one was allowed to go and see them However, Paul Münster had given me a graphic description of how, when he was out the other day with the other cadets, they suddenly came upon them, and their captain called out to know whether any among them could speak English. Paul Münster at once came forward and was then told he might say a few words to them.

He said the poor men were so pleased when he asked them about their homes and where they had come from, etc, and when he mentioned several places in England he knew well himself, they at once became most friendly.

This, of course, fired me with the idea to go there. I knew it was impossible without an officer in uniform, and I asked one or two I knew if they would go; but they all said it would not be allowed, and might be misconstrued, and all the usual reasons which were forthcoming when any interest in the English was shown. However, I knew my good-natured brother-in-law would do anything I asked, so we three sallied forth.

It was dinner-time when we arrived, and they were all lying about in the heat of the blazing sun, in a sort of fenced-off waste of sand. They were a most unkempt lot, I must say; but, poor men, it was not their fault. They were laughing and joking among themselves, and one of them was reading out what evidently was a very amusing story, judging by the peals of laughter that it caused. A very nice official came and spoke to us, and while he and my husband talked, I began very cautiously to make my way up to the wire railing, and then I said to them, "How are you; is there anything I can do for you?" I shall never forget the look on those poor men's faces when they heard these few words of genuine English; they all crowded up to the wire fence, each wanting a word said to them. I had to be very careful, as I knew I might be stopped at any minute. They had nearly all been prisoners since last August or September, and seemed so weary of it.

I asked which battles they had been in, and one man said to me, "I was wounded at Less Skates." My brother-in-law, who was standing near, said, "What does he mean?" I said, "He says he was wounded at the battle of Le Cateau," and this really was the first time it dawned on me how different the descriptions and names of battles and everything must sound when spoken of in England—when I think of Less Skates and Wipers, for example.

I could not tell them I was English, although I longed to, but I knew that would be quite fatal, so I went on making desultory conversation to them, my brother-in-law joining in at times, but they did not rise much to his conversation. They saw he was a German officer, and spoke broken English, so they were more cautious and suspicious, and kept their eyes fixed on me, with a smile on their faces, as much as to say, "We see you are a friend and that you are English."

I asked if they got parcels from home. Some said sadly, "No," but one told me that he got them regularly every week. I asked what regiment he belonged to, and he replied "Royal Fusiliers," which rejoiced me, because it was the regiment my mother had undertaken to provide for, and her own hands may have packed them.

My husband then came up, and as his English is perfect, and as he was only in the uniform of the Knights of Malta, they opened out to him at once. He asked them if they had any complaints, and whether they had all they wanted. They replied that they had plenty of food; that they heard regularly from home; and that they liked working on the roads as it helped to pass the time.

So my husband said, "Well, that's all right. I am glad you are happy." But they replied, "We want to be in England, that's all we want. It is the only wish we have, to be once more back in good old England." And underlying every word they said one could read downright genuine home-sickness. The poor men said it with such feeling that it made a great impression on me.

Then a sentinel called out in a very loud voice, "It is not allowed to talk to the prisoners." So we drew back instantly, but continued our conversation *at* each other in a way, I talking to the interpreter so that they could hear, and they talking to each other so that I could hear.

One sentence I remember specially. A very rough-looking young soldier, who was lying in his shirt-sleeves on the sand eating his dinner, said to his neighbour in an audible voice that I could hear: "I wish the dickens she'd get them to send me a pair of boots; how the deuce I am expected to work in these blessed things I don't know" (these blessed things being a sort of clog sandals). I looked at him and laughed and did my best to send him these boots, but never heard whether he got them or not.

We then moved away, all the men smiling at me as I went. One very young sailor boy struck us so much, he looked so unutterably sad and ill, and he was the only one who stood up to attention and saluted when we left. I have tried since to find out his name, but have never been able to. I longed to say some little words of comfort to the poor youth.

We then went to a little wayside inn and had our lunch in the garden outside. The prisoners' dinner-time was now over and they were all back at work on the tram-line on the road. It was an historic sight I shall never forget, the surroundings so typically German, and these ultra-English men working in their shirt-sleeves all along the line, and whistling and talking to themselves quite oblivious of the rest of the world. I am glad to say they seemed on most jocose and familiar terms with all the foremen who were working with them. I gazed out on this scene and felt as if I were in some land of dreams.

After our luncheon we went home by tram and had to pass along the line where these men were working. Their delight at recognizing me again in the tram was really most touching; they all looked up and waved their hands and called out "Good-bye" to me, and I felt I had left a few more unknown friends behind me, whom I shall probably never see or hear of again.

Many months afterwards I heard from the English chaplain who visited them that they still talked of my visit, and they had managed to find out who I was and all about me, and they told him what a happiness it had been to have a little breath from the Old Country, as my visit had seemed to them.

The *Times* has published some evidence extracted from Bavarian deserters, who vouched to have witnessed the shooting of English prisoners, whether wounded or not, under supervision of a Bavarian officer. I was in a great state about this and wrote to a friend of mine, a Bavarian officer. His reply is as follows: "I think the whole thing is perfect nonsense. . . . I expect the deserters were short of money, and made it by telling sensational stories, the Dutch reporters being most anxious for information of that sort. I know many instances of that kind . . . a deserter is never a very trustworthy person."

He also drew my attention to the fact that in a fight it is very difficult to say when the "action" has come to an end and when captivity begins. Very often a man, I suppose, may be ready enough to surrender and yet must be killed because the man attacking cannot stop to take him prisoner. A man saving a prisoner may be forfeiting his own life by being hit while doing it. So the Frenchman, of whom a friend told me, was killed by a man who would have liked to save him when he heard the words, "Ayez pitié de moi, j'ai une femme et six enfants."

I sent the article out of the *Times* to Prince Löwenstein, who was at the Bavarian Headquarters at Comines. He answered that the "Deserters' story" had been thoroughly investigated, and that no such men existed at all as the two names given as the eye-witnesses, and that he and others with him considered it a Press fabrication from beginning to end. The Bavarian Crown Prince expressed great astonishment that any one should even think they ever killed prisoners. He said, we want prisoners who can talk and tell us something; there would be no point in killing them.

.   .   .   .   .

How easy it is to talk about atrocities, and how few people pause to weigh the full meaning of their words when adding their quota of horror to the tale. In Berlin, for many months after the beginning of the war, we heard nothing but tales of torture and barbarities inflicted by Belgian women and *franc-tireurs* on German soldiers. Then came stories of French *franc-tireurs* and the bad treatment of prisoners in French camps. These were outdone in horror by the wave of feeling against Russia, whose atrocities were said to exceed in cruelty all those perpetrated by the Belgians. Germany punished the Belgians ruthlessly, but dared not adopt such drastic measures with Russia, as too many Germans were in her power on whom she could wreak vengeance.

Next came England—"Gott strafe England!" The

hatred of England, English measures, English culture, is beyond description. Germany has never been able to record British atrocities that would stand the test of proof, nor even cases of unjust treatment of prisoners; yet I am convinced that if a Belgian, a Frenchman, a Russian, and an Englishman were placed at the mercy of a German, he would kill the Englishman first. Why is it? I think they truly believe that England entered the war from greed of gain.

The hatred has intensified of late. There has been a silly story going about of King George offering £1 to any one who would bring him a German. The Bavarian Crown Prince, on reading this, is supposed to have replied, "I think I had better offer the same sum to any one who does *not* bring me an Englishman" I don't suppose there is a word of truth in this, but it has encouraged the idea strongly that the Bavarians are urged to murder their prisoners, and may be responsible for several stories.

.   .   .   .   .   .

It was reported some time ago in the papers that Prince Max of Hesse had been wounded, and since then I and many others have been trying every possible means to get definite news of him for his mother, who is distracted with grief. He was the Emperor's nephew, aged 18, and now appears to have died of his wounds received in October 1914. He had been living in England, and left friends and relations there to come and fight for his country, and to face these friends as enemies on the field.

His mother, Princess Margaret of Hesse, was for three months without any definite news. The Emperor himself wrote asking the Americans to find out about him, but without avail. At last, through the searching inquiries of the Pope and the King of Spain, the tragic news of his death was announced. He had been carried into a monastery near Mont des Cats that was in the hands of the English that night; he was a prisoner then, mortally wounded, and was attended to by two doctors,

Dr. O'Brien Butler and Dr. Johnson. Dr. Johnson is now at Crefeld, a prisoner.

Dr O'Brien Butler spent the night with the Prince, who knew he was dying, and who gave Dr. O'Brien Butler a locket for his mother and his last dying message. Next day Dr. Johnson inquired of Dr. O'Brien Butler about the Prince's last moments. Dr. O'Brien Butler said he had received so sacred a message from the dying Prince for his mother that he felt he could confide it to no one else, but must tell the Princess himself. That day he was killed—so the poor mother, who is broken-hearted, will never know what her boy had meant for her to hear. It is a most tragic story.

A friend has informed me that one of the nursing sisters in Boulogne told him that Prince Max is buried near the monastery, his body having been picked up by an old priest or monk, who intends to keep the burial-place a secret until he is paid for the damage done to his church!

Royal relations are not supposed to correspond with each other in belligerent countries in these sad times, but of course (like all of us) they feel for those in sorrow. Queen Mary sent a graceful message through the Crown Princess of Sweden, expressing her great sympathy with Princess Margaret, and returning the Prince's locket, which had been sent to the King, and which she had tied up with her own hands.

BERLIN, *June* 18, 1915.—I have been fearfully busy about the Reprisal Question, which is that, as it is said, Winston Churchill has ordered all submarine prisoners to be kept apart in England, and not to be allowed to associate with the other prisoners of war. Germany, on hearing this, needless to say, went in for reprisals, and ordered 39 English officers to be put into solitary confinement at once. They chose 39 out of the Guards Regiments and from among the best-known names among them. Princess Münster, Princess Pless and I were told that, as we all had relations among the number chosen, we could write to England and state the case, and tell them that these 39 officers would be released when Winston Churchill rescinded his decision. We therefore drew up a statement together, and I being the only one at the moment in Berlin, it was decided that I should beard Mr. Gerard in his den, and get him to send it through to England to our most influential relations.

I wrote it out in the form of a circular, as I knew the answer I should have got if I had asked him to post a letter. I went to the Embassy and asked to see the Ambassador, and was requested to wait a minute. We ladies were by now quite accustomed to being treated like ladies' maids seeking situations when we went to the Embassy to inquire for our missing relations; however, this time I was not kept waiting long, and as I walked into the room I was greeted with the words, "I can't post any letters for England, if that's what you have come to ask me to do." I felt inclined to reply, "Wait till you are asked"; however, I realized that it would not be a good beginning if I intended to get this document posted, so I only replied, "That is not what I want in the least" (being exactly the thing I had come for), but calling it a circular I knew would change the nature of the request; so I showed him the list of names and the circular, and said that if he could see his way to sending them to my mother, she would do the rest. He was tremendously interested as he read it, but of course dared not say so in so many words, as it might have been misconstrued into "an unneutral act on the part of an ambassador." He simply said, "What is your mother's address?" I gave it and withdrew, without asking any more questions.

Of course we have never had the satisfaction of knowing whether we *did* shorten the time of solitary confinement for these officers or not, but we certainly managed to improve their treatment during their time there, as very shortly after I had a letter from my cousin, saying that they were now being allowed certain privileges, that they were allowed to be together all day, and that the commander was quite a nice man, who tried to improve their position as far as he was permitted to do.

Within ten days Princess Münster had received an answer through a third person from one of the Cabinet Ministers, and I had received one from my mother saying she had sent the matter to the fountain-head; and also we heard that the American Consul in Cologne had been dispatched to report on and improve the condition of these officers.

KISSINGEN, *June 22*, 1915.—We spent a night in Dresden on our way to Kissingen, and met there several Austrian relations who were staying in the same hotel (Continental).

Prince and Princess Lobkowitz came from Bohemia for one night on purpose to see us. They have their three sons out and in daily danger. Their views on all the usual subjects were varied. They considered the sinking of the *Lusitania* a ruthless and somewhat inhuman event, but dare not air their views on this subject. They (unlike most Austrians) criticized their own General Staff, and were loud in praise of German organization and generalship.

Staying with us also was Prince Lobkowitz's widowed sister (Gebhard's cousin) Princess Ratibor and her son Ernest, who is a young naval officer aged 23, and who is now on three days' leave from his submarine. Princess Ratibor has already lost her youngest son in the Carpathians, and at this moment is in very deep grief about him; she has also another son in an exposed position on the East front, and her eldest son is lost in Canada; at least he was there when war broke out, and she had heard nothing about him since

Another interesting visitor at this hotel is von Mügge —of *Emden* fame; he is just on his way home after all his adventures, and is treated like a hero wherever he goes. There is a crowd outside the hotel always to watch him go in and out, and he is followed everywhere in the streets, and has continual bouquets of flowers presented to him.   M. Hoyos and C. Lobkowitz and I have just been watching his departure for the station.

He seems a smart, simple, good-looking youth, and is most bashful at the excitement he creates.   He was quite overpowered by the admiring crowd that followed him to the station just now, and which inundated him with magnificent flowers and much cheering; but certainly, if he was embarrassed by it, his poor old mother who was with him fully appreciated it all, as I have never seen such an expression of perfect happiness and pride as I did on that poor woman's face as she walked with him and helped him to carry the numerous bouquets of flowers with which he was laden.   He is indeed a hero, and I know he is looked upon as such by people of all countries.

His story is as follows:

He was conducting a landing party of about 60 men on to one of the Pacific islands, when the *Emden* and its captain and the rest of the crew were captured by the English.   So von Mügge and his 60 men were left stranded.   They eventually succeeded in capturing a sailing vessel, put some of their quick-firing guns from the *Emden* on it, and sailed across the Indian Ocean to Bombay, and there, it is said, they held up a British steamer. They later on landed in a Red Sea port south of Aden, worked their way across the Arabian desert, and had to fight several tribes, during which they lost some of their men, and eventually reached Damascus, where they took train for Constantinople, from whence they eventually reached home after many thrilling adventures.

.   .   . .

But to return to the Ratibors, with whom we spent our time whilst at Dresden.   Ernest, the naval lieutenant, told me much interesting news about his life in a submarine. Of course, I asked him whether he was the one who had wrecked the *Lusitania*.   He said he was not, though he knew who had done it, but no one is allowed to say.

He began to tell me all sorts of wonderful things he
had seen in the English illustrated papers, *London News,
Graphic,* etc., so I asked him, "How do you come to be
so well informed as to the pictures in English newspapers?" and he replied, "Oh, English fishermen give
them to us sometimes when we have to capture their
boats."

He told me of some quite amusing conversations he
had had with some old fishermen. On one occasion, when
they had ordered these men to clear off everything and
take away anything they liked off their fishing trawler
before they sank it, the men were all so frightened that
they said—no, they *wanted nothing,* they would come
away just as they were; but when they were in their
boat and got into conversation with these young submarine officers, and saw that they were not so alarming
as they had at first thought, one old sailor came up to
Ernest and said, "May I just go back for one thing?"
and on being given permission they all waited for him,
and wondered what this one treasure was going to be
that the poor old man could not leave behind. In a few
minutes he reappeared carrying a bottle of whisky under
his arm, and as he passed Prince Ratibor he said, "It
did seem a pity to leave that behind!"

I continued to draw this youth out on the subject of
his submarine experiences all the time we were together,
because it interested me more than anything else, as his
life all these last months had consisted in prowling round
Scotland under water.

He, to tease me, said on our morning of departure:
"Aren't you jealous of me? I go to Scotland every
week. I will pick you a flower there, and if you like to
give me a letter for your sister, I will pin it on a Scotch
cliff next time I touch it." I replied, laughing, "Don't
you boast quite so much. You will touch Scotland once
too often, if you don't take care!"

"Well," said he, "anyhow, there are only two things
that can happen to us submarine officers; there are no

half measures about our fate as about others. We either go to the bottom like a stone and are drowned instantly, or else we come back victorious." I saw such a sad look come over his mother's face as the laughing boy said this, and as he was leaving that day to rejoin his submarine, I tried to answer in a more hopeful tone than I really felt, and said, "No; I feel *you* are just the sort who would bob up like a cork when every one else is drowning."

.   .   .   .   .   .

How little I knew that within a month of my making that remark the very thing would have happened. In the beginning of August his mother received an official notice from the Admiralty that the U27 had been sunk off the coast of Scotland, and that Prince Ernest Ratibor and three others were all that had been saved of the crew of 45. We heard afterwards he was picked up out of the water just as he was sinking and in an utter state of exhaustion. He was taken to Edinburgh Castle, where he was a prisoner for some days, and where he was very miserable and ill; he was then moved to Duffried Castle, North Wales, where he is happy and very well cared for, and where my family have now undertaken to look after him and provide him with all the comforts that are permitted.

.   .   .   .   .   .

KISSINGEN, *June* 26, 1915.—We arrived at Kissingen on June 20. It is a beautifully peaceful spot, but as there is no peace to be had anywhere, what difference does it really make whether the surroundings are pretty or not? In a place like this one misses the foreigner more than anywhere else, and the shopkeepers make no secret of how they loved and miss the English. The Russians, perhaps, were not so much loved, but were equally indispensable to the finances of the place. Five thousand Russians left last year when war was declared; one, when bidding adieu to his car-driver, who was

bemoaning the parting, replied tactfully and consolingly:
"Ah yes, you will see us again. This time next year
we shall be back again in Kissingen playing football with
the Germans' heads in the streets!"

There were not many people we knew doing the cure
there. A few days after I arrived Countess Henckel and
her sister Princess Löwenstein came, and I spent most
of my time with them; but we did a very half-hearted
cure, and agreed that in times like these cures begin and
end in the post office.

Baroness S—— and I became friends, and used to
drive and walk together every day. She told me of a
mirage she had seen which interested me enormously. It
was in the beginning of July 1914, when she and a number of friends were on a private yacht on their way to
Kiel for the regatta week. One evening the captain called
them all to the side of the ship and pointed out a mirage,
and she said they all stood transfixed with the beauty
of it. In the distance, all along the water, they saw
all sorts of beautiful hazy scenes and coloured mists of
every describable hue and shape floating along the top of
the water and gradually up into the sky, where they
disappeared. "A mirage is always the sign there is a
great war coming," said the captain, "and those
coloured shapeless mists are said to be the souls of the
fallen going up to heaven" They were struck with
the beauty of the idea, but laughed at the suggestion
of war. They then went on to Kiel, where they began
to enter into all the gaiety of the Kiel week, when
the telegram arrived announcing the murder of the Archduke and his wife. So perhaps the mirage had its
meaning after all.

This is by no means the only portent which has come
to my ears. A lady who has been staying in Westphalia
told me that she had made acquaintance with one of the
villagers, a sickly delicate man, who had spent his life
in studying Nature, and had made a fine collection of all
the different kinds of birds to be found in that part of

the world. He had shown her proudly all these specimens prepared by his own hands, the last of which was a small bird which she had never seen before.

"You won't know this bird, lady, for I never saw it before in my life, but the spring of last year, before the war, suddenly whole flocks of strange birds appeared here. I managed to catch this one, and looking in my books I found out what it was, and that these birds hardly ever appear in Germany. They come from the north, and only in great flocks, before a war."

I spoke to Dr. M——, who is a great authority on birds, and he too had noticed the Silk-tails or Chatterers here for the first time. He said there had always been an old tradition existing amongst the people that the Silk-tails were a foreboding of war.

BERLIN, *July* 12, 1915 —I left Kissingen on the 9th without much regret, except for saying good-bye to the Henckels, who had been true and good friends to me there. The day before I left I went on a pilgrimage of discovery, to see the Way of the Cross that I was told was on one of the mountains. It began at the bottom of one of the lower mountains, and the stone stations lay about 100 yards apart all the way up the winding mountain path. It was so picturesque.

As I wended my way upwards I now and again came upon a little cross hidden in the grass, and on reading it found that they were graves of soldiers who had fallen there in the year '66 during the battle of Kissingen. "Here lie two brave Bavarians and three Prussian soldiers," etc., etc. These were enemies then; and now, not long after, are fighting as friends.

On reaching the summit of the hill I sat down on a little rustic seat below the Calvary, and hidden in the grass by my side was another little solitary grave and wooden cross with the inscription "Here lies a brave but unknown hero, who died fighting," and then vividly before my eyes came the picture of that other battlefield in Flanders, and what that will be like in years to come; how many such crosses of unknown heroes will lie there hidden in the grass, and what strangers will pass them by, and what impression it will make on them!

BERLIN, *August* 1, 1915.—Another month has passed away, and we seem no nearer Peace than we were at the beginning, except that in the papers to-day they say that England now realizes that Russia is useless for offensive purposes, and that the Pope has written an Address to all the belligerent Powers appealing to their chivalry; and as up till now he has always said he would not make a move until the right moment presented itself, this gives some little hope that behind the scenes some one has made a move.

The American Note crisis is still the great subject of discussion, and in yesterday's paper the heading was "Renewal of Submarine Warfare," which seems to mean that Germany is snapping her fingers at America.

A new light was put to me on the subject yesterday by a German officer, who told me that really it was England's interest to keep America from going to war with Germany, as directly she did so she would probably have to fight Japan, and therefore would have to keep all her ammunition, supplies, ships, etc., for herself, and could no longer assist England to the extent she had been doing.

We had a very interesting talk with a Lieut. Pauley, a wounded German officer here, who came to dine with us. He was one of the exchanged prisoners returned from England, so I pumped him with questions, and he spoke most enthusiastically of the kind treatment he had received whilst in hospital in England.

WILDBAD, *Thursday, August* 5, 1915.—It is said that the outer forts near Warsaw have been taken and that at one spot the Russian army is nearly surrounded.

The Russians have been obliged to send reinforcements from their Southern army, thus leaving a weak spot for the Austrians to try to break through.

The Germans have taken Mitau, a town in East Prussia.

On the West there is silence, except it is said the English took a few houses and a trench near Hooge, but these are believed to have been retaken, and many dead were found in the trench, and some prisoners taken.

G—— has gone for a long walk up into the mountains with a friend, so I have been spending my day typing letters about the missing.

At three o'clock suddenly all the bells in the town began to ring, the band struck up the usual refrain of "Deutschland," the hall porter appeared on the roof to put up the Würtemburg flag, and all the people suddenly burst forth singing the national anthem; so I very soon realized that something unexpected had happened, and am told that Warsaw has fallen. It is great news, as it was not expected to fall for another ten days.

I try to enter into the rejoicings, but inwardly my heart is heavy, and my thoughts flew quickly and selfishly, I suppose, to the question, How will it affect England? I realize only too quickly that it means that thousands of German troops will soon be released to go to the Western Front, and will swell the forces trying to break their way through to Calais.

DRESDEN, *September* 1, 1915.—More German victories in Russia. Can there be any more forts to fall, any more Russians left to be captured, and more big guns and ammunition to be taken? Judging by the figures in the papers there cannot be many. But a few millions more or less in the Russian army does not seem to make the slightest impression on it. I read to-day some of the official statistics from a Russian source, in which it says that the losses in the Russian army since the beginning have been five and a half millions. In the same paragraph they add that they have just raised a new army of a million men, and although they admit their present reverses they seem in no way discouraged by them.

.   .   .   .   .   .

A few days ago I went to the Opera with the Landgraf of Hesse and Baron and Baroness Schenk and her sister. The Landgraf, who is blind, is connected by marriage with the Emperor, and with the Queen of Greece and Princess Margaret of Hesse. He feels the war and the estrangement with England and his English relations terribly, as he had been accustomed to spend six months every year in England, part of the time in London and part at Eastbourne, where the Queen of Greece and her sister also were. They were actually there when war broke out, and had to hurry off home, like so many other Royalties.

GLÄSERSDORF, *September* 11, 1915.—From Dresden we came on to Gläsersdorf, Count Ballestrem's castle in Silesia, a beautiful place, so quiet and peaceful, except that one is reminded of the war at every turn by the absence of men servants, of the master of the house, of motor-cars, and by the family being in mourning for the brother who was killed in June.

As I sit at my window I can watch the prisoners working on the farm. They have twenty-four Frenchmen and one Russian as farm labourers. The Frenchmen look so funny working away in their bright red trousers; it seems cruel to have sent them to the front in such a conspicuous get-up.

.   .   .   .   .

News has come this evening that the German army are now only 100 miles from Petersburg It is wonderful certainly, as they still maintain they do not intend to go there. What then is their object in this speedy advance?

Lord Kitchener in his opening speech in the House, which is reprinted in the German papers to-day, sounds confident and hopeful. As to the Russian retreat he takes the line that the German advance into Russia is not really so fine or rapid as people think, that they are now only advancing two miles a day instead of five miles, as they did at first. Of course, those who read this speech here say, "Sour grapes! Doesn't he wish he could advance two yards on German territory!"

ECKERSDORF, *September* 1915.—We are still on the move, and are now staying for a few days with Count and Countess Magnis, and a whole housefull of children. There are 18 in all, including the visiting cousins.

The chief subject of discussion is the feeling between Austria and Germany. Princess Starhemberg, who is here, is Austrian, and is always ready with her bristles out in defence of everything Austrian; and on the other hand the Germans of the party take credit for all the victories without admitting that they had any assistance whatever from Austria. One cannot help being slightly amused to notice how the point of the whole war is forgotten in the greater interest of internal jealousies. I asked Princess Starhemberg one day whether there was much hatred against England in Austria. "Well, when we have time to, yes, we do hate them; but we are so busy hating Italy and criticizing Germany that we don't think of much else at present."

ECKERSDORF, *September* 24, 1915.—We went to lunch with Prince and Princess Radolin in Breslau, and there indeed we found a different spirit and different views from any we had met for a long time in Germany. Nothing but downright hate and abuse of Germany and the German authorities, and, being people with a grievance, their bitterness was all the greater. It is, of course, difficult to form an opinion, but one could not help feeling pity for them in their treatment.

Prince Radolin had been Ambassador at Paris, had been one of the favourites at the Court in Berlin, and was also on intimate terms with the late Empress Frederick and with Queen Victoria; but since then, evidently owing to Court jealousies and intrigues, his and his wife's reputation had been gradually nibbled at and undermined. Besides the discourteous way in which he had been turned out of his post as Ambassador, he and she had both, at various times, received small insults from various Royalties and officially from the German Court. Therefore they were ready to air their grievances on the smallest provocation.

A German regiment and staff were billeted on them, the head of which was General Bernhardi, now a well-known General. He was one day abusing the French to a quite unnecessary degree. Princess Radolin burst out into defence of them. He turned to her and said, "Madame, you seem to have some French sympathies"; at which she, most indiscreetly, flew into a passion and said, "Well, of course I have French sympathies. My mother was French, and as I was ambassadress in Paris for so many years I have many good friends there." He did not say much in reply, but reported her to headquarters, and from that moment all sorts of petty tyrannies and underhand watching began. One day they found the telephone room in their own castle, where they were then living, locked, and when she asked the reason, a young officer answered her in a most insulting manner, telling her that she had been suspected of tampering with the telephone, and of having given warning to some Poles. Imagine her indignation!

Her letters were also being privately opened, and in consequence of an indiscreet reference to military matters she was put under police supervision. She was not allowed to receive or write a single letter, even to her husband, without its being read, nor was she allowed to leave Breslau without special permission; and she was even asked to return all her orders and decorations received during the term of her husband's office. This is such an unprecedented insult or disgrace that no German would ever get over it. (The decorations have since been returned to her.)'

Prince Radolin up to then had tried to keep a dignified silence, but at this last insult to his wife he turned, as only a deeply wounded man can turn, and became even more bitter than his wife. It seems so sad for an old man of 70, who has spent his life working for his country, to think that the last few years should be spent thus!

ECKERSDORF, *September* 28, 1915.—There is a feeling of depression about every one to-day, and of wonder at the silence from the Western Front. Has there been an offensive? Could there have been a reverse? A sudden silence like this generally means that something is not going as it was expected to.

Many things have made us begin to wonder. First, in the official telegram of yesterday it was said that the Germans had been obliged to evacuate two front trenches after hard fighting against the English, and that there were fearful losses on both sides. To admit this in an official telegram means that there must have been a decided reverse, as small defeats are unmentioned and ignored.

To add to this, several men in the village, who had returned on short leave, were hastily summoned back to the West immediately. Then a letter from a doctor to a friend in the village says that things are not going at all well in the West, and finally a telegram has just been received from Count Franz Magnis, brother to our host, saying, "Safe and well." As he never telegraphs, and as he and his regiment have not been near the fighting line for ten months, this causes much consternation, as they know it means that his regiment has suddenly been called into action.

ECKERSDORF, *October* 2, 1915.—Our presentiment was right then; there was a great battle going on on the 28th, and the Allies were nearer breaking through in the West than they have ever yet been, and are now occupying the third row of German trenches.

They seem to have made one enormous offensive the

whole way along the line.   There was incessant drum
firing (120 a minute) for 60 hours continuously from
the French and English lines, and the noise alone sent
many out of their minds.   Then they used poisonous
gases, which the Germans were not prepared for, and had
therefore not got their masks ready, and the losses in
consequence from this alone were enormous.

The Germans really were taken by surprise this time.
I think they had for so long looked upon the English and
French talk of a big offensive as nothing more than a
threat, that they had begun to think it would never really
come off.   But it did, and on so gigantic a scale as to
surprise even the Germans.

It is said the French had 25 army corps, the English
23, and Germany 23 engaged at the front.   It is also
said here that the Commander of the 8th German Army
Corps made some mistake which occasioned a terrible
loss of life, and he has been removed from his command
in consequence, and that there had been a fearful row
between him and Prince Rupprecht of Bavaria, who had
sent hastily for reinforcements, but there were none ready
to send him.

One colonel, who has just returned here since, says his
regiment alone lost 70 per cent in a few hours, and the
few stragglers returning wounded, caked with blood and
mud, were a most pitiable sight to see.   The losses on
the German side were 20,000 prisoners and 40,000 dead
and wounded.   The names are only just beginning to
come out, and the suspense in consequence is terrible to
witness.   Germany is still confident of success, but their
anxiety everywhere is beginning to be felt, although they
will not put it into words.

.   .   .   `   .   .

In a quiet way the shortness of supplies is beginning
to show   The price of milk was increased on October 1,
and it is said that soon very little butter will be allowed
to be used.   It seems a funny thing to have run short,
before bread, for instance, but it is said that milk will be

scarce; firstly, because too many calves were killed in the spring, and also because the cows could not be fed properly.

Another thing that they are getting anxious about, although they would not own it if you asked them, is material for making ammunition. A circular has been sent round to every house in Silesia and in Austria, and I think here, ordering an inventory to be made of all copper, brass, etc., that they have in chandeliers and on roofs and everywhere   It is pathetic to see the house-holders making lists of their household gods, wondering sadly when the moment will come when they receive the order to tear them down and have them melted into ammunition.

.   .   .   .   .   .

BERLIN, *October* 1915.—At dinner last night we met a Mexican minister who had been to Paris, Brussels, and other places, and who told us that he did not at all think the Balkan question at an end; that England would leave no stone unturned to get Greece and Roumania, and that he did not consider the neutrality of Greece by any means so safely settled as the Germans do.

He did not agree with the German view either, that the war will be decided with the Balkan campaign. He said that England and France were so strong in the West, and had made such tremendous preparations, that they meant to sit there till doomsday rather than give in, whatever Germany might do elsewhere

He then talked of the terrible verdict that had been passed on the three spies in Brussels. He told me that Brussels was like a smouldering furnace, and that this act of cruelty has excited people almost as much as the *Lusitania.*

.   .   .   .   .   .

A few days ago I went to tea with the wife of Prince Christian of Hesse, whose mother had just got back from America. She, Mrs. Rogers, had remained some hours at Kirkwall on the way, where the ship was held up by the British. So she had much to tell us of all the examination of papers and questions they had to undergo before they were allowed to continue their passage.

Her daughter also showed us a very interesting snapshot photo her husband (a naval lieutenant) had taken at Zeebrugge, of a Zeppelin being fired at by three English Dreadnoughts, and the photo showed it just falling into the sea, broken and ruined. He himself had an appointment on the coast there, and he said that particular spot was bombarded by English ships almost daily, and they do much harm.

.   .   .   .   .   .

As to the actual war news, it is difficult to say anything the last few days. All the talk is now whether Greece is going to be drawn in, and also Roumania.

Bulgaria has evidently quite decided to throw in her lot with Germany and Austria, and this seems to cut the Allies off from using Roumania, even if she did decide to go with them, unless Greece is persuaded to change her intention of keeping firmly neutral. For the last few days she seems quite bent on keeping out of it. Wise country!

BERLIN, *October* 11, 1915.—There is once more one of the usual rumours of peace by Christmas; but this time, they say, with more reason. I wonder whether one can allow oneself to begin to have a gleam of hope. It is based on the fact that the English are withdrawing their troops from the Dardanelles, and had attempted a landing at Salonika. But as, so far, the Greeks have shown most decidedly that they do not intend allowing that, it looks as if there is nothing left for the English to do. If they cannot get to Nisch, as the railway has been destroyed there, they are cut off.

Perhaps they will bring all their troops to the West Front, and what appalling loss of life there will once more be there if they do. I believe, if they and the French went on long enough, they could break through, but the loss of life would be terrific.

One knows that when the Peace negotiations begin, one scratch of the pen will settle those few yards of territory more decidedly, and with much less suffering, than all this fighting can do. So why not do it that way now? The heart for victory is taken out of every one on all sides.

The losses the last ten days at Loos must have been stupendous on both sides, and bits of information about it begin to come in. An officer told us last night that one regiment had had every single officer in it killed during the one day's fight, and that the regiment in front of them had been absolutely wiped out, and their dead bodies had filled a trench, so that the incoming regiment had to fight standing on these dead bodies the whole of one day.

Dr. Ohnesorg, the American Embassy doctor, said he had yesterday visited some wounded at Bayreuth. Among them were three wounded Englishmen, one belonging to the Black Watch, one to the East Surrey, and one to the Royal Engineers, and the description they gave of these days' fighting at Loos was appalling. One of them said his regiment had had to follow a Kent regiment, which had been completely mown down, not one single man of it left standing   Another of them said he had lain for three nights and days outside a trench, where he fell when wounded. Shortly after he had received his wound, a German doctor had crawled out to him and bandaged him up, and from that moment he had lain under incessant artillery fire, and the English troops and Germans had swayed backwards and forwards over near where he lay, the ground changing hands four times during those three days as the waves of victory varied. He had a haunted, anxious look in his eyes, they said, which made one sad to see; but otherwise he was comfortable and well cared for, and was in a large ward with French and coloured wounded prisoners, all from those recent fights.

BERLIN, *October* 14, 1915.—I must note down two interesting stories I have been told to-day, of two German officer prisoners of war just returned The one officer arrived a day or two ago with the latest batch of wounded, who have been passed by the doctors as no longer any use for military service, having proved to be deaf, dumb, and blind from shock. On arriving here he very soon began to talk, and said that he had faked being deaf, dumb, and blind for seven months continuously, and that no one had detected he was shamming.

The other story was of a naval officer, also just arrived back, who had been one of those who jumped overboard from the *Dresden* when she was sunk by the British. He had been picked up by a Swedish vessel, where he passed himself off as an English sailor, and was taken by them to Sweden and then on to England, where he passed himself off as a Swede, and was employed as a common dockyard hand in the London docks for four months. He then returned to Sweden, and from there got back to Germany, and is now once more established in his position as a German naval lieutenant.

BERLIN, *October* 23, 1915.—At the beginning of the week we dined at Excellency Solf's (the Colonial Minister), where we, as usual, met a great many interesting people. Baron Jagow, the Secretary for Foreign Affairs, took me in to dinner, and as he is personally acquainted with many well-known Englishmen, we soon found that we had mutual acquaintances.

He said that he had heard a rumour of the resignation of Sir Edward Grey, and then went on to tell me that in his opinion Sir Edward is innocent of much that he is accused of. He considers that the "villain of the piece" is Sir Arthur Nicholson, but that he is cute enough to keep behind the scenes. Suddenly, in the middle of the dinner, he turned to me, remarking: "But is there nobody who will shoot Lord Northcliffe? He is his own country's worst enemy, as well as ours. And he is more answerable for all this bloodshed and carnage than any other single individual throughout the world."

After dinner my husband had an interesting conversation with Helfferich, the Finance Minister, who was the hero of the evening, as all were complimenting him on the success of the second war-loan. He told my husband that he could not help being amused at seeing himself caricatured in the English papers as "Helfferich the pickpocket," and of having been accused of docking the salaries of the poor.

At first sight this may seem to have been the case, and probably refers to the different Sparkassen that contributed their deposits to the war-loan. It is Germany's system to use money that she must pay back to herself, so to say. Of course the poor people get 5 per cent for the war-loan money, whereas "Sparkasse" deposits only pay 3 per cent, and the Government is naturally security enough from their point of view.

But the chief topic of conversation throughout the evening was the diplomatic success over the Balkan question, and every one was congratulating Herr v. Jagow on the clever way he and his colleagues had "pulled it off." And even I personally could not help feeling pleased that they were coming in for a little praise at last, as the poor Foreign Office has really had nothing but "kicks" for such a long time past.

But even whilst listening to all the laudatory remarks, I could not help thinking of a conversation I had heard only that afternoon in a military circle: "Yes, we can let the Foreign Office enjoy this triumph for once, but we know nothing succeeds like success, and that it is in reality our great military achievements that have influenced Bulgaria's choice, and (maybe) will influence still more important countries before we have done!"

After dinner, conversation was about the copper collection. One lady said she had sent all the copper she had, and was sorry to have to part with her lovely copper kettle. Another said hers had been sent back as not wanted at present.

I ventured to suggest that the scarcity of copper might bring about an earlier end to the war. Cries of indignation arose. Germany's organization required this collection of copper, just as the so-called "Brotkarten" (bread tickets) were issued to control the amount of bread consumed. They only wanted to see how much copper they could lay hands on, and had so much already from kettles, pots, pans, etc., that the supply would last them three years. Even the telephone wires have been reckoned on if it should be necessary!

My heart whispered that this must be "bluff." It is an interesting sight, though, to see cartloads of old pots and kettles and candlesticks, door-handles, chandeliers, etc., being driven along the street, and a poor woman or schoolboy carrying a copper kettle or brass lamp to the collecting offices to be weighed and paid for. For the Government pay well, and many people are tempted to be quick about getting rid of old copper for a good price. I heard a man the other day say that if he could get 100 tons of copper to sell, he would be a rich man for life!

Then we talked of the terrors of submarine warfare. One officer present described how his submarine had been caught in one of the English net traps. There he and the crew had to remain for hours under water, like rats in a trap; no possibility of escape and a death of starvation. They eventually managed to break through, but many don't. He said they could live for seven hours below the sea before dying of suffocation, and shuddered, poor man, even then as he spoke, at his recollections.

.   .   .   .   .   .

The same evening, my brother-in-law, Gustav, dined with us, on his way back from Warsaw. And we made him tell us about his life there.

He said that it was very little different from here,

there being hotels as luxurious as the "Esplanade," with music every evening, and that it is only outside the town that one realizes what the Russians have done. They have killed all the animals and removed everything out of the houses, even down to the brass handles on the doors; everything that might be of any possible use to the Germans.   On my asking him, "How about the inhabitants—can you go about in the streets without being met with a look of loathing and hatred, every time they pass you?"   "No," he answered quaintly in his broken English, "it is not as bad as that; they are as one might say, 'civil, but not enthusiastic.' "

A few days after that I went to the American Embassy.   Princess Braganza (American, with an Austrian husband) and another American lady with a German husband were there.   So, with my English self, we were rather a mixed party, and war conversation on these occasions is supposed to be avoided.   Nevertheless the question of the American Note cropped up as usual, and the Ambassadress said that if ever she heard the words "American Note" or "Ammunition" mentioned after the war, she would probably "shriek"!

Then the other American lady joined in with, "Yes, what a dreadful time we have had all this summer, and just as we were beginning to feel a little 'cosy' on the subject of the *Lusitania,* those old Germans must go and sink another whole boat-load of Americans."

I could not help smiling at her husband at this very pointed remark, which was such a proof of the saying that "Americans step in where angels fear to tread."

BERLIN, *October* 1915.—I have not so far ventured to utter my views about Miss Cavell, for the simple reason that if I once began I should say too much, and should probably be too candid on the subject.   I think it one of the most dastardly deeds of the whole war, and I am not by any means alone in this opinion even in this city itself. It is extraordinary that the German Government (*i.e.* the military authorities) should continue to ruin their cause by making repeated diplomatic mistakes like this. They argue that she was guilty, that she was a spy, that she had been smuggling dynamite to blow up bridges, that she had been signalling to the English troops where to land, that she had a regular code of signals with fliers; but, I ask you, can one woman do all those marvellous things, especially in a town like Brussels? I know what it is like even here; if one sneezes out of tune one is accused of signalling to the enemy; how, therefore, could it be done in an occupied town like Brussels, where every second man is a detective?

Maybe she was guilty, but of what exactly? Of helping wounded soldiers of any nationality to hide, to get into a place of safety, perhaps to get across the frontier back to their own country. What woman with a woman's heart would not do this? Would we have any woman of our acquaintance act otherwise? Even if it were the act of a spy, will the Germans *never* learn the lesson of "Mercy to season Justice"?

And then, why was it done in such a hurry? And why were all the others forgiven, and only she executed? Was it, as it is hinted here, due to private and personal malice because she was English? All those who were forgiven were of another nationality. Well, it is a blot; in fact, another blot, to be quite exact; and as a German officer said sadly to me to-day, when the war is over, and in the years to come, however distant, these blots are the things that will be remembered and go down to history, and all the brave deeds and wonderful feats that our troops and armies in the field have done, and all the many individual acts of heroism will be forgotten, and only such episodes as these will stand out.

The Emperor is as usual getting the entire blame for the crime in all the neutral and other papers, but it is probably true, as they say, that he was really in ignorance of it until it was too late. It is declared emphatically, that on hearing of the sentence he wired ordering a postponement for further inquiry. It is also said that the Empress received a telegram the evening before from the King of Spain, begging her to use her influence, and only replied that if women behave as men they must be punished as men. I can hardly believe it, but it is a fact that it is the Empress who dislikes England and the English, rather than the Emperor, whose English "interest," as they call it, has aroused jealousy here ever since the beginning of the war.

    .   .   .   ,   .   .

There are so many rumours current as to who really is to blame for the sentence of death being carried out on Miss Cavell, that I hardly know whom to believe. Until now, I always thought it was Bissing who had insisted on it; but I have heard from officers who were there at the time, that it was not so, that both Bissing and the Kaiser were against it, and that the latter even made use of his prerogative for mercy, and sent a pardon at the last hour, but the messenger arrived half an hour too late.

It seems she had boasted too much at her trial of having helped English and Belgian soldiers over the frontier. Baron Lancken, who wished to acquit her, tried to make her speak in her own defence, which she refused to do, and thus she sealed her own fate. Major Sauberzweig, who confirmed the judgment as head of the court-martial, is accused of having hurried on the execution, in spite of the fact of Baron Bissing pleading for her acquittal in Berlin at the same time, so the onus of her death must fall on him.

BERLIN, *October 29*, 1915.—The most interesting conversation I have had to-day was with Prince Munster, who told us that the hopes of peace were all shattered once more. He related that an Englishman had arrived in Hamburg, having got through with an American pass, and went to see Ballin (the Hamburg-American Line manager), who has so many English friends. In an unofficial way he volunteered the remark that Grey and Asquith sent their greetings to Ballin and wished to know his views as to the prospects of peace. If, for instance, Germany would enter into negotiations on the basis of giving up Belgium, England, he suggested, would be ready to do the same.

The answer was, "Das glaube ich!" which is about the same as, "I've no doubt she would." And there the matter dropped.

BERLIN, *October* 1915.—I have got some more news about Roger Casement. He came here to-day from Munich for a week, and I saw him for a moment. People here have very mixed opinions about him. Some think he is an English spy and only pretending to be a rebel, whereas others laugh at him as at a man who has failed.

He tried, as usual, to talk me round about Ireland. I told him Ireland to me was like a little terrier biting at the heels of two great mastiffs. "Why," I said, "if he loved Ireland so, had he come to Germany?" He wanted to stop the recruiting, was his reply But that, I told him, could have been done more effectively by having remained in Ireland or having gone to America. "Why stop it?" I asked him. "The Irish had proved such splendid soldiers and had even won an entire battle by themselves."

Then his pride in the Irish soldier showed itself, proving that in reality he does not know what he wants. But when he begins airing his opinions in too self-satisfied a manner, it makes me want to repeat to him the words I had heard lately from the lips of a German lady about him. "If you ask me," she said, "what I think of Roger Casement, I think him a blot on the earth!"

.   .   .   .   .   .

I happened too to meet a lady who knows the man who invented poison gas. His wife, it appears, was a

doctor of chemistry too, and they used to work together.
When the war came, and she saw what use was being
made of her inventions, she committed suicide.   Her
husband, though, is proud of the valuable service he is
doing for the Fatherland, and says he is even proud that
he was called upon to sacrifice his wife to the cause.
How different human beings are!

BERLIN, *October 29*, 1915.—Prince Alfred Salm dined
at the "Esplanade" the other evening. He was interesting
to talk to about Poland, whence he is just back. He is
the head of the Warsaw Nurses' Association, and organ-
izes everything there. I asked him whether he associated
with the Poles at all. He said the Polish ladies were
most amiable, and invite the Germans to smart dinners,
and are very charming to them. Then after dinner they
begin to touch on politics and think the Germans won't
see through it. They have only one wish, and that is
to know who is going to be king of Poland!

Old Count Metternich was there too, much flattered
at the rumour that he was going to be made Ambassador
at Constantinople. He had retired from public service
after leaving London, and every one looked upon him
rather as having been put on the shelf, and too old, and
so on, so that he was pleased at having suddenly been
unearthed.

He has since really been appointed. He was telling
me about his journey with Solf to The Hague. He met
ever so many old acquaintances from England there,
and was deeply hurt at being cut by them all.

BERLIN, *October* 1915.—So English submarines are
busy in the Baltic, and ships are bombarding the Bulgarian coast. Is the navy coming out at last? I can't
deny that I have been rather disappointed in the English
navy, and the Germans are as much astonished at the
little the navy has done as they are at the unexpected
size, ability, and bravery of the English army.

I hear the scarcity of cotton may influence the fabrication of ammunition. It makes my hopes for peace rise to think of it. As Prince Munster says · "If you want to see Countess Blücher smile, tell her the Germans are running short of ammunition!"

Personally I wish the world would run out of ammunition for ever.

.   .   .   .   .   .

A scare has broken out again among the Americans. The feeling to-day and yesterday has been almost as bad as after the *Lusitania*. The German attachés are not to be given a safe escort home, which is a thing unprecedented in history, it appears, and the Germans are furious about it. These attachés are supposed to have instigated others to blow up ammunition factories, but the Americans cannot lay their fingers on an actual proof.

Anyway, the attachés are to return, and no guarantee for safety! There were 150 dining here yesterday, and each single person took a different view.

Ten days later.—It is amusing to read all these discussions and at the same time be sitting with the heroes of it at the same table. Herr von Papen, from Washington, is here now at the "Esplanade" and was introduced to us last night. He says all the stories were much exaggerated. It is true that his cheque-book was taken away from him; but most of the letters were pure invention.

I was interested too at meeting Mr. and Mme. Dumba on their return from America. (Dumba, it will be remembered, had given his letters about the German ammunition factory workers to Archibald to take to Austria, and as it came out, America asked for him to be removed.)

They dined here at the "Esplanade." Dumba seemed to feel things rather; but it was quite evident that Mme. Dumba was delighted at finding herself so notorious on her return.

.   .   .   .   .   .

I overheard an interesting remark to-day. They were speaking of the taking of Warsaw "What is there to celebrate?" said a young officer. "We had to ride over the bodies of our comrades to enter the town."

I believe this young officer was one of the first to enter; but I remember at the time of the fall, each young man we met from that part had been *THE FIRST,* and it amused us to keep account of these firsts. We got to very near 100!

.   .   .   .   .   .

A German friend, Baron H——, who had been living in England for many years, told me that though he knew nothing of soldiering, when war was declared he had had to leave his office-desk in London, and come straight out to join his regiment. He and his regiment (cavalry) were sent straight to Belgium, and for the first three weeks of the war they just rode about scouting. One night, after a 36 hours' continuous ride, just as they were lying down to a most welcome sleep, they were roused and ordered out to take a village. They set out wearily and very reluctantly, and rode into this village, clearing it and driving all before them. *Months after, they were told that they had taken part in the now famous battle of Mons.*

How different is a battle, how different is war, from what we "stay-at-homes" picture it!

BERLIN, *November* 15, 1915.—This morning the English papers are full of the butter riots in Berlin. The accounts are, of course, exaggerated. There is absolutely no question of "200 people dead"; one or two slightly hurt is all that can be faithfully reported. Absolute silence on the subject is imposed here, and not a word is allowed to slip into the daily papers. I suppose they think this is the best way to suppress further disturbance.

What really happened was the following. About 200 women trooped down the Linden, calling out "Frieden,

Frieden" (peace), and at once 150 mounted police appeared on the scene with drawn swords to disperse the crowd. This they soon succeeded in doing, though they are supposed to have said themselves that they hated such drastic measures towards women, and a common soldier on leave said that if the infantry at the front were to hear that their wives were being treated thus in their absence, whether they demanded butter or anything else, they would refuse to continue fighting.

Anyway, on the day of the Reichskanzler's speech the town was prepared for a regular riot. They had closed the gates of the Linden, and taken all precautions, but, strangely enough, hardly anything occurred. I have since heard that the crowds were immediately met by mounted and other police at the gates, and so many of the foremost women were taken prisoners that the others dispersed. The women have been sentenced to a fortnight to three weeks' imprisonment.

The disappointment at the Reichskanzler's speech is very great—every one expected something tremendous from him, something that would alter the aspect of things. And he has said nothing. So people shrug their shoulders, and general depression is in the air. I, personally, do not see what he could have said, unless he had openly declared that Germany will give up Belgium. Every German now says, "Of course, we are ready to give up Belgium"; and the English say, "We'll make peace if Germany will give up Belgium." So there they are facing one another, but no one will take an actual step towards opening negotiations.

Berlin, *November* 1915.—A friend just returned from England tells me that the Zeppelin raids have aroused England's anger tremendously. The English will never show fear of any kind, but their faith in the impossibility of any enemy reaching London has been shaken, and a certain tradition has been broken and every Englishman is roused.

At the same time there is a lighter side to the raids. In the fashionable shops you can see nightdresses and dressing-gowns advertised as "Zepp nighties," "Robes for Raids," etc.

This to the German mind appears the zenith of superficiality, frivolity, and English arrogance (arrogance in their belief that nothing can touch them). They are much too ignorant of the English character to realize that an Englishman (or woman) might feel a pang of fear, but with his last breath he would say, "I don't care."

The English could not have chosen a more effective way of showing the enemy the uselessness of these raids than by jeering at them.

.   .   .   .   .   .

The pathetic tales one hears wherever one goes make the heart bleed. A poor woman in the train the other day was holding up her hand and counting the fingers on it slowly—one, two, three, four, five—over and over again. The passengers gradually began to smile at her, until at last the man sitting next to her looked up and said simply, "Don't laugh at my wife, ladies and gentlemen. I am taking her to the asylum. Her wits are gone. She has lost her five sons—all killed in action."

Another tragic story is that of a boy who felt like a wild beast caught in a trap when forced into active service. He went to the front, almost lost his wits, and wrote distracted letters home. His parents, beyond themselves with despair, left no stone unturned to get him sent home. At last their petition was granted; they knew their boy could come, and on that very day came a wire from the front: "Your son has committed suicide."

Stories of this kind are not few and far between, and my heart cries out that it is natural, for those who are truly civilized cannot lightly set out to kill their fellow-creatures.

What happens when they do, shows how war brings out the brute in man. Men in Flanders are sent into the houses to get firewood; furniture is taken, boards from the flooring. "Why, then, of course, let us smash up the whole show," they say. They pass their bayonets through the pictures, and destroy whatever is useless. Crockery is taken along to be used first; after meals, when the cups and plates are dirty, it is easier to throw them out of the window than to go in search of water to wash them. There are plenty more cups and plates for to-morrow in another house!

No German soldiers may force the inhabitants to give them food without a receipt that is to be as good as cash after the war. So out they come, the poor Flemish women and Polish men. They offer milk, poultry, cheese, and the soldiers willingly give them bits of paper with a few words which they treasure up as carefully as if they were worth their weight in gold. The words on the paper are usually the following: "A thrashing to this old woman for her excellent cheese"; "Three blows to the bringer of this paper for his fine eggs," and so on.

They do not mean to be brutal, these German common soldiers: it is their idea of a good practical joke. "Who," they say, "is to pay all this after the war? We shall not. Their own Government will not. It is all a farce; let us do it in style!"

BERLIN, *November* 1915.—Germany will be a very difficult country to live in after the war, as, whether she wins or loses, the Socialists are going to revolt—*I* feel quite sure of that. It is the German custom to nip everything in the bud, and to use such drastic measures that whatever goes on in the soul of a man or party never rises to the surface, but is left fermenting in suppressed silence.

It seems now, though, that the war is going to alter this state of affairs. The tremendous enthusiasm at the beginning for a struggle that each German felt was not of his desiring, but imposed on him, and which called forth all the loyalty as well as all the military instincts of the race, left no room for discontent or contradiction.

As the German army passed from victory to victory the people were lifted off their feet with surprise at their own strength, and all party discussion seemed drowned in one great unity. What was said by the English Press about the revolt of the Socialists was absolutely wrong —Germany was united as perhaps never before.

But now the war has been going on for a year and a half, and it has not been possible to suppress the losses, the suffering, the horrors. The long lists of casualties have developed into great thick volumes; more and more men are being called up; women are realizing the enormous burden imposed upon them. They have to do the men's work as well as their own, and when they have earned their pay it all goes into the pockets of others who sell them food at enormous prices. Naturally they begin more than ever to say: "Why should we work, starve, send our men out to fight? What is it all going to bring us? More work, more poverty, our men cripples, our homes ruined What is it all for? What do we care whether we have a bit more land added on to our big Germany? We had enough land. We'd rather fight for a more just division of the goods of this earth. For whether we obtain land or money for the 'Fatherland' after this war, *we* shall not see any change in our lives; the wealth will not come our way. The State which called upon us to fight cannot even give us decent food, does not treat our men as human beings, but as so many screws in the great machine of the German army. If one screw drops out or gets bent, there are plenty more; we cannot stop to pick up the lost ones, or straighten the crooked."

A young officer returning from a fight in which he had had to watch his men being literally mown down by machine-guns, went up to Headquarters to report. There he found the highest staff authorities sitting at a banquet and discussing the war in a flippant way. "I could have killed them all," was his remark. And men going out to the front after recovering from their wounds have been heard to say: "We've been hurt once and are half cripples; they think it better to send us back as 'cannon fodder'; we can get killed off and no loss to the State."

Everywhere you can hear it murmured: "We are forced to keep silence now; but wait till the war is over, then our turn will come."

How must a mother feel whose only son is in daily danger, when, going into some hotel like the "Esplanade," she sees people feasting in splendour, smartly dressed, talking and laughing, and in every way living in the lap of luxury? Will she feel anything but hatred for these thoughtless, indifferent creatures? Will she not say: "Is this what we are sacrificing everything for? Is this the great country, the culture that is to redeem the world?"

What about the way the officers live, when not in action? Pheasant served on slices of pine-apple, with champagne, is a mere item in a long menu, whilst others are starving. The bread they get is so hard that they cannot bite it, and often there is not even that. The injustice of all this is bound to make them cry out for equality and fairness, not that they should be sent out to fight other men, called enemies, who are just in the same plight as themselves.

The authorities act the whole time. They keep up appearances, revel in victories, praise their organization, and never a word is breathed amongst them about the sadness of the losses, the sufferings of friend and foe alike.

.   .   .   .   .

Germany with all her mental and physical progress has suffered this military autocracy for a hundred years. Maybe she will now wake up to realize that this is not the right government. How will the people's awakening manifest itself? Will they wreak vengeance on those who are really to blame, or will they make all of us aristocrats responsible for what we could not avert?

Will a new Radicalism arise—not destructive this time,

but constructive and creative? Will they realize that
might is not always right? That a clear vision, sound
principles, and work side by side with one's brother man
are what is lacking in this up-to-date civilization that has
fallen so low, and is bleeding to death now where the
Great Powers are demonstrating their methods on the
battlefields of Europe?

BERLIN, *December* 1915.—In referenec to what I have
last written, a man looking in at the "Esplanade" the
other night, his face pressed against the glass of the door,
showed an expression of hatred and disgust at the elegant
public within at their supper, in which there were few
signs of the frugality expected in times such as these.
How well I can understand this, though; or that a man
returning from the front, where he has seen all the horrors of war, when meeting a lady in the Berlin streets going to some concert or theatre, should try to waylay her
and impress her with a sense of her wickedness. It must
strike them as frivolity in the extreme, and heartless
wantonness; and yet—"life must go on as usual"!

Disappointment about the expected response to the
Reichskanzler's speech from England is great here, and
hatred of the English is surging up again. There is no
doubt the speech was prepared with the intention of holding out the olive branch. And now?—England answers
by ridiculing the offer. To them it seems as though
England were like a gambler who has lost all, but hopes
to regain his losses and win besides by a continuation of
the gamble.

Is it that really? Or is there more going on behind
the scenes? Does Germany ask too much for the
other Powers to be able to accept without sacrifices that
cannot be made?

Germany says she will not keep Belgium; England
says she will make peace if Germany will give up Belgium.
And yet no attempt at a truce and negotiations is made—

at least so it appears to us who have only censored newspapers to satisfy our thirst for knowledge, and a word
dropped discreetly or indiscreetly here and there.

If only the Emperor were able to enforce his will!
He is so terribly misunderstood and misjudged His
position is too difficult, as he is always being suspected
of pro-English feeling.

He has done two great things lately—I only wish
people knew. He has forbidden the air raids over
London, and has tried to oppose von Tirpitz's submarine
warfare. I know for a fact that von Tirpitz has had to
resign and is not in favour. He declared the German
navy could only be effective by submarine warfare and
had to resign practically by order of the Emperor.

.   .   .   .   .   .

A lady I know was telling me of her experiences in a
"Stadtbahn" railway carriage the other day. There
was a poor Galician peasant girl who couldn't speak a
word of German, and who had been told to go to her
home and to leave Hamburg. She had a piece of paper in
her hand with her name and address, and was weeping
bitterly all the time.

This naturally started the people in the compartment
talking, and as it was a third-class carriage, comments
were pretty free

One man said out aloud: "We can't talk now, but wait
till our turn comes; we're not going to sacrifice all our
blood for the rich. They'll be surprised at what we shall
have to say when our turn comes!"

When is that turn of theirs to come, I wonder?

BERLIN, *December* 15, 1915.—Christmas is approaching, and in every heart is a fervent prayer that the season
of peace and good-will may in some way become the term
appointed for a final step towards the end of all this
bloodshed. "The Christ-child will help us," as the
German children say, and so we are making our scanty

preparations for the festival, with an undercurrent of hopefulness in our souls.

Berlin, or what we call "Our Berlin," seems as full as usual. The members of the Reichstag are arriving for the opening of the session, and troops of officers are flocking in on their Christmas leave.

Prince Löwenstein is back from Lille, Prince Salm from Warsaw. Prince Lynar and many others are here. They do not speak much of their experiences, but one gathers a great weariness of all the horrors of war. There are so many uniforms here, in fact, that some one said the other day: "Could the enemy look in at the Esplanade Hotel and see all the officers sitting here, they might think it a good moment for attempting a fresh offensive."

.   .   .   .   .   .

We are still suffering from disappointment over the Entente's reply to the German Chancellor's speech with its peace feelers, and the reactionary outburst of hatred against England. It is especially the women who hate so intensely, the women who cannot vent their feelings in action, as men can, but are forced to remain suffering passively, after having fostered the hope somewhere in their subconsciousness that things were about to change, and that their sons and brothers and husbands, who are with them now, might soon be spared to return to their normal duties.

It is ever the old refrain we hear—England is guilty of keeping on the war—England with her arrogance and inhumanity is responsible for all the oceans of blood being shed. Often enough I ask myself despairingly, "What *can* England do?" My soul is weary of the carnage, and I crave for peace at almost any price—and yet I see, or rather I *feel*, why England cannot stop now.

It is the old experience that the alien world has often wondered at, and has never understood, and never will understand. The English never know when they are beaten, and in the face of all odds go on. An American expressed it very aptly, if somewhat naively, in a few words which he had heard in the English War Office only a week ago : "How can *we* make peace now ? We are not yet victorious, and may win still if we continue fighting."

This is the whole situation in a nutshell, and rightly or wrongly it is characteristic of England, and demonstrates a quality too often neglected in the calculations of her enemies, and is just what is so infuriating Germany at present

The energetic pushing Prussians so often scoff at the English and use bitter words about their so-called decadence. England has been asleep, they say, resting on the laurels gained by her forefathers. England, gorged with colonies and surfeited with riches, has grown old and impotent; too much play and too little work has ruined her vitality!

The shadow of a fear flits across my mind at these words. At any rate, she is awakened now, somewhat roughly as it seems And it remains to be seen if the long decades of prosperity have really quenched that fire which glowed so hotly in the blood of the old seafarers, or if the British grit which so often won battles in the past will still hold fast where it has once bitten, and not lose hold until one of the opponents lies exhausted on the ground.

I, who am endeavouring to see both sides of the question, cannot refrain from asking myself why Germany is so keen on making peace at present. Is it solely from humanitarian reasons? or is it rather that her strength is waning, and although she may be able to hold out a good time yet, she cannot advance any further?

If solely from a humanitarian point of view, why did she reject the feelers for peace offered some months ago by the other side, on the plea that they were an insult to her, at the height of victory and success? Did she then foster any feelings of humanity for the sufferings of her opponents and their countries? Is her present humanity born of the fact that she may sink no more *Lusitanias*, and cause no more wholesale slaughters by means of her Zeppelins?

No, I am afraid if ever humanity played a part in the

warfare of past times, it certainly forms no consideration in the wars of to-day. Germany needs peace, and is probably ready to sacrifice some of her former aims and ambitions, arguing that having so far been victorious from a military point of view, she hopes to reap the harvest of her conquests, whereas, should the war continue, she may from growing exhaustion lose her grip on the treasure-trove, and in the end be forced to sacrifice more than she would wish.

But to return to the question of hatred, which has to-day assumed such biblical dimensions that it can only find expression in the words of the Psalmist. "If England be well hated here, America is hated still better," as the Bavarians would say.

Their hatred is in fact so intense that many Germans will not be seen speaking to an American. They assert that if it had not been for America continually supplying the Allies with munitions and money, they would have been financially ruined by now, and the war over long ago. One gentleman the other day likened America to a great greedy vulture, feeding on the carrion of the battle-fields of Europe, and growing ever grosser and more complacent as the masses of its gory food increased.

BERLIN, *December 27*, 1915.—Well, Christmas is over, without bringing any fresh development in the old state of things, but also without bringing any new catastrophe, as some of us half expected.

For weeks past, the town seems to have been enveloped in an impenetrable veil of sadness, grey in grey, which no golden ray of sunlight ever seems able to pierce, and which forms a fit setting for the white-faced, black-robed women who glide so sadly through the streets, some bearing their sorrow proudly as a crown to their lives, others bent and broken under a burden too heavy to be borne.

But everywhere it will be the same; in Paris and London too every one will be gazing at their Christmas-trees with eyes dim with tears.

We made some joint efforts to celebrate Christmas for others by preparing small gifts for the soldiers and for the poor. The shops made some rather futile attempts at Christmas sales, which were peremptorily forbidden, and the crowds which had collected from all parts of Berlin were dispersed without having made any purchases. No textile goods might be sold in special sales!

On Christmas Day I went to assist at the celebration of the festival at the Hedwig Krankenhaus, now turned into a Lazarett for soldiers. The hospital was beautifully decorated with Christmas green, each soldier having a Christmas-tree of his own, under whose branches the small gifts of love lay spread which every German treasures like a child.

The solemn Christmas songs were sung, touching the hearts of all those present, and we ladies did what we could to bring some touch of gladness into the hearts of these men who have sacrificed so much for their Fatherland, and many of whom will never be strong and active for any fight again.

But infinitely more heart-rending and pathetic was our visit next day to the blind soldiers' Home, those poor men whose lot is assuredly the hardest of all. The rooms had been decorated in exactly the same way as at the hospital, at the express wish of the poor fellows, who could only see it at all with the eyes of memory.

It was extremely touching to see how they tried to convince themselves that everything had been done exactly as if they could see, and how they felt their way round the room, lighting up small branches at the candles on the trees, so that the smell of the burning pine should more forcibly suggest all that they could not perceive, whilst their dead eyes reflected the tiny lights which they would never see again.

In the meantime the snow had been falling unceasingly, and as we all went off together to Midnight Mass at the Convent Hospital, the silent streets and houses lay shrouded with pure white snow. The church was

crowded with wounded soldiers, nurses, nuns, and pale-
faced, heart-broken women, and as the solemn music
slowly wound its way through the dim shadows of the pil-
lared aisles, it seemed to me as if our fervent prayers
must meet in union, and rise like a cloud up to the very
feet of God—prayers for the dying and dead, for comfort for the bereaved, and for ourselves, that we might
never again spend such a Christmas of anguish and suspense; prayers imploring "the tender mercy of our God
to shine upon them that sit in darkness and the shadow
of death, and to guide our feet into the way of peace."

BERLIN, *January* 1916.—Berlin is not a city of romance. There are none of those dark winding by-ways,
filled with the memories of past centuries, which are to be
met with in Paris or London. The spirit of it is intensely
modern. Its streets are broad and straight, unromanti-
cally clean. There is no room for imagination, which
loves the shadows and crooked alleys of the past

The architecture is new and painfully varied, almost
every building bearing the stamp of some man who at
the moment was seeking to make his impress on the
sands of time. There is no one great master-mind, but
many lesser minds struggling for expression

And so we meet with a strange incongruity in the styles
of the different streets and houses. Gothic stores and
classical bank buildings, renaissance villas and baroque
churches, Nuremberger houses and theatres conceived in
the spirit of Greek tragedy: these all greet our eyes during an hour's walk.

Our Hotel Esplanade is none of all these. It represents exactly what it was intended to be, a centre or
gathering-place for the great world of Berlin in time of
peace: royalties, statesmen, diplomats, officers and high
officials, and last but not least, the great financiers who
are supposed to hold the wires of the affairs of the world
in their two hands. At present it has become a sort of
caravansary for all the homeless exiles of position and

influence, who have been driven away from house to house by the great tidal wave of the war.

All people of any repute passing through Berlin take up their abode here, princes and nobles, and impecunious millionaires, who somewhere or other possess the accumulated treasures of an Aladdin, but who for the time being exist here on the reputation of these treasures, which seem to have disappeared just as mysteriously as they did in the *Arabian Nights.*

All the heroes of the war meet their wives and friends here, very much astonished to find themselves suddenly grown famous overnight. American diplomats prepared for instant flight, should the scales of peace and war suddenly weigh down on the wrong side; American princesses and duchesses, of the characteristic lightheartedness, some married morganatically but carrying off their position with a high hand, bring a fresh breezy and inappropriate tone with them, which gives a touch of comedy to the general tragedy of human life at present.

I sometimes sit downstairs in one of the beautiful reception-rooms, and wonder with a great wonder. Everything looks the same, nothing has changed outwardly. And yet it is all so different.

There is the same spacious lounge with the luxurious carpets and furniture, the huge arm-chairs inviting to meditation and repose; the vast reception-hall, with its groups of flowers and plants; the quiet corners, where in the screen of sheltering palms grave questions of state or those of a lighter nature may be discreetly discussed.

The wide flight of steps leading up so gracefully into the brilliance of the dining-room; the exquisite proportions of the oval-shaped apartment; the pillars of grey-veined marble; the white festivity of the flowered ornaments on ceiling and walls; the soft luminance falling from the crystal chandeliers on the rosy redness of silken curtains and screens—style of Louis XVI.—what an enchanting setting for those gay festivities of but a few short years ago!

I close my eyes, and again the gay pageant arises before me. The stiff ceremony of the Court receptions over, it used to be the custom for us all to throng here. How well I remember it all! The soft brilliance of the rooms seemed but to enhance the beauty of the women. The exquisite robes, creations of some great artist of European fame; the radiant eyes outshining the radiance of gleaming jewels on white arms and necks; the ripple of glad laughter, and the rise and fall of many voices in gay conversation. Men with the clear-cut features and characteristic expressions of those bearing the burden of authority, silver-haired and showing many orders on their coats; and young men in the flower of their youth and strength, the perfection of manhood, who in the splendour of their court-uniforms conjured up visions of the knights of King Arthur's round table.

Where are they all now, those proud Lancelots, and brave Sir Galahads and Percivales of the white uniforms and gleaming cuirass? Done to death most of them—their bodies lying unburied perhaps, mouldering and decaying in the bloody foulness of some distant battlefield, or at the best condemned to spend the rest of their days as cripples, the beauty of their manhood marred for ever!

Style Louis XVI.! In the light of past events, it seems to me now that there was a sort of similarity existing between our festivities and those of that ill-fated Court at Versailles. "Après nous le déluge," we too might have said, had we been able to gaze but a short space into the future. But we, like the rest of the world, were visited with a great blindness, and there was no prophet amongst us to read the Mene Tekel perhaps even then written on the walls.

And now to return to our life of to-day. The greatest simplicity in dress is of course the universal order—black, relieved by dull-coloured shades of brown and grey. Most of us still wear the clinging robes of before the war, and only the Americans make futile attempts to exhibit the strange eccentricities of fashion on their own persons.

Conversation is quiet and subdued generally, although there are of course those who still seem to regard life as a mere chance of having a good time. "Let us eat, drink, and be merry, for to-morrow we die," seems to be the guiding principle of their doings.

But for most of us the pain and suffering of humanity have eaten into our souls, and as for love? Is there room for love in any one's soul nowadays? The dainty, delicate, rainbow-hued god of the past can have nothing to do with the agonizing hurried embrace in between two battles, which love means at present.

In spite of my varied interests and occupations in connection with the war, I sometimes feel terribly lonely. Not the loneliness of being alone, but the loneliness of being one in a crowd, in a country where every one's sympathies and opinions are so terribly in opposition to my own.

I sometimes feel fairly rent in two, between love of my family and native land and love and loyalty to my husband and his country for his sake.

I remember one day last spring, when the hatred began to turn against America, how an American friend came up to me, her eyes filled with tears. "I thought I knew what you had been suffering all the winter, but now that they are beginning to vent their hatred on us, I realize for the first time what you poor women have been enduring. It is not so much what they say, as the cold scorn of their faces, when they look at us."

There are a good many ladies amongst us, like myself, who are internationally married. Some people say we ought to be labelled and ticketed to say where we all come from, and to what country we belong, as otherwise it restricts conversation.

Well, without going so far as that, I will describe some of those who are here, as we are rather like people in a besieged town, and have been in daily intercourse with one another for more than a year. There are Princess Münster, Princess Pless, Baroness Roeder, all

English like myself. Of Americans, there are Princess Braganza, the wife of Prince Miguel, who is son of the Portuguese Pretender (she was a Miss Stewart); Princess Isenburg, Countess Götzen, the Duchess of Croy, who was well known as Nancy Leishman in Berlin when her father was American Ambassador; Baroness von Rath, a war-bride, who is considered quite the prettiest woman among our set; Baroness Barchfeld, the morganatic wife of Prince Max of Hesse; Countess Seherr-Thoss, who was Miss White, daughter of Mr. Henry White, formerly American Ambassador at Paris; Baroness Sternburg, and several others besides. Princess de Biron is French, and there are a few ladies of Polish and Russian extraction.

Amongst the men there is a Major S—— with his bride of last year. He is an officer of the 1st Garde Regiment and was all through the awful reverse on the Marne. She is always pointed out as the only wife in that regiment who is not a widow, as she was married after the appalling slaughter took place. Talking of this regiment, its losses have been so fearful that the whole regiment has been entirely renewed five times since the beginning of the war, and this particular officer has never been able to rejoin it owing to break-down of nerves from the experiences he witnessed.

Then there is the ex-Turkish Ambassador, Muchtar Pasha, whose wife, a great friend of all of ours, is sister to the Khedive of Egypt. So she, like the rest of us, is torn in two with divided sympathies.

Then there is Count Flotow, ex-Ambassador in Rome, who, when Italy came into the war, had to leave Rome, and at the same time obtained temporary divorce from his Russian wife, as, according to Russian law, she would have had to sacrifice all her great fortune if she had been the wife of a German during war-time.

Then the following come and go from the front, as the Herrenhaus sits or as they obtain leave: Prince Pless, Prince Salm, Prince Münster, Prince Lowenstein, Prince

Lynar, Prince Braganza, Prince Furstenberg, Prince Lippe, Prince Taxis.

Besides the international clique, there were of course many other residential friends of ours in the hotel. For instance the clan of Hohenlohe; so numerous are they that it would be impossible to name them personally. Prince Hohenlohe, the head of the family, better known as the Duke of Ujest, was always treated somewhat as the princely owner of the hotel, and sat at a large round table in the centre of the room around which were clustered smaller tables of different members of the family like satellites revolving round a central sun. Needless to say, the said solar system was not entirely devoid of financial attraction.

Also among the groups were to be seen Princess Max Taxis, who finds Berlin society somewhat narrow after her gay international life, and her mother, Princess Metternich, who was a famous beauty and is still attractive at the age of 70.

To descend to some less conspicuous but equally attractive members of Berlin war-society in the hotel, come Mr. and Mrs. Jackson, he already well known internationally for his organization of the Prisoner of War Department, and she for the kind-hearted hospitality she showered on all of us. Also, lastly, Mr. Lay, the American Consul-General, and his wife. He has earned a word of gratitude for the sympathetic help he rendered to prisoners of war in an unofficial way, and she will always be remembered among us for her friendly, openhanded entertaining, which we always enjoyed in her pretty suite of rooms above us in the hotel.

. . . . . .

Most of us are pretty fully occupied. Our mornings are filled with self-imposed war duties. There is nursing at the hospitals; soup kitchens to be helped; women's guilds and workrooms to be visited, where destitute women are provided with sewing, and given tickets for clothes or food; the Red Cross office, and correspondence

My special department, and that of my English friends, is the British prisoners and research of the missing. We sometimes type for three or four hours on end, or spend the day looking through the inquiry lists at the American Embassy or the Red Cross office.

Then again, many destitute governesses and maids, banished from England with £10 in their pockets, and who have often been deprived of their letters of reference at the Customs, come to us for help, and we try to get them employment again, which grows harder every day, as the German employment officials object to finding them work, reproaching them with having gone to England in time of peace, and only returning when they had no choice.

During luncheon the latest news from the front is discussed, extracts from letters are read, the *Berliner Zeitung,* the midday paper, is brought in; and as it has had the whole morning to fabricate its lies, it is generally more thrilling than the morning paper.

My husband is always very popular at this hour, for he brings the English papers from the office, just two days earlier than any one else gets them, and as he has to return them in one and a half hours, there is something like a scrimmage to get a glimpse at them.

During luncheon American diplomats often look in on their way home from the Embassy, and they are generally laden with news, which, as it comes uncensored straight from England and America, is always of burning interest for us. But they are not always in the mood, or are forbidden to impart it.

We regard these Americans as a kind of political barometer, whose demeanour generally informs us pretty well as to the state of the impending Notes between Germany and America. Some days they come in smiling and affable, mentioning little bits of news as if by accident; and we know that the political clouds are clearing up. But on other days they pass by without seeing us, a Sphinx-like expression on their faces, and only talk amongst themselves. Then we know there is a crisis pending. But when they become directly aggressive in appearance, and keep to themselves in a general atmosphere of glum gloominess, we know that the crisis has become critical, and the American ladies here who are married to Germans take turns in trying to pump out of them what the exact state of affairs is.

I suppose the position of these men is rather difficult, but I think they might be more sympathetic sometimes. One would imagine they had no family ties themselves, by the way they seem to freeze into silence at the mention of any affectionate interest in one's relations in England.

In my own mind I class the Americans at the Embassy under the headings "the kind-hearted and sympathetic," and "those who simply regard the whole situation from a business point of view."

Every fortnight one or other of them travels to London, and they might realize how much good they could do our aching home-sick hearts if they would only bring one little word from home, even if it were only an anecdote about London, or what the weather was like, and how people were looking; instead of which the whisper goes round that some one is going to London, but the ladies are not to know, for fear of their having commissions for them.

But all our lives, we shall remember those few with gratitude who sacrificed themselves a little in our interests.

After lunch we sit about until 3 o'clock, or some one of us gives a tea in her private rooms for a select few. Dinner is at 8.30, a repetition of lunch, followed by the visits of ministers, military authorities, court officials, or, more interesting still, men going to or returning from the war.

And every one brings news of his or her corner of the world, or of the world-war; and I hear everything, and sometimes grow quite dazed at the manifold and contrary opinions and judgments I hear expressed, until at last

I believe nothing at all, but can only sit still with folded hands, in a state of abject despair.

BERLIN, *January* 1916.—The day before yesterday we had dinner with Prince and Princess Braganza and met the Duke of Mecklenburg. He is the first man who entered Nisch He has now gone to Bagdad to take command there for a year. That does not sound like an end of the war.

.   .   .   .   .   .

The American scare is worse than ever. We have been told to be nice to the Americans. They are hardly the sort to be taken in by sudden amiability on the German side.

Colonel House, the American pacifist, was here at the time when the Note arrived. Strange that is, for his Government surely must have known the lines on which he was working here at the time. Bethmann-Hollweg was to meet him; his mission was one of peace, and he was going round from one belligerent country to the other, preaching it, whilst the American Government behind him was threatening war.

.   .   .   .   .   .

On returning from a luncheon-party to-day, my husband told me that the feeling between the ministers and the military and naval party is growing from bad to worse. It all turns on the burning question of unrestricted submarine warfare, which its partisans say will be the turning-point in the war for Germany. The Admiralty are all in favour of it, prophesying that it will starve England out in six months, and so bring the war to a speedy end. Ludendorff and Hindenburg are against it, as they say they can win the war without it, and Ludendorff complains bitterly of the indecision of the responsible statesmen in this matter. The Kaiser and Bethmann-Hollweg are absolutely opposed to it from feelings of humanity.

BERLIN, *January* 22, 1916.—The excitement about the

Baralong is tremendous. We had tea with Baron Jagow, and of course it was discussed. They think this cold-blooded answer from England worse than anything.

My husband explained that the very fact of England's suggesting a court of arbitration and judgment by American naval officers showed that the English did not intend greater offence. He told them that at the Foreign Office too, and Solf and Jagow said, "Germany must send back as cold an answer." Whereupon G. said, "Why not have a court of arbitration? Any kind of negotiations between the two countries might lead on to peace in the end." On the strength of this argument Germany's answer was kept back for twenty-four hours, but as the Americans refused to arbitrate, the whole thing fell through.

Somebody told us that the Note had been worded thus by England so as to make the German answer an impossibility, the cases brought up against Germany being too dangerous Grey, he said, had had nothing to do with it. Balfour had worded the Note.

There are two parties now—partly through the *Baralong*—the Foreign Office versus the Admiralty. As for von Tirpitz, he is so angry that they can hardly keep him in the Admiralty. He has handed in his resignation twice already, but it was not accepted, so he remains, but has lost all interest.

He says he was just in full swing with his submarine warfare when he was stopped by the Emperor suddenly. He says only drastic methods are of any avail; but the Emperor has a spark of humanity left and won't have this, although he is not credited with it.

Disagreeables are going on in the army too. Hindenburg wants more troops, and von Falkenhayn and the others are jealous of his popularity and success, and will not let him have all he wants. So he can only remain on the defensive. It all seems incredible.

Much discussion has been going on about the Reichstag and Herrenhaus debates. One little bit I must mention here, as it was not allowed to leak out into the news-papers. One of the Princes rose and made a speech in which he said that Germany must go on with the war until she can make peace at her own terms. She must keep every inch of the conquered country and get every penny of the expended money back.

A regular tumult arose, and another Prince answered him, saying that in a speech of that kind he was not only jeopardizing Germany but the throne itself. The thing for Germany to do was to know when to stop.

"If America keeps on," the Germans say (some of them, of course), "we're done for. America is actually keeping things going. If America will stop providing the Allies with munitions, we can still win."

Who knows? Anyway, all seem to agree that Bismarck would have managed things better. He would have known how to draw Germany out of the matter gracefully after a few months, and the other countries would have been able to imagine that they had played the game all right, as well!

There is an intrigue going on to get Bethmann-Holl-weg out and Bülow in. So there are jealousies every-where. If it would only bring the end a bit nearer, there would be some hope in it all.

BERLIN, *February* 1916.—We were dining at Countess Henckel's the other night. Count Henckel is just back for a few days' leave. She being Austrian, her parties are generally a mixture of R C. Austrians and Germans —just the one little set of Larischs, Tattenbachs, Löwen-steins, etc.

This evening the Austrian Ambassador, Prince Ho-henlohe, and his wife (an Austrian Archduchess) were dining there, and as we were sitting down to dinner I was surprised to hear her call out across the table to me in English (which is always a shock nowadays) :

"Guess whom I had a telegram from to-day?"

It was not difficult to guess, judging by her beaming

face and her animated remark, seeing that as a rule she is a quiet, retiring little lady who never utters a word. And so I knew from this that it was from her sister Princess Salm, who had been with her husband a prisoner in Gibraltar, to say they were on their way home after a year and a half's absence.

BERLIN, *February* 20, 1916.—Yesterday evening we met and had a long and most interesting talk with friends, among whom were Prince and Princess Salm-Salm, whom I have just mentioned.

I have been most interested in Prince Salm's fate, and had heard all about his internment in Gibraltar. It was quite a different matter meeting him personally, and I proceeded to put several questions to him about his treatment by the English.

I was touched at the Archduchess' (Princess Salm's) gratitude to me. She told me that my message about her children being well was the only news she had received of any sort for the first six months of the war.

I felt particularly proud, as I know that the King of Spain and many others had been trying to get messages through to her and her husband, and had not succeeded. I wrote to my family, who communicated with Sir Lewis Michell (a great South African magnate), and he got this message through. She says she will never forget her feeling of joy when, as if from the air, the words came: "Countess Blücher told me to tell you your children are well and send their love."

Prince Salm's treatment in Africa was the worst part. He was put into a camp with eighty other men, mostly farmers, in the pavilion of a cricket ground; and no distinction whatever was made. Then, he said, there were constant risings against the Government, and the prisoners were sent up to Johannesburg. Hardly had their train started than the lines were destroyed, and they were cut off from every kind of communication. He could not even hear from his wife.

After that they both left South Africa and were transported to Gibraltar, where Prince Salm was again interned, but this time in a better fashion.

He was fairly comfortable and could see his wife frequently, but had only a yard to walk in, so got very little exercise, and he is certainly quite unlike the old Prince Salm who rather longed for war and adventure. In fact, it was in search of the latter that he went off to Africa, so missing the former! He is to go ·out to the Russian front to-morrow and is feeling doubtful as to how he will stand it, as his long internment has made him quite soft and unused to bodily exertions of any kind.

The Princess had quite a good time in Gibraltar. She is gay and fond of company, and made many friends there. She had plenty of change, and heard news and opinions from every side. She made friends too with the English ladies there, and read her copy of the *Times* every day. In fact, they had nothing to complain of. Prince Salm even raved of the English cooking!

Princess Salm went twice to see the King of Spain. The Duke of Alba, it appears, is somewhat pro-German (in fact, half the country is); and they get so excited about politics that she told me two Dukes actually fought a duel in her presence, one being pro-German and the other anti. Very Spanish that scene must have been!

On their return voyage they stopped at Tilbury. It was strange, he said, to see the change. All the sailors go about with life-belts slung over their shoulders, ready to be torpedoed any moment. Three wrecks were floating about near the docks, and as they passed along, they heard the distant roar of the guns.

. . . . .

I can revel in my husband's fame once more. Prince Salm said that wherever he went in South Africa he was always asked if he did not know Count Blücher, and that he heard his praises warmly sung on every side.

. . . . .

I heard an amusing story to-day. A Catholic soldier

here refused to go to confession. "Why," he said, "what is there to confess? Stealing is permitting, and killing a duty."

It seems to put the situation pretty clearly. A letter too from a "Kriegsfreiwilliger" this morning contained the following observation: "Why take life seriously? If a man were to ask you to do what life asks of us, you would say, 'He's a fool; don't take him seriously.' Why then life?"

BERLIN, *February 27*, 1916.—I sometimes smile at the mixture of friends I have here. It is all like a great play at the theatre. Outside there is apparent comedy, and below the surface a strong current of feeling, a passion of contradiction!

For instance, yesterday I had a tea-party, and the conversation changed in "tone" according to which nationality happened to enter. The first was Countess Moltke, the American wife of the Danish Consul. Her duty orders her to be "neutral," or guardedly pro-German, out of deference to her husband's official position. She is a very clever woman, and politically there is nothing she does not know.

Then came Countess Platen; she is half Dutch, half English by birth, and now married to a German. At the beginning of the war her views were fairly cosmopolitan. Now she too has to be most guarded, not only for her husband's sake, but for her daughter, who has become engaged to Baron Stumm, a rising member of the Foreign Office.

Countess Tattenbach then joined us. She is a Bavarian and, like all who are not Prussians, somewhat critical of the ultra-Prussian! I always try to tease her, and so get her off her guard and hear her say unpatriotic things. A sure method is to say or even imply that Germany forced Austria to declare war against her better judgment. This time I tried quite a new tack. I said: "I hear that negotiations are going on between

England and Austria for a separate peace," and I produced the *Morning Post* of February 8.

This remark caught like wildfire, and all immediately
set off on that topic in the most animated and heated
manner.

Princess Metternich, Prince Bismarck, Countess
Dohna, Baroness Sternburg, Mrs. J. Lay, and Mrs. Grew
then came in by degrees, and we had to keep clear of war
until the party was over.

That same evening when my husband and I were
dawdling over the evening papers before dressing for
dinner, Prince Alfred Salm, Prince Münster, and Count
Magnis all looked in at separate intervals on "their way
up to dress." They had all three just returned from the
Herrenhaus and had news to tell us that was a great
deal more interesting than all the women's gossip of the
afternoon, the most important being that Germany is
growing weary of being humbugged by America, who is
making her terms more and more difficult for Germany
to accept, and that the Herrenhaus, the Military, but
above all the People, are beginning to tire of it, and want
Germany to declare war on America, instead of waiting
for them to go on "haggling about terms."

The Foreign Office, they said, had—figuratively—gone
down on their knees to implore them not to make such
an appalling error as to break with America. Peace
must be maintained with America, they say, *at any price!*
The military authorities do not see this; they are still of
opinion that "Right is Might."

We have a sure sign of impending trouble with America, for the "Stormy Petrel" has reappeared. This is the
nickname given by us all to Mr. Morgan, the American
Consul at Hamburg; for at the most crucial moments of
the American crisis he always turns up suddenly, and
to-day—well, I came up in the lift with him!

BERLIN, *February* 1916.—One daily hears stories
which show the weariness of killing on both sides. A

youth, just home on leave for the first time, was telling his sister the other day his experience   He had been out since the beginning and had been on every front in turns, but he says his time in Belgium at the very beginning was the most fearful of all, and the *franc-tireur's* warfare the most ghastly part of it.

One night, when they were just settling down to sleep after a hard day's march, they were ordered out to take a village where the inhabitants were supposed to have been shooting on the troops. No very definite inquiries were made as to the truth of these statements, but for safety's sake it was thought best to burn the village. And so these young officers were given the order to march into it in the middle of the night, and to kill every one they met in a house with a light in the window. In the first house which he entered with his men they met a woman coming down the stairs. They had to carry out their orders, and killed this woman, and so on throughout. Next morning a hundred men were brought out, and the order was to stand them against the village walls and shoot every tenth man.

The wives, the mothers, all the women of the village were there imploring mercy, but no mercy was allowed to be shown. These men, who were not even permitted to be blindfolded, were shot before the eyes of their womenfolk.

And this boy returns to his family to "enjoy" his few days' leave, and his family are disappointed that he does not seem to enjoy it, that he seems preoccupied, that the things that used to amuse him now no longer seem to interest him.

BERLIN, *March* 5, 1916.—Here we are in March, and in ordinary times we should be rejoicing that winter is nearly over and spring coming, but now one feels nothing but dread, for it means that the armies will come out of their winter quarters and slaughter will begin once more.

March 2 has become a real nightmare with me, it being the date of the opening of the new submarine campaign. The description I have heard of the large German submarines makes me tremble. So confident are the Germans of their success that they say they can even bear the brunt of battle with America, for they are strong enough to cross the ocean and return in safety. Many are even hoping for war with America, so that they need exercise no consideration, but torpedo every single thing on the sea without discrimination or warning. Shocks are in store for us all, I fear. One cannot pretend indifference.

.   .   .   .   .

Verdun is the chief subject of interest at present, and in Germany it is now looked upon as likely to be one of *the* decisive victories of the war. They say it is only a matter of a few days before the whole fortress is taken, and that the terrific losses among the French fill even them with horror. Whereas on the other hand one reads in the English papers "that the Verdun attack has been a failure."

.   .   .   .   .

Ossip Schubin the novelist (she is a Bohemian, with all the Bohemian hatred of the Germans and Hungarians) told me a terrible story. Some Bohemian soldiers were ordered to enter a Serbian village and shoot all the inhabitants, including the women and children. They tried to refuse, but a second detachment was called up to urge them on at the point of the bayonet. The lieutenant who had to carry out this order went out of his mind at the horror of it. The soldiers then turned on the captain and shot him, saying, "Do your dirty work yourself."

That reminds me of another episode, equally horrible. There are a number of Austrian Serbians, that is to say, Serbs who have become Austrians by migrating into Croatian territory. Now, as Austrian subjects, they have been called upon to fight against their own race.

One day, in a house where they were quartered, they assembled in a room—sixteen of them—to discuss the matter. An Austrian heard them say that it was a hard job for them, and the sixteen were shot to a man! . . . Is this not the reign of terror?

.   .   .   .   .   .

Mr. Dresel, an American friend of mine, has been to visit the Bavarian prison camps, and tells me that the prisoners are much better off now than at first. One commandant told him that he knew how well the German prisoners were being treated in England, and so they were trying to do the same here.

I feel very proud, because he told me that all the officers asked after me and sent me messages. There is quite an amount of freedom allowed them. They go into the town and to a gymnasium there, and the German and English officers have grown quite friendly towards one another and say it is about time both countries made concessions. I asked him if he had been allowed to see them alone, and he told me there were now new rules permitting them to go for a walk with any of them singly, if they wish.

He had gone out with one or two, "but," he said, "you know what the English are; it is a long time before you can get an Englishman's confidence. If you do get it, you get it for ever, but they are reticent and dignified. You can't get an Englishman to complain!"

It is good to hear that, isn't it? It isn't that I don't know it, but I love people to tell it me. Mr. Dresel told me he noticed a new class of men getting into the English army now—rankers that have risen.

.   .   .   .   .   .

We lunched at Count Moltke's yesterday. He is the Danish Minister. The Jacksons were there and several other Americans; we were about thirty in all. The tension between Germany and America is so great now that no one dared venture on the subject at all, even at a so-called neutral party like this.

BERLIN, *March* 10, 1916.—There is great political news this week. Admiral Tirpitz is going—he has sent in his resignation and it has been accepted. Out of all the obscurity one thing appears to be certain, viz. that there are two parties, one headed by Tirpitz and his friends, the other apparently by Bethmann-Hollweg and the Emperor. I want the Emperor to get his due in this matter at least. He has long been against these very drastic measures, and does all he can, it seems to me, to prevent any avoidable cruelty. Now too it is distinctly difficult for him, and many say he is actually jeopardizing his throne; for Tirpitz has Bülow with him, and they are both strong men with many friends. Of course Tirpitz is being regretted by every one officially, as he is looked on as the maker of the German fleet and the creator of the modern submarine, which he has always regarded as the only effective weapon for modern naval warfare.

The military and naval authorities are furious with the Foreign Office, and call them half-hearted; but their reply is that one must take into account the position of Germany after the war. The Foreign Office also says that submarine warfare has not been a success from the beginning, and that England was not in the least on the way to being "starved out" after the first submarine blockade. To accomplish this they would have needed at least 200 submarines, sufficient to form a chain round England; and then if England had invented something to break the chain, as she has actually done, the enormous expense and sacrifice would all have been in vain.

I think a good deal of the Foreign Office. They seem to me to be smoothing things down, and will do much towards a better understanding between Germany and other peoples. As for Tirpitz, they say his fury is indescribable. They gave out as the reason for his retirement that he had broken down and needed rest; so he walked with his wife up and down the Wilhelm Strasse for two hours to prove to the crowd that it was not true, but that he was in the best of health. The next day he appeared in tall hat and frock coat, to show that he had been "deprived of his uniform" (or rather to let the people think he had), and talked to his wife in a loud voice so that the crowd should be able to hear, and even addressed them. If this is true it points to trouble. It is a little as though Tirpitz and Bülow were trying to threaten the Emperor.

I hear that the Emperor went to Verdun to see how things were going, and saw a whole company of men blown up by a French mine. The sight was so terrible that he had a nervous shock and has been ill since.

    •   •   •   •   •   •

We met old Zeppelin at a party the other night He looks a dear old man. They say he flies over Munich and drops flowers on to the heads of the people below! A lady said she would not relish bombs dropped instead of flowers. "Oh," said Zeppelin, "I am sure I wish I could always drop flowers."

BERLIN, *March* 12, 1916.—There is great excitement here to-day about the *Möve*, and the Commander, Count Dohna, whom we know well, has just arrived back and is staying at this hotel.

He is much fêted, he has received the "pour le mérite," and looks splendid, just like an English officer. It is interesting to watch how proud they all are of him, from the lift boy upwards!

Both the steamers that conveyed Prince Salm home— the *Malojah* and the *Mecklenburg*—have been sunk by him. One took the Prince to Tilbury and the other to Holland. No wonder Prince Salm noticed that all the men had life-belts slung over their shoulders!

    •   •   •   •   •   •

Some one came in to-day and told me that there is a so-called "cripple brigade" near Verdun. Men that have lost a finger, or who are disfigured but able-bodied, are used at the front again for odd jobs of one kind or an-other. This "cripple brigade" had the sad task of burying

4000 corpses outside Verdun! Some of them go out with the feeling that as they are not much more use, they may as well be shot dead out there. Poor fellows, it is so tragic!

BERLIN, *March* 14, 1916.—I have been in bed with what people say is influenza, but I feel inclined to call it "Ersatz" illness. Every one is feeling ill from too many chemicals in the hotel food. I don't believe that Germany will ever be starved out, but she will be poisoned out first with these substitutes!

Just as I write this, some one comes in from household shopping, a thing I never have to do, being in a hotel. She looks quite unhappy, and says that really England is succeeding, as food is getting so dreadfully scarce. Her butcher told her that he is seriously thinking of closing down. She could get no potatoes, no sugar even. The shopkeepers told her that the soldiers don't get meat more than three times a week now, and even vegetables are scarce!

Then again one hears that so much is due to over-organization. The "Magistrat" forbids the selling of butter, sugar, etc., until all has been bought up and distributed equally and justly. In the meantime masses of butter and other stuffs get spoilt. So, they say, the Bolle dairy gave their butter to a big soap factory for the making of soap, as the butter had got bad through lying by so long, and in this way it was not entirely wasted. And potatoes and such-like lie by waiting to be bought up, and the poor clamour for food. It is all terrible, and what it is going to lead to no one knows.

. . . . . .

My husband has just returned from a journey to Vienna. He stayed there a week and saw the "whole of Austria," so to say, in that short time. The chief topic there, he told me, is the hatred of Italy—the smart thing is to go to the Italian Front. The hatred of Russia is not great enough to call forth any enthusiasm on that side

The other topic is criticism of their ally—Germany. There does not seem to be any love lost between those two allies, and they say that Turkey too is getting restive and tired of the whole thing. Erzerum was a very hard blow to the Turks, and they do not appreciate being left to their own resources. This I heard from the former Turkish Ambassadress, who lives here.

.   .   .   .   .

Prince Ernst Günther (Duke of Schleswig-Holstein and brother to the Empress) sat next to me at dinner the other night—we were dining with Count and Countess Colloredo. He told me of his experiences at the Western Front. It was he who picked up Captain Ivan Hay and drove him in his car to his destination, a prison camp. They could not help laughing at the fact that, had there been no war, they would have met that very month shooting in Silesia, as guests of Prince Pless.

He just missed seeing the Duchess of Sutherland when she was nursing in Brussels. He said they were very old friends, and he would have liked to see her in her capacity of nurse. He gave directions for her to receive special treatment and every possible attention, but did not know if these orders had been carried out.

Once, too, he nearly came face to face with his cousin and great friend, Count Gleichen, a relation through the Hohenlohes. They were in command on opposite sides and quite a few miles within sight of each other.

Poor Prince Ernst Gunther spoke so sadly of all the friendships with his relations in England being cut off. He said: "One feels it, when those whom one has looked upon as intimate friends speak openly of their hatred of one's relations. How could Lord Charles Beresford say of my brother-in-law: 'The head of the assassin, William the Kaiser, should be hung from the highest tree in Potsdam as just retribution for all his cold-blooded murders'? Do you think in your heart that a man like Lord Charles really and truly believes that the Emperor is personally responsible? I can understand the people still thinking that kings are all-powerful, but surely no one else does."

I murmured some inane reply, for what could I say? But I should have loved to quote the words my husband used some days ago: "All governments nowadays are pacifists naturally, but frightened of their own peoples. Monarchs and governments are literally shaking in their shoes for fear of what the people will do, who have been called upon to make such superhuman sacrifices. The Emperor is the only monarch who did assert his authority, even until half-way through the war, though even he cannot do so any longer; but as he was the only one who ever could do so he is now blamed for all."

By the way, it was amusing to see Prince Ernst Günther take his "bread card" from his pocket and put it on the table beside him. It showed how deeply what the French call the "discipline de l'appétit" has sunk into the heart of the nation!

BERLIN, *March* 1916.—Here are some extracts from a private document, supposed to be a true account of the state of England and English feeling at the time (January 1916), compiled by a so-called neutral, but in reality a German, who obtained a passport and went over to England for the purpose.

His foremost impression was that it is the people who are now keeping on the war, in spite of the Government being fully ripe for peace overtures. The latter have lost control of the nation, and are simply tools in their hands.

Goethe's well-known verse:

Die Geister die du riefest, die wirst du nicht mehr los,

may be aptly applied here.

Lord Derby is the hero of the hour, his working of the conscription question having made a great impression for the time being   They say he was very sceptical himself at first as to the results.

Sir Edward Grey, like so many of the responsible men in the history of the war, is not strong enough to face the stern and immeasurable actualities which now confront him. Some say he is only a puppet moved by stronger and more unscrupulous wills. He is said to believe in the possibility of an eventual understanding with Germany, although here he is almost the most unpopular Englishman alive.

His position is growing more and more untenable, as the people are in such a state of inimical excitement that anything smacking of leniency towards Germany is looked upon as un-English and treacherous.

A parallel might be drawn between his case and that of Bethmann-Hollweg here in Germany, who is being almost as impatiently and thoughtlessly criticized as Grey in England.

The Cabinet of twenty-two seems to be the object of an increasing dislike and aversion on the part of the people, who are expressing their opinions more forcibly and less refinedly every day. "You have led us into the mess, now pull us out again!" I can imagine how gladly the "22" would pull them out if they only knew how. It certainly is easier to get stuck in the mire than to get out of it again.

Lord Kitchener, the "butcher of Omdurman," as he is usually called here, has lost prestige on both sides of the North Sea. Those small affairs which he was formerly engaged in must have been like playing at war compared to this world conflict.

The pacifists, it is said, meet with small regard on the part of the people, and tend more to excite the belligerent instincts of the "great unwashed" than to pacify them. I could imagine that open-air meetings of the pacifists, systematically arranged all over England, would be the best means possible for winning over the people, including "conscientious objectors," to accept compulsory service.

John Bull, reborn as St. George, radiant and beautiful

in shining armour, goes out to destroy the venomous dragon of "German militarism" by force of arms, and one of the hugest jokes of history is exhibited to the astonished world!

The names of Sir Aldyn (*sic*), Morley, Bryce, as well as McIver, Middleton, Lorebourne (*sic*), Aberdeen, Gladstone, Beecham (*sic*), and Charles Mosterman (*sic*), are mentioned as leaders in the pacifist movement!

The most popular figure, says the report, is Lloyd George, the munition-man, who has donned the mask of a ferocious man of war, haranguing the masses, and assiduously providing food for the iron beasts of war, all for the sake of his own private ambitions.

Bonar Law is described as being a connecting link between the fanatical Unionists, who are clamouring for a general election, and the much harried Parliament, who, in their reverential awe of themselves as divine instruments for working out England's salvation, are still glad enough to cling to his strong personality, as a middleman in the dizzy whirl of events.

Will there be a general election or not? is said to be the burning question of the day. Should a new Government come in, we may expect the war to last another twenty years, which may the gods forbid.

. . . . . .

I have heard the reason why such a huge number of unwounded prisoners were taken at Verdun. It was because they were rendered senseless by a new gas bomb invention. I was pleased at what seemed to me quite a humane use of this terrible gas, but I was soon disillusioned. I was told that the same thing had been done a little while before with 700 men, but a day later only 100 were still alive; the 600 had died from the after-effects of this gas—their lungs had shrivelled up and prevented breathing, so suffocation had set in and killed them!

. . . . . .

The people continue to be very restless; I hear that in other towns they have resorted to energetic measures

for getting more food.   In Cologne the mayor had to un-
lock the market twice in the middle of the night; once they
hung a dead cat before his door, with the eyes gouged out,
and an intimation that that would be his fate if he did not
look after the people better.   They also tried to mob the
Town Council when sitting.   The peasants now jeer at
the town-breds, who have to spread their bread with
Kunsthonig (artificial honey), while they, the peasants,
have a thick layer of their own butter and a slab of ham
on top!

My sister-in-law in Bonn gives a description of disturbances much in the style of those in Cologne.   She
says: "Yesterday there was a fearful mob and a fight in
the Rathausstrasse for lard.   It was the day for waiting
outside the stores for this article; the town provides it for
the people on certain days, and who arrives first is first
served.   A carriage with rich people in it drove up, and
the inmates were served before the others, which caused a
riot.   The policemen had to use their swords, for the
crowd nearly lynched them.   The mob broke the windows
of the police station."

BERLIN, *April* 1916.—Last night we dined at Baron
von Jagow's and met the Dutch Minister and his wife,
M. and Mme. Gevers.

As a change from the everlasting American crisis,
which is becoming monotonous, a Dutch crisis had just
sprung up; so it behoved us to avoid politics, and we
crept delicately round the thin ice of the dangerous topics
which were on the tip of our tongues

It seems that England has just been proved to have
sunk a Dutch merchantman, and is adopting a somewhat
threatening attitude towards the neutrality of Holland;
which is all very well in its way, but a Dutch neutrality
in favour of England would be so very much better, seen
through insular spectacles.

We were again struck by the difference between England's and Germany's diplomacy.   If Germany happens

to sink a ship, protected by American guardian-angels, the whole world knows of it at once, and the inevitable crisis springs up. If England, on the contrary, sinks a ship belonging to one of the long-suffering neutrals, by mistake, the matter is hushed up at once, and only some obscure notice of it appears in a list of shipping casualties, and the regrettable accident is lost to sight.

English diplomacy is certainly marvellous. The Germans call it by other names sometimes, not very nice ones, but would give a good deal if they themselves could catch the knack of it.

The practical, hard, matter-of-fact "uprightness" and "downrightness" of the Prussian character in general misses those finer lights and shades of what is generally known as tactfulness, and in its exaggerated form often leads to the virtue (or vice, as you take it) of a somewhat blundering form of diplomacy since the giant Bismarck resigned his post of steering the ship of Germany through the stormy seas of history.

A few days later we lunched with Dr Solf, the Colonial Minister. Herr von Zimmermann, the Under Secretary of State, was there too. The policy of these two men is to refrain from taking any part in the war of abuse carried on by the Press against England, in wise forethought of the critical colonial question for Germany in the future.

Dr. Solf is one of those clear-seeing men who understand how complicated every phase of the struggle becomes through the vindictive vituperation of the Press. For this reason he is himself very much abused by certain members of the military party. For men like Kessler and Falkenhayn the sword is the only solution possible, and all methods of a milder nature are regarded as signs of effeminate weakness.

A friend told me that the Kaiser is practically kept under supervision by men like Falkenhayn, who never allows any one to speak to him alone, he always being present at every audience. Prince Münster tried to do so in vain. They are afraid of the Kaiser's kind heart. At dinner one night the Kaiser said to Prince Munster: "Münster, I have had a letter from Lady O——, asking me to find out where her missing nephews are." A peal of scornful laughter arose from the other guests at table. A German Kaiser, they said, had other work to do than to search for missing English officers   The Kaiser remained silent, but on rising from the table asked Prince Münster to try and get some news for Lady O——.

.   .   .   .   .   .

The other day an article appeared in one of the daily Berlin papers, entitled "Englische Krankheit," and warning men in high positions not to allow themselves to be influenced by English women who are married to Germans, *as English women seem to have a dangerous knack of getting the men to look at things from their point of view.*

Of course, every one here is wondering which of us is meant, and we are ourselves very much amused at this candid homage to the fascinating powers of English women, in spite of their being so often condemned as utterly under-educated from the German schoolmaster point of view. It is in any case not very complimentary to German women.

The fall of Tirpitz has been ascribed in some quarters to Princess Pless's influence over the Kaiser, on the ground that she had talked him over into using less drastic measures towards the English.

This is, of course, nonsense, as Princess Pless has never seen the Kaiser alone since the beginning of the war. And as for her being admitted to Headquarters because she is English, that is another ridiculous exaggeration. She was once at Headquarters, it is true, but as they happened to have settled them at her own house, they could not really turn her away. She had, however, to keep entirely to her own apartments, and had no intercourse with the Staff at all.

BERLIN, *April* 4, 1916.—I was suddenly rung up on the telephone by Sir Roger Casement, saying he must see me at once. I was somewhat surprised, as I thought he was ill in bed at Munich. He was, a few days ago, when we heard of him last.

However, although I was not keen on seeing him, I telephoned back to say that I would do so for a few minutes. Little did I think what a scene was before me.

The poor man came into the room like one demented, talked in a husky whisper, rushed round examining all the doors, and then said: "I have something to say to you, are you sure no one is listening?"

For one moment I was frightened. I felt I was in the presence of a madman, and worked my way round to sit near the telephone so as to be able to call for help. And then he began: "You were right a year ago when you told me that I had put my head into a noose in coming here. I have tried not to own you were right, and I did not like to tell you when you kept on urging me to get out of the country, that I realised from the moment I landed here what a terrific mistake I had made. And also I did not want to tell you that in reality I was a prisoner here I could not get away. They will not let me out of the country.

"The German Foreign Office have had me shadowed, believing I was a spy in the pay of England, and England has had men spying on me all the time as well.

"Now the German Admiralty have asked me to go on an errand which all my being revolts against, and I am going mad at the thought of it, for it will make me appear a traitor to the Irish cause."

And at these words he sat down and sobbed like a child. I saw the man was beside himself with terror and grief, and so I tried to get a few more definite facts out of him, and told him there *is* a way out of every difficulty if he would only tell me more.

But he said, "If I told you more, it would endanger the lives of many, and as it is, it is only my life that has to be sacrificed." I made all sorts of suggestions, but all he would say was: "They are holding a pistol to my head here if I refuse, and they have a hangman's rope ready for me in England; and so the only thing for me to do is to go out and kill myself."

I argued him out of this, and at last he went away after giving me a bundle of farewell letters to be opened after his death. As he went out of the door, he said: "Tell them I was loyal to Ireland, although it will not appear so."

He asked to see me again, but as I am watched like every one else here, and as there was evidently some political intrigue on, I had to refuse.

BERLIN, *April* 1916.—Last Sunday we lunched with Prince and Princess Christian of Hesse (Barchfeld), and there we met the great Count Dohna, of *Möve* fame, and I had an opportunity of speaking to him for the first time.

He is a very nice man, and quite like an English naval officer. He told me many interesting things about his trip, but of course not as much as I wanted to know.

The one thing we are always trying to find out is where he coaled during the voyage. It is a great mystery and no one knows, not even his own sailors on board. They stopped to take in coal at some port, and it must have been Ireland or Scotland or somewhere where they were taken for English sailors.

I asked him if he had seen English Dreadnoughts, and he said he had seen the smoke of some, but that he was not going to tell me a word more, and that he had seen Scotland; but how much of Scotland he had seen he also said he must leave to my imagination.

He so simply described his surprise at finding himself a public hero on his return. He had no idea, he said, that his adventure would have taken the public in the way it had done. And he told me his unmarried sister was still more surprised. She went one evening to a theatre in Frankfort, unknown and a nonentity, and came out a heroine, as in the middle of the play it was suddenly stopped and the manager came out and announced the news of the wonderful feat of the *Möve*, and the ovation was so intense that the play could not be finished   No one was more surprised than this sister of his, as she did not even know that her brother was Commander of the *Möve*.   I was glad to think that this young officer, like Captain Müller of the *Emden*, had behaved as a true sailor and a gentleman in all his actions with us.   If the submarine commanders had done the same, what a difference it would have made to Germany's reputation throughout the world.   As it is, generations will hardly suffice to wipe out the memory of her piratical deeds at sea.

At this luncheon party also was Prince Lippe, one of the reigning Princes.   Such a nice, simple man.   He told me much about his time spent on the West Front with the English opposite them for months, and said that such a friendly feeling had grown up among them all that they and the English used to exchange hot coffee and cigarettes and books to read in the trenches.   For weeks the trenches were only seventeen yards apart, and they could hear the conversations in each other's trench quite plainly.

He, like Prince Löwenstein, was one of those who had been so good about trying to get news of missing English officers, and identifying the graves, and getting news of the wounded in the hospitals at the front. And he said that his only disappointment was the very little consoling news he had managed to obtain for the relations.

While on this subject I feel I owe a special word of gratitude to Prince Löwenstein, who was on Prince Rupprecht of Bavaria's Staff, as he was the means of procuring many comforts and concessions for some of the English officers during that trying period between the time they were captured and the time they reached their prison camp.   As this has, through all inquiries, proved to be the time when most of the ill-treatment is said to have occurred, one realizes that any one who would be the intermediary at such a time deserves thanks. Prince Löwenstein, who can speak English perfectly, and perhaps has spent more time in England than some of the captured officers themselves, who may only have landed there once on the route from Canada or Australia, was able to give the captives a hint or two which helped to soften things. For instance, on one occasion when he offered a newly captured officer some food, the young Englishman (straight from Canada) stood with his hands in his pockets and a huge pipe in his mouth, and simply grunted a reply. Prince Lowenstein quietly said to him: "As you are on your way to Germany, and may have to be there for some time, I should like to give you some advice which may help to ease your time of captivity, and that is, when addressed by a superior officer, if you took your pipe out of your mouth and your hands out of your pockets, you would be more likely to be well treated than if you do as you are doing now, because our customs differ in that respect perhaps from those of your country."

BERLIN, *April* 28, 1916.—I wonder if my friends in England can see the sky as blue as it is here, the sun as bright, and the green (of the Tiergarten just round the corner) so intense. The green this year seems so bright that, in spite of the wonderful spring-like beauty, it strikes me as out of tune and out of place.

Sometimes I seem suddenly to notice the greenness and the sun, and I wonder that it can be spring once more—that the winter is really over, and yet the warmth has not begun to melt the hearts of those makers of history—those monarchs and ministers that still think it necessary to send hundreds of men each day to their deaths.

.   .   .   .   .   .

I have not yet said anything about Asquith's answer to Bethmann-Hollweg's long tirade. How the people here waited for that speech of Bethmann-Hollweg. There was a gasp of expectation running through the population. When it came people shrugged their shoulders and said: "We hoped he would say more."

Then came Asquith's answer, and the nation rose in indignation. "What did he mean by the crushing of Prussian militarism? Could he not have answered Bethmann-Hollweg's words in a different way?"

A defence of the latter immediately commenced, and England of course is blamed once more as the arch-enemy.

But how can the Allies destroy militarism? They cannot beat Germany to such an extent. It is from within alone that this militarism can be shaken. The Allies may say that without their efforts the people of Germany could never be brought to an understanding of their military government. But however that may be, it is only the German *people* who can destroy it and who *will* destroy it slowly, for they get wearier and wearier, from day to day.

.   .   .   .   .

A good example of the mismanagement of affairs which causes so much discontent, is the following. When paraffin oil became scarce people who had to work by lamp-light were encouraged to use methylated spirit. Most of the poorer classes went to the expense of getting their lamps arranged for this purpose. Now they do not even see the word "Ausverkauft" for methylated spirit, but are simply told that all of it has been confiscated by the Government for military purposes.

Materials—woollen and cotton—are supposed to be getting scarce. Ladies *will* wear skirts of five to six yards in width. Officialdom does not go so far as to forbid this, but lays a hand of iron on the working-class by ordering every dressmaker who employs more than one hired worker to report to the police, who thenceforth control her expenses and receipts, etc., allowing her but a certain percentage of profit and a certain number of hours for work, so that she cannot use up too much of this precious cotton and woollen material.

Was Bismarck right in saying that officialdom in Germany would end by stifling Germany with its own weight?

And yet there is a humorous side to the whole thing. If we want soap we can get 100 grams a month; but only if we present our bread ticket. I read an amusing tale of a child who was sent to buy 50 grams with her bread ticket. She came home with it; it was a bit dark. Her mother put some precious butter and even meat sausage on it! When her husband proceeded to partake of it, lo and behold it was 50 grams of soap the child had brought instead of bread!

BERLIN, *May* 1916.—On returning to Berlin after a peaceful Easter spent with Princess Münster in Derneburg, we were horrified to find the streets surrounding our hotel in a great state of excitement. The hotel even seemed to be in a state of siege, being surrounded by a cordon of police and a rather threatening-looking mob, who, it seemed, had already stolen the bread supplies for the hotel, evidently supposing that we were living in a superabundance of luxuries, whilst they were wanting in everything. As a matter of fact, our supply of bread is limited to the same allowance as every one else's in Germany, 1900 grms. a week, including 400 grms. of flour.

It was in fact the "red" May 1st, and a few turbulent Socialists had tried to get up a passing agitation to celebrate their day in the usual manner, on which occasion Liebknecht, the notorious quarreller in Parliament, was arrested for attempting to disturb the public peace, and is now safely under lock and key.

May was decidedly in the sign of general discontent and complaints at every one and everything The barest necessaries of life were wanting, and many people kept Easter in the face of an empty larder.

The unexpected duration of the war has led to unfore-
seen complications in the economic administration, so
that all sorts of changes are taking place in the Board of
Provisions; added to which the keeping back of food-
supplies by speculators for the purpose of demanding
exorbitant prices reached such a climax, that it almost
seemed as if a revolution on a small scale were threatening in Berlin.

The butchers' shops were closed for two to three weeks
on set prices being denominated by Government for
meat; vegetables were not to be had; butter almost unknown; whilst soap had become so scarce that regula·
tions were enforced forbidding white dresses to be worn
in some parts of Germany. Every one is now allowed
1 lb. of soap for washing purposes a month, and 100
grms. of toilet soap extra.

Long processions of women waiting for hours before
the butchers', grocers', and bakers' shops were to be seen
everywhere, and gave rise to the name of the "butter-
polonaise." These women often got up in the middle of
the night, to be first on the scene, and took camp-
stools with them, working or knitting, and seemed rather
to enjoy this opportunity of unlimited gossiping, evil
tongues said. One industrious woman was even said to
have taken her sewing machine with her!

Things have since grown better Delbrück, the
much worried Secretary of State, who with seventy-
five Privy Councillors managed (or mismanaged, as his
opponents say) the organization of the food-supplies in
Prussia, grew sick with the weight of his responsibilities
and resigned his onerous post, and in his place a dictatorship of three tried men has been placed, who are cour-
ageously commencing the struggle with the existing lack
of everything.

Our daily rations are at present: ½ lb. of sugar,
½ lb. of meat or lard, 1 lb. of potatoes, with 100 grms.
of butter per head weekly. Eggs are hardly to be had,
two companies having bought them all up in the province

of Brandenburg, and they cost 32 to 30 Pf. apiece, if available at all.

We can hardly complain of starvation, but the whole population is being under-fed, which of course, in the long run, means a deterioration of physical and mental forces in all classes.

.   .   .   .   .   .

The German answer to the American Note was just pending, and we found Mr. Gerard, the Ambassador, and all our friends practically sitting on their boxes waiting to leave at a moment's notice, should a rupture take place between the two countries.

The answer of the German Government was a relief to the greater part of the population, who are intensely anxious to avoid any further complications For the time being the dispute has been laid, who knows for how long?

.   .   .   .   .   .

In Silesia we heard of an old Latin saying mentioned by a Catholic priest, which is especially applicable for this year :

> Si Marcus pascham dabit
> Et Joannes Christum adorabit
> Totus mundus vae! clamabit,

which, being translated, means: "When St. Mark's day falls in the Easter week, and St. John's in the Octave of Whitsuntide, the whole world will wail and lament" —which is most certainly the case at present, when in addition to the losses of the past, the last precious goblet of the wine of life is being poured out at Verdun Every one seems to be losing their last relations there.

How right Kitchener was in his prophecy that the war would last three years, and how strangely short-sighted now seems the light-hearted saying of the Kaiser to the troops in 1914 that they would be home again with their families before the leaves had fallen from the trees.

.   .   .   .   .   .

I was not very much astonished when at Derneburg

to hear the news of Sir Roger Casement's arrest on the west coast of Ireland, and of his being taken to the Tower by two armed constables, just at the time when Easter sight-seers were "doing" the place! But I hardly realized to what a disastrous end fate was leading him.

Very little of the affair leaks through the censorship here. On the whole no one will say a good word for him The Germans, who are not partial to traitors, even if they use them as tools, scoff at him as the impotent leader of a lost cause, and the Americans and other neutrals despise him, whilst the few English hate him

It is certain that the Germans in their own minds looked upon him as an English spy, and it was only when he happened to fall foul of a certain naval officer that they concocted their scheme of handing him back to England for England to do her dirty work herself. But between the time he was "handed back" and the time of his arrival in Germany, that is the time when I had the opportunity of seeing the man drink the cup of humiliation to the dregs, penniless and starving, friendless and hunted, should I have been a woman if I had not given him a meal at times, or on the last day, when he was going to a certain death, and came to me abject with terror and evidently out of his mind, could I have done less than promise to use what influence I had to ask for mercy for him? With this object I have written to a friend in England, but have little real expectation that it will save him from his fate.

BERLIN, *May* 1916 —To our great astonishment we have been asked to undertake a little peace movement on our own account. They want me to write to the Duke of Norfolk, as the head of the Catholics in England, and find out if they are in any way associated with the Pope's well-known efforts for peace.

In answer to my objection that my letter would probably never pass the English censor, they replied that it would not go by post at all, but by special messenger, and that I could see the very man who would personally place my letter on any writing-table in London—a curious proof of how the censor may be evaded

They actually seem to have succeeded moreover, for after I had with considerable qualms of conscience committed myself to the letter, a reply reached me in due course which I will not quote. It was of a very guarded nature, and threw grave doubts not only upon the prospects, but upon the expediency of peace at present.

BERLIN, *June* 1916.—This month began with such unusual excitement that I was quite stunned by the overwhelming nature of the catastrophe. A great naval battle —a great German victory! People celebrating it with champagne, the streets gay with flags, church bells ringing, schools closed in honour of the event, and every one flushed with pride that at last the great day had come, when the German David should smite the English Goliath a deadly blow.

The suspense was awful, as I could not at first get any English news which might contradict or supplement the triumphant German reports I knew perfectly well in the depths of my heart that these were exaggerated, and that even if they had managed to do the British fleet a great deal of harm, they must have suffered enormous losses themselves.

I think for those few days my soul must have visited England sometimes, for I experienced so keenly everything that must be going on there. I saw the thousands of anxious women besieging the Admiralty for news of husbands and sons, and the wave of disappointment which must have swept over the whole country at the news which the papers have since called "A great victory which the Admiralty announced like a defeat."

All the naval men here were at once called back to Wilhelmshaven, and the Emperor hurried there too They say that the sight of the procession of coffins, dead bodies, and wounded being carried through the streets was enough to suppress any feeling of rejoicing which may have been felt elsewhere.

And then came the news from England, and I read that England regards the battle of Skager Rack as the most notable victory achieved since the battle of Trafalgar, which may have results only less momentous than Nelson's, and that the German fleet was chased back in disorderly retreat into its ports.

England's losses seem irretrievable, including no less than 300 officers, and are said to be seventy per cent greater than those of Germany. Everywhere people are saying that the English Navy was in every way excelled by the German Navy, which is said to be the only one able to fire at full speed. The superior air-service, *i.e.* the scouting done by the Zeppelins, helped them to play havoc with the enemy's ships.

Kind friends who knew that I should be sorrowing in the midst of the universal rejoicing came to see me, such as Countess Henckel and Countess Tattenbach— women whose silent sympathy does one much good in the midst of the derision and jeers of the mob.

And then came the fresh shock of Kitchener's sudden death; which is appalling and startling, coming as it does on the top of the naval victory. Here there are rumours of his having been killed in the great battle, but I suppose the *Hampshire* was really sunk by an English or Danish mine.

This month brought a great scene in the Reichstag, when the Chancellor, Bethmann-Hollweg, at last stood up to his political adversaries and revenged himself for all the petty attacks of which he is so often the victim, by turning and rending them in a very fine speech.

.   .   .   .

Since I wrote last, I have heard much more about the terrific naval battle of the Skager Rack. A German naval officer, who was in the midst of it, described it to a friend as "Hell in the sea and air." Dr. Ohnesorg and Mr. Dresel from the American Embassy have been down

to Mainz to see the saved English naval prisoners.
Unfortunately they could not get much out of them.
At some of the camps the Commanders refused to allow
them to be spoken to, and at other places the English
officers refused to speak.   There certainly seems to be a
mystery about the whole thing.   Baron von Rath told
us that his brother-in-law was chosen to conduct the
English naval prisoners to their camps   He said they
were very haughty, refusing to speak, or to give any
information whatever.   At last a happy thought struck
him, and he told them that he was born in Scotland
and lived there for some years; then they began to thaw
a bit. They entirely refused to believe that Lord Kitchener
was dead, even when shown the German newspapers.

.   .   .   .   .   .

A German friend remarked yesterday: "What I ad-
mire about the English is that they own to their mis-
takes, and that is their strength."   I should like to see
Germany own up to their mistakes in the way Sir Ian
Hamilton did in his Dardanelles dispatches, or Lord
Beresford, when he criticized the naval battle.

The account of Baron von Rath's brother-in-law of
the battle at the Skager Rack is most interesting.   He led
the whole of the Destroyer Flotilla, and stood for fifty-
seven hours on the bridge.   One of his destroyers saved
140 Englishmen (?).   This is an interesting statement,
as by English accounts the Germans ran away, and could
not have saved an English crew during the battle.

Count Colloredo has just returned from Wilhelmshaven
He described having seen the whole fleet returning, and
added that it was the most historic sight he had ever
seen.   He had all sorts of interesting details to relate.
One cruiser had rammed an English destroyer and the
result was simply terrific, as the ship turned a somersault
over them.   He also remarked that the most impressive
sight was the 32 English Dreadnoughts, which formed a
kind of wall across the North Sea.   They shot at a distance of twenty miles away, and as they fired incessantly

one after the other, it seemed to form a continual streak of light—a most imposing sight to watch.

BERLIN, *June* 15, 1916.—At present nearly all the talk is about the Austrian reverse, which was quite unexpected.   The Archduke and his staff had been thinking more of sport, whilst the Russians surrounded the Austrian army, and made 62,000 prisoners, which really means 120,000 with dead and wounded   The Archduke has been sent away.   As a consequence there is great gloom here, as German troops have to be sent out.

I have just received messages from Captain R—— and Captain A——, thanking me for having had one of them sent to Switzerland and the other to another camp.   It is such a satisfaction to know that one has been able to do some little good in this way, and that it is appreciated. Soldiers on the whole are very grateful, and as I am on the subject I should like to relate a little story of a German wounded prisoner in England, who was so grateful to the nurse he had that when he returned home he could not praise her nursing and devotion sufficiently. He regretted after his recovery having had to fight against her countrymen.

The dispute as to who gained and who lost the Jutland battle is keener than ever.   The chief argument put forth by the Germans at present is, that they were the last to leave the zone of the battle, having remained to pick up the sinking and drowning sailors, as is proved by the number of English naval officers and men in their hands.

BERLIN, *June* 20, 1916.—There is a great depression over the Russian offensive and the evacuation of Czernowitz.   The Germans have had to form two new army corps, to send to the aid of the Austrians, and the rather bad feeling between the two countries is not improving in consequence.   What makes matters worse is, that the Austrians had to stop their offensive against the

Italians, and withdraw their best troops to send to the
Bukowina.

I think the bad feeling between the two allies is in
part owing to the great diversity of character. The
Austrian soldiers are easy-going, especially the officers,
and consequently there is a great want of discipline. A
lady heard the other day at one of the stations here a
conversation between an Austrian soldier and a civilian,
in which the former complained bitterly of the negligence
and indifference of his superior officers.

The German and especially the Prussian soldier is perhaps not as sociable or agreeable as the Austrian, and
might at times be somewhat of a martinet; but on the
other hand he has a great sense of duty, and practises
the severe discipline not only on others but also on
himself.

But the present depression reigning here is in part
owing to the worry over the food question, which is
increasing daily. We were told the other day that the
authorities intend closing the schools for three months,
as they want to keep as many women and children as
possible out of the towns on account of the food-supply.
A great difficulty is the scarcity of fodder for the cattle,
which means less milk and butter. One would expect
that all this shortage would prove a very serious question
in regard to the prisoners, but as a matter of fact they
are really better off than we are, as "The Prisoners' Aid
Society" sends 58,000 packages from England weekly to
the prisoners, and 10,000 loaves of bread from Switzerland. Each prisoner receives his package and loaf, and I
must give the German authorities their due as to the
proper delivery of these parcels.

The English Government sent an official inquiry as to
some complaints they had received, and the answer proved
that only one cigarette had been missing out of one box
in one week; and considering the number of parcels that
come from England for the prisoners each week, it does
not seem so bad. Mr. and Mrs. Lay have just returned

from Switzerland, where they were able to see the bakeries, and also the loaves which are sent every week from there to the English prisoners. The flour is sent to them from England. Mr. Lay played golf with eleven different nationalities, and he said that the war-talk between them was pretty lively at times, and that the war-talk here was child's play to their conversation.

KRIEBLOWITZ, *September* 1916.—For some three months I have written nothing, for it has been my lot to be the centre-piece in such an unusual series of events, following so fast on one another, that I found neither leisure nor inclination to sit down and write any account of them, or of my own feelings.

I had made up my mind to a quiet uneventful sojourn for some weeks alone in Berlin, when suddenly, on July 8, an event occurred which changed the whole course of our destiny. My father-in-law was killed by a fall from his horse, during a sudden attack of giddiness, whilst out riding in the park at Krieblowitz.

It is not easy to describe the difference which suddenly took place in our lives After having existed for more than two years in a bed-sitting-room in a hotel, we all at once found ourselves in possession of several beautiful castles and estates, a palace in Berlin, and many rich acres of land in the country. In fact it all seems rather like some new phase of the *Arabian Nights,* as by reason of the unusual relations existing between the members of the Blücher family, we had not until now in any way shared in all these desirable things, and it seemed almost magical to wake up one morning and find oneself the owner of them.

The funeral of my father-in-law, which my husband attended, brought about a sort of reconciliation (or was intended to do so) between my stepmother-in-law and the other members of the family, then all meeting together at Krieblowitz for the first time for twenty-five years. On July 23 we officially left Berlin for Breslau, where we stayed in the Ballestrem Palace, which had been lent to us by Graf Ballestrem, until we could take up our residence in Krieblowitz, which was not made possible for us until September.

Every one else seemed to be leaving the "Esplanade" at the same time, either going off to Switzerland or retiring to their country places, tired of the ever-increasing scarcity of food in Berlin; and we shall probably never again reunite in the same manner as during the last two winters in Berlin, if only on account of this difficulty.

On our at last taking formal possession on September 9 of Krieblowitz (the estate presented by the nation to the old Marshal "Vorwärts"), we met with quite a solemn reception at the entrance to the castle, where all the household were assembled to greet us, each one presenting me with a bouquet of flowers; while the officials, in frock coats and white gloves, each delivered a separate speech of welcome to me. The widow and her family met with a similar ovation in farewell, and departed, leaving us to settle down in earnest.

It is impossible to describe all the beauties of my future home; it is such a lovely old place, with its marble staircase and magnificent banquet-hall, its cloisters and vaulted arcades running round the castle, and the glorious views from the windows, over beautiful lakes and woods. And the people are so simple and natural in their kind way, with no display of bitterness or hatred towards the English nation; only full of gratitude for every kind word offered them, and resigned submission to their own personal losses in the war, eighty men having gone from the village of Krieblowitz alone, of whom no small number have already fallen.

The whole place was in deplorable need of repair; painters and decorators took possession, and began laying on electric light, putting up bath-rooms, etc., with the greatest speed possible, although, on account of the want of workmen and the shortness of all materials caused by the war, all sorts of delay were inevitable.

One of my husband's first acts was to create a chapel, as an offering of thanksgiving, and in memory of all our relations and friends who have died or fallen during the war. It is intended to form a place where perpetual prayer may be offered up for them all, and it will indeed be an exquisite little place of worship when finished and decorated, being formed out of a room already existing near the entrance to the castle, and which probably was originally intended as a chapel, having a vaulted Gothic roof and Pointed doorway.

It is as if some invisible curtain had fallen, separating us for ever from our nomadic life of unrest in Berlin, with all its political perplexities and vexations as to "fats and greases" (or rather the want of them), and the constant irritating absence of everyday needs. Here we are living on the fat of the land, as the monks of old themselves most probably did in this very same monastery. We are in fact self-supporting, which means that my husband and the keepers supply us with all manner of venison and game, such as wild duck, hares, partridges, and pheasants. We buy no butcher's meat; the farm supplies us with milk and butter, flour and bread, and the garden keeps us in vegetables and fruit. As elsewhere, these things are more or less "beschlagnahmt," but after having experienced what it is to be starved, we can appreciate all these luxuries well enough.

KRIEBLOWITZ, *September* 1916.—I have put off until now writing an account of a thrilling experience which I went through, and which sounds more like the plot of a shilling-shocker than an actual occurrence of every‧ day life, although there is very little love in the story and a great deal of ill-feeling and hatred. Well, every one has to have some little affair in connection with the war, and so I have just had "ma petite guerre à moi," and feel rather elated than otherwise, as I have decidedly come out of it with flying colours and routed the enemy hip and thigh.

Some ten days before the old Prince's death, I was suddenly and peremptorily summoned to appear at the Kommandantur, the centre of military legislation in Berlin. On my arrival there I was informed that my husband was not allowed to enter the room with me, so that during the two hours' investigation of my crimes which followed he was left to wait in an ante-room, not knowing what was going on, or if I was not going to be sentenced to the same fate as Miss Cavell for some unknown treason on my part.

On entering the room I asked for an interpreter, and was then put through a minute cross-examination, which amazed me more than anything else; most of it seemed to have so little do do with any possible reason for my being there.

I was informed that I was accused of having criticized the German treatment of prisoners of war in an unjustifiable manner. This had been overheard by a female informer, and I was asked to repeat what I had said. I was for the moment taken aback, for I could not recall having ever spoken of the matter to any one but my husband and my most trusted intimates. Wishing, however, to be perfectly truthful, I agreed that I might perhaps have discussed the matter at some time or other, upon which they proceeded to assist my memory by telling me I had been heard to use the words "unglaubliche Unmenschlichkeiten" (incredible inhumanities) to Mr. Gerard, the Ambassador.

I pointed out that this was palpably false, as not only did I not know what the words meant, but I could not even pronounce them had I done so. Having convinced them of this through the medium of the interpreter, a very nice German officer, who took my part the whole time and thought the whole matter a storm in a tea-cup, they proceeded to question me on all sorts of vague things which had nothing to do with the affair at all.

They were greatly interested not only in my own

age, but that of my parents as well, and were very curious about my mother's maiden name and the date of my father's birthday; after which they suddenly sprang back to real business, and we did a little light fencing as to the exact position of the tables and chairs and the coffee-cups on a certain memorable night in the "Esplanade" garden, when my treasonable incrimination of the Prussian methods of treating their prisoners was supposed to have taken place. When we had agreed on these various points the matter was settled as follows: Scene laid in the illuminated gardens of the Esplanade, my husband and myself sitting on the terrace drinking our coffee, as we always did in the evening; later enter Prince and Princess Braganza, and Baron and Baronin von Rath, who joined our party, as was their habit after dinner; conversation general and vague until the arrival of Mr. Gerard on the scene. One of us asks him to tell us something of his doings that day, to amuse us. Mr. Gerard, in his customary abrupt way, replies: "If I told you what I had been doing to-day, there would be a long article in all the German papers to-morrow, accusing me of being anti-German and pro-English. But I can tell you one thing," he added, "there will be food-riots in some of the prison camps very soon."

I: "Food-riots? How can that be? I thought they got such splendid parcels from home!"

Mr. G.: "Parcels from home consist of groceries. I should like to see you living on groceries."

And I really could not remember anything more having been said after this, although I was alleged to have poured forth volumes of wrathful criticism on the subject. I was then not only questioned on the family history of my husband and myself, but also on that of Prince and Princess Braganza, of Baron von Rath and his wife, as well as of Mr. Gerard.

I was thereupon informed that the matter was finished, and returning to the hotel at once ran to my friends' rooms to laugh over my experiences, and was at

the same time rather amused to hear that one of them
had just been summoned to the Kommandantur too.

For the next ten days I had not much time to think
of the matter, as in the meantime old Prince Blucher had
died, and I was laid up in bed with influenza.   Then,
on the very day when my husband was away at the
funeral, I received a second order to appear at the
Kommandantur.   I at once rang up my doctor, who
wrote out a certificate saying that I was too unwell to
appear.   My judges gave me two days to recover, and
on my then presenting myself I was curtly informed that
I was to quit Berlin within three days.   For the moment
there was nothing to be done but obey, as no one knows
what procedure this military dictatorship may employ
next.   But once established in Breslau, my husband
immediately proceeded to set all strings in motion to get
behind the matter and have the sentence rescinded.   He
drew up an appeal to High Quarters, and travelling back
to Berlin demanded imperatively to see General von
Kessel personally.   He was put off with all manner of
excuses for several days, when losing further patience
he sent in an "ultimatum" to the Commandant, saying
that if he did not see him within twenty-four hours he
would go personally to the Kaiser.   He then took the
next train for Breslau, but before even arriving there
telegrams and telephone messages came raining in from
terrified officials begging my husband to return at once
and see the General.

Some one who interviewed him at that time on the
subject told us that the General had realized his mistake
when it was too late, but was unable to draw back.
On being directly asked what my real offence was, he
was obliged to admit that I had not said the things I
was accused of, but that I had shown anti-German
inclinations; and on its being put to him that this was
not a grave military offence, he agreed, but said, "I
mean to teach German princes not to marry English
wives."   Wonderfully diplomatic, is it not?   On the

other hand, in High Quarters they say: "We want the foreign wives of our nobility to be encouraged to live in our country, and not to be driven out of it one by one."

By this time all the figures who had been dancing to General Kessel's tune began to see their mistake also, and proceeded to try and mend broken pitchers. One of the principal marionettes, the woman who had stooped to play the part of an informer, wrote and apologized, saying that she had "overheard incorrectly"; but she met a well-deserved fate, and having served their ends, she and her husband were flung aside by the military authorities like tools of no further service. They were, of course, cut dead by every one, and had to leave the hotel, and the husband had to resign his post on the Staff into the bargain. The General, who was by this time in a state of abject fear, implored my husband not to let the affair get to High Quarters, and he would rescind the sentence at once. But it was already known there, causing intense indignation. I received all sorts of nice messages and letters from High Quarters, and from various high officials, apologizing for the idiotic affair and regretting the inconvenience it may have caused me. I am therefore glad to be able to express my appreciation of the kindly, chivalrous feeling existing amongst many men of the highest position in this country.

The conclusion of the affair was rather amusing than otherwise, for General von Kessel, feeling he had put his foot in it rather badly, became quite friendly with my husband, and in a moment of confidence told him some interesting details as to their methods of watching the doings of women of foreign birth. He said that we were all under strict supervision, and that descriptions of our lives and doings were all entered in books for this purpose.

Gebhard asked him what proofs he had of my so-called "anti-German inclinations." He thereupon produced a letter which I had written to my cousin, Captain Trafford, four months ago. Two incriminating sentences were marked in it, and the letter had been sent by the Commandant of Crefeld to the Commandant at Münster, who was so shocked that he sent it on to Kessel, who, still more shocked, showed it to Bethmann-Hollweg, who, however, was obliged to admit that he could not see anything so very terrible in them.

The inoffensive letter had, however, grown into a State affair, and they had all been pondering deeply on its meaning for the last four months. The two extracts run as follows:

1. "The Tennis Club is now open again, and we sometimes go there in the afternoons; but it is not amusing as it was last year, as every one seems in low spirits and has no energy or keenness for anything." German note at the end: "The writer evidently means to convey to her cousin that the German nation is depressed about the ultimate result of the war."

2. "When the happy day of peace arrives, what a lot of new nephews and nieces you and I will have to be introduced to when we meet again in England." German note: "The writer seems to be discontented with living in Germany, and intends to go back and live in England as soon as she possibly can, and seems to infer that she would like peace at any price, so that that moment should arrive for her."

It seems hardly possible that so much fuss should be made about such harmless little sentences, and many *Germans* laugh at it themselves. I myself can hardly help being amused, although I am so angry. But if this is all that they can bring against me after two years, I feel rather complimented than otherwise, particularly when I think of the things I might have been accused of saying, which perhaps it would not have been so easy to explain.

KRIEBLOWITZ, *September* 1916.—The great topic of interest which is hypnotizing the mental powers of all Germany, and putting great strain on the national sagacity, is the best way of preserving human life on a minimum of albumen and farinaceous foods. Letters received from friends reveal the desperate plight they are in to cope with the necessities of the day. We hear too of food-riots in Berlin and other big towns, but in order to prevent a panic they have all been hushed up.

Prince Friedrich Wilhelm, a nephew of the Emperor, and the Landrat not very far from here, was shot at last week, the people blaming him for the shortness of food, etc.; and an official in the Board of Provisions here told my husband, a month ago, that if the war lasted another six months it would be impossible to keep the people in hand at all, the disquietude is increasing so alarmingly.

There has been food enough during the last year, but it seems that so much has been stored up that whole cart-loads have had to be thrown into the Rhine, as it has all gone bad. This is what enrages the people so fearfully.

.   .   .   .   .   .

Although the battle on the Somme has proved to be of much longer duration than any one expected, no decisive action has taken place up to now. Bloodier and more costly as it has proved to be than any other phase of this murderous war, Germany remains determined not to be crushed by the Allies, as these in their turn are shrill with assertions of its being the final move towards her destruction.

An officer back from the front told us to-day that the flyers in the West are causing the most appalling havoc there. The French flyers come down to within 300 metres of the lines, and throw bombs on to transport and hospital trains. Only the day before he had himself seen an engine blown up, and the engine-driver killed together with all the other occupants of the train. How thankful I feel that my husband no longer accompanies the wounded on the transport-train, as the very one he was on has to go into the thick of the fighting in the West. In fact, no one is safe anywhere, it seems, and only to-day we heard of English and French flyers being over Brussels, and German flyers over Portsmouth.

.   .   .   .   .

The death of Prince Emanuel Salm affected us deeply. It was only a few short weeks ago that he was relating to us his experiences in an English concentration camp, and how kind every one had been to him there   He had been a prisoner for some eighteen months, his friends working hard the whole time to set him free; and on this finally being accomplished, he was at once sent to the Russian Front, where he was killed within a very short space of time after his arrival.

.   .   .   .   .

The relations between Austria and Germany are becoming very strained, the Germans complaining that the Austrians lose all the ground gained by the Prussian troops, and the Austrians grumbling that they are never given credit for any victories, but are always accused of muddling and making mistakes.   The Austrian Arch-dukes, who invariably arrive too late on the scene, are the most popular butt for the criticisms of the German comic papers.

The Austrians, on the other hand, affirm that Germany would have been in a sad plight now had they not stopped the Russians from pouring into Silesia in the commence-ment of the war.   The agitation in Bohemia and Lower Austria is said to be increasing alarmingly, the people clamouring for bread and peace, even at the cost of handing over Galicia or any other territory to Russia, if they only be left unmolested.

The feelings amongst the people here in Germany, in the interior, are a mixture of stoical submission to their present desperate plight, and a certain conviction that Germany can never be really humiliated.

.   .   .   .   .

Hindenburg's promotion as Commander-in-Chief in the place of Falkenhayn was a very popular step, the latter being regarded as a man of personal ambition,

whose own ends were at least as important as those
of his country. It is said that Hindenburg made it a
condition of his accepting the post that no further actions
against Verdun should be attempted.

.   .   .   .   .   .

A great movement is being organized to ensure the
co-operation of the Reichstag in the field of work especially monopolized by the Foreign Office until now. In
fact, a more democratic form of government on English
and French lines is being dreamed of and worked for
already by the more liberal party in the Reichstag.

To-day is one of the critical days in the Reichstag,
as the Socialists are going to speak, which generally
means more street riots. Men coming home from the
front are beginning to murmur, and the authorities are
in fear of their causing disturbances. We also hear that
Herr von Jagow, the head of the police, has been suddenly promoted (?) to the same post in Breslau, on
account of the Emperor's displeasure at the drastic measures taken by the police during the last bread and peace
riots in Berlin when women are said to have been
wounded. The Emperor said he would have no more of
it, and that some other method than that of shooting
women must be found for quelling street-riots.

.   .   .   .   .   .

The unprecedented English artillery fire on the Somme
is filling the hospitals more than ever, all those on
the Rhine being over-filled, so that wounded are being
transported straight from the front to the Tempelhofer
Hospital in Berlin, which has never occurred during the
war before. Cases of overstrained nerves and temporary
insanity are the order of the day. Only yesterday I
spoke to an official who told me that within the last week
both of his sons had been sent home insane, having gone
out of their minds at the awful things they had witnessed.

.   .   .   .   .   .

An incident which caused much rejoicing here was
the successful crossing of the merchant-submarine boats,

the people looking upon it as the commencement of a new era of commercial enterprise and success.

The reduction in pay of all officers in the German army, from the Minister of War down to the youngest lieutenant, though regarded with satisfaction by the civil population and the rank and file of the army, has been received with very mixed feelings by the officers themselves. They look upon the moment as too critical for such trenchant measures, and those who have had to bear the whole of the hardships of two years' fighting feel themselves very much injured. To the simple looker-on the system seems to be one of burning injustice.

KRIEBLOWITZ, *September-October* 1916.—The air raid on Karlsruhe was hushed up, but a witness told me it was terrible The aeroplanes were so high that nothing was to be seen; one only heard the uncanny buzz in the air and watched the fire drop. The man who described it was a watchmaker, and very indignant at this attack on an open town. "Well," he said, "I wonder what we shall do in return—a few more attacks on England!"

On September 1, all people having meat in any form were required to send in an exact return of the kind, amount, etc. Several society ladies of a certain kind immediately gave big dinner-parties, saying, "We would rather let our friends eat it than give it up to the authorities as we did our stores of sugar." There is a peculiarly unpatriotic undertone there, whereas the following is a case of misplaced patriotism. A man back from the front on leave was asked in the train when he thought the war would end. "Why," he replied, "when the Emperor has to eat bread and jam like us." A lady who heard this had the man arrested. The poor devil meant no harm, though of course he should have been more guarded, but he was tired and fresh from horrors that I should have liked to send the patriotic lady to share.

A friend of mine wanted to buy some woollen under-wear, and her experiences are typical of war-shopping now in Germany. She saw what she wanted in a shop and went in. The girl who attended her was very obliging and got everything ready, but when the bill was made out she turned to my friend and said, "Where is your 'Bezugschein' (permit of purchase)?" "Oh," said my friend, "I have none." The girl told her it was a trifle, and that she would reserve the goods for her until she had obtained one; she need only go to the police station. Off went my friend, and when she arrived at the police station they told her to go to a stationer's, and get a form which is filled in as a kind of control when one moves about So she departed and returned with this form. "What shall I write on it?" she asked. The answer was, your name, your age, where you were born, what subject you are, and last, but not least—not how much material do you want, but what faith do you profess? My friend filled in all this, whereupon the official stamped her paper, which meant that he guaranteed for the truth thereof, and then sent her off to the place where she might receive the permit. This was a good walk from where she was, and she decided to go next day. When she got there at 4 o'clock in the afternoon she was told the office was only open from 8 to 1 o'clock. Patiently she trudged home, to start again next day. When she arrived this time she was asked what the permit was to be for "For three pairs of combinations," she told the official (there are no discreet secrets from officials here in war-time). "What!" he exclaimed, "you want three pairs? You cannot have more than two, one to wear while the other is in the wash!" Shopping becomes a strange thing when con-trolled by Prussian officialdom.

Cheese has run out—why? There has been a quarrel with Switzerland, whilst Holland exports to England, for Germany will not pay enough. Germany says: If we pay so much for cheese, the public must pay so much too; the poor will then not be able to buy cheese. The rich, however, will. Then, as the poor consider cheese their right, they will revolt if they see that only the rich can buy it; whereas if there is no cheese at all, there can be no cheese riots!

. . . . . .

Roumania has declared war on Austria, and the Austrians are in despair. Their freedom is gone anyway, for they cannot defend themselves against all these enemies alone; and, after all, is it so much worse to be under England's sway than under that of Germany, which seems their only prospect? Austria wants peace at any cost.

. . . . . .

War Commandment: Thou shalt not slaughter cattle without a special permit.

One dark night the village policeman passes a butcher's house and hears queer sounds; he also sees a light streaming through the chinks of the door. He determines to knock and ask what the butcher is doing so late at night. The butcher's wife says she is getting her meat ready for the next morning. The next day he appears at the same butcher's, and lo! there he finds a freshly slaughtered calf. "What!" says the policeman. "This is forbidden. You will have to pay a fine." The butcher's wife protests perfect innocence; her neighbour had called her in to kill the calf, for the poor beast had been climbing a ladder, got its head between the rungs, and hung in awful agony. It was a good excuse, but the policeman decided that a fine must be paid, and that calves which climb ladders must be left to hang until the permit for slaughter is procured!

This is not an exceptional case, and no wonder evasion goes on. The greater the number of prohibitions, the greater the amount of swindling.

. . . . . .

Prussians were much disappointed on their journeys

to the Bavarian Alps this year. The Bavarians never had any food when Prussians were hungry!

.   .   .   .   .   .

A soldier home on leave tells me about the life the officers lead. Why, he said, the officers were having the time of their lives even now. Every day for dinner the tables are decorated with flowers; the officers have butter in quantities, eggs, meat, all most beautifully prepared, and the table laid as if they were in a first-rate hotel. Following each regiment there is always sufficient baggage among which are crockery and glass, forks and knives of the best kind One officer had even his dishes in silver. His view was, I suppose, that it was less breakable! The men get nothing of all this, neither butter, eggs, nor forks and knives; but that was just it—war!

They had bad losses near Verdun. The Major had got the Iron Cross 1st Class—why? Because he had remained in a protected position and received the ammunition from a lieutenant in a protected position on the other side. Between these two was about 300 yards of ground over which the waggons had to go backwards and forwards with the ammunition, and each journey cost so many lives which were rewarded by the Iron Cross the said Major received for *his* bravery. This seemed to me very like a suppressed grumble, but actually there are no more faithful and loyal soldiers than these stolid Prussians, whose sense of duty and obedience is indomitable.

KRIEBLOWITZ, *January* 1917.—We are all growing thinner every day, and the rounded contours of the German nation have become a legend of the past. We are all gaunt and bony now, and have dark shadows round our eyes, and our thoughts are chiefly taken up with wondering what our next meal will be, and dreaming of the good things that once existed.

All labour resources are being organized for military purposes, which means that every man will be called upon to serve his country in some way, and even those who were passed as physically unfit a few months ago are now being trained for military service.

One curious feature in the mental condition of the people is the way in which feeling towards England and everything English has veered round. Men who were scoffing and railing at England twelve months ago are beginning to express their admiration, and even dare to display a certain affection and attachment publicly. A popular speaker, addressing a large assembly the other day, declared that the talk about Germany's splendid organization was all nonsense; she was nowhere in it with England, and that England was the only country which could organize at all. Another acquaintance, Count B , offered help for English people to the emergency society here, declaring that he had only learnt to love England since the war, and that he would never allow a word to be said against her by any one in his house.

The truth is, the soul of the people is sick unto death of the useless carnage and hateful sinfulness of it all. In the Reichstag the same old bombastic phrases still bring down a volley of applause, so that the quiet observer is astonished at the childishness of these representatives of the nation; but the man who would bring peace and not war would be hailed as a real leader and king One intrepid Socialist, goaded to despair at the artificiality of the speeches, shouted out the truth in the face of the whole assembly: "The people don't want war; what they want is peace and bread and work"—but he was only snubbed by contemptuous derision in reply.

.   .   .   .   .

Herr von Jagow's resignation of his post as Foreign Secretary was a great sorrow to us. He was a personal friend of ours, and a clever, cultivated man, a pacifist, which, of course, rendered him abhorrent and suspect to the military party. In his own quiet way he contravened many ruthless orders of the militarists, and regretted many more which he was helpless to prevent. He is probably a victim of inimical forces over which he had no control. He was not relentless and uncompromising enough for the military party, and he did not trouble himself enough to play to the democratic party which is daily acquiring power. He was too much a diplomatist of the old school, and lacked the power of forcing his own personality on his hearers when speaking.

Perhaps one of the most pathetic central figures playing on the stage of the European War is the German Emperor, brilliant as his rôle may seem to superficial lookers-on. In reality he is but a lay figure, crowned and clad in shining armour, and moved here and there at the will of the military power which he has created.

I think people in England hardly realize the covert scorn with which people speak of him here. The remarks made often astonish me. "Let him talk as if he had won these victories, and let him believe he is running the whole army." "Send him to the East when there are some prisoners to march past, and he will be pleased; and again to the West when there is a little success to show him, and he will be as pleased as ever." Whilst the Emperor himself complains sadly in the same words: "I never know what I am going to do from one day to another," he says. "To-day I am packed up and sent off to the East, and to-morrow to the West."

Summing up his character it may be said of him that he is to a certain degree a tyrant, and is not always to be depended upon to keep his promises. As regards his friendships, he takes people up easily and drops them again just as easily, and further possesses certain qualities which go to make up the bully. Yet in spite of these drawbacks he has a great charm of manner which endears him to all those who really know him; and his real friendships are genuine and lasting, and if he only possessed the courage of his friendships he would be a happier man.

As for the Emperor's six sons, there are many malicious remarks and criticisms rife amongst the people; and all the touching anecdotes of the sacrifices of the Empress in sending six sons to the front, where other mothers had only one to offer, have long disappeared from the papers. The monster of war has always had a way of passing over the six princes, and preferred the only son of a widow. People are beginning to murmur that they are being too carefully guarded; and granted that they did run into danger at the beginning of the war, they always seem to be now more or less on the Staff—and, funny as it may seem, a great many people seem to take it specially amiss that one or other of them is always getting married. "The fact of the matter is," said one of the ministers in a very high position here not long ago, "one of the Kaiser's sons ought to be sacrificed—to appease the people."

BERLIN, *February* 1917.—After an interval of peace and quiet in the country for six months, Berlin again with all its unrest and harrowing problems. Krieblowitz, with its docile Silesian peasants and their somewhat cringing manners, characteristic of the mixed breed of Slav and the East German race, was a soothing experience.

There is intense cold here as there, such as has not been known for more than half a century. But there one had the wide expanse of ploughed acres walled in by great game-haunted forests, whilst here there are shivering throngs of hungry care-worn people picking their way through the snowy streets, and anxiously watching for some isolated waggon of briquettes, which may offer a chance of buying ten or twenty, and thus having a warm room for at least one day.

Coal, or at least the want of it, is the one subject of the moment. It seems suddenly to have disappeared from the face of the German empire; or is at least not available, and is lying shunted off in innumerable waggon-loads on obscure side-lines somewhere or other in the coal districts.

Imagine the result! Everywhere people staying in

bed and refusing to be comforted, or hurrying off from their own flats to meet with a very frigid reception in the hotels and pensions where they seek refuge.

Of course, there is a perfect epidemic of burst water-pipes all over Berlin, and as there are no plumbers to repair the damage, people are beginning to think that the torments of Dante's *inferno* are capped by the hardships of this deadly winter of 1916-17.

Berlin the cleanest town in Europe is of course a thing of the past   The snow lies unmolested until the boys' schools are turned out to shovel it away, or some few enterprising females do their best to aid in making the roads clear

There are practically no motors to be had, and the few antediluvian droshkies are being dragged wearily along by half-starved beasts, who, if they happen to stumble and fall, don't even attempt to rise, but lie still, humbly thankful for the respite from work, on the cold frozen ground.

As for the mood of the people, the heroic attitude has entirely disappeared. Now one sees faces like masks, blue with cold and drawn by hunger, with the harassed expression common to all those who are continually speculating as to the possibility of another meal.

If by chance one does happen to dine well it is always with more or less of a bad conscience, as everything is in reality forbidden and belongs to the nation at large.

At Krieblowitz we tried now and again to kill one of our pigs, but it won't do as a rule. There is none of the feasting and revelry which generally accompany this solemn ceremony. The whole province of Silesia watches the act with hungry faces, counting how many mouthfuls we each appropriate for our own share, and Hindenburg stands sternly in the background, demanding a portion of it for his munitioners, whilst we are deprived of our meat-tickets for weeks to come as a punishment for the few succulent morsels we may manage to get.

The fowls are exasperating and will not lay any eggs,

so that if we are lucky we are doled out one egg every three weeks. Our bread is being "stretched" in every way possible, and is now mixed with some of those numerous subterranean vegetables coming under the rubric of the turnip, of whose existence we never dreamed before.

On our return to the "Esplanade" we met with a very cold reception, for some of the men who attend to the heating apparatus had refused to leave their beds, saying that their food-tickets had been appropriated for the guests and they intended sleeping until they were restored to them. The whole hotel was in a great state of excitement, moreover, several of the managers having been arrested for appropriating food and butter entrusted to them for the wounded soldiers, and selling them at an enormous profit to guests in the hotel.

On the whole, all the conscientious scruples which really did hinder many people from storing up underhand supplies of food some six months ago have disappeared before the pangs of hunger, and the feeling prevalent in all classes is: every man for himself and the devil for us all!

The princes have come up for the opening of the Herrenhaus which is about to meet, and my husband's first appearance there is looked upon as quite an event, the seat having been in abeyance for twenty years.

Prince and Princess Münster were here for a few days, she rather depressed, as her eldest son, Freddie, is being ordered off to the East Front after being at home on sick leave for one and a half years. But now practically every one who can manage to creep on all fours is being called back. And as her second son, Paul, is also leaving Lichterfelde and going out later on, the Princess will be in the painful position of seeing her husband and sons joined in fighting against her own relations and countrymen.

Nancy (Duchess of Croy) is alone here as well, as her husband has had to go back. And Princess Braganza

(Anita), whose husband is now in Warsaw, has only just returned to say good-bye to Mrs. Gerard, one of her oldest American friends.

One small spark of pleasure amongst us has been the engagement of Countess Pourtalès (the widowed daughter of Count Bernstorff) to Prince Johannes Löwenstein. Such small faint rays of happiness light up the lives of us exiles who have been sharing one another's lot for two years and a half.

.   .   .   .   .   .

The Great Headquarters have, we hear, been changed from Pless to Creuznach (?), as it is expected that the decision will come shortly in the West. It is a somewhat exposed position for flyers, and fears are expressed for the person of the Emperor.

Every one is excited about the submarine question. We all know and feel that Germany is playing her last card; with what results, no one can possibly foretell. The resolution for sharpening up the submarine war was received silently by the commission in the Reichstag. The middle-class Chauvinists and the Pan-Germans hail it as an infallible step to a final victory; whilst the pessimists and wise men who are discontented with the war assert that God has struck the German nation with blindness before utterly ruining it, and predict that all the neutrals will follow the lead of America, who has just handed over her Note threatening war.

One astute man declares the whole move to have been purposely provoked by England, who intentionally phrased her refusal of the peace proposals in such insolent terms as to provoke Germany into doing something rash in retaliation.

We, however, think the situation looks pretty serious for England, as the U-boats can starve her out partially. On the other hand, rumours are rampant as to the mysterious inventions presumably planned by England for frustrating the devilish workings of the submarines.

The excitement amongst the Americans here is intense,

and yesterday, when news of the rupture of diplomatic
relations was announced at the Embassy, during a
luncheon-party there, several of the women lost all control over themselves, and faints and hysterical weeping
seem to have been the order of the day.   The American
ladies married to Germans, who have undertaken to pay
their princely husbands' bills, are in a sad plight, as all
financial connections will be broken off between the two
countries.

Mr. Gerard, the Ambassador, will be regretted by few.
He was a man of disagreeable, tactless manners, and
managed to offend every one.   In fact, he was not the
person to have been chosen to act as negotiator between
two hostile powers at such a critical period of the world's
history.   Mrs. Gerard, his wife, on the contrary, will be
regretted by all of us.   With her quiet tact and patience
she endeavoured to gloss over the many breaches of good
manners committed by her incorrigible husband.

Mr. and Mrs. Grew were very popular here.   She, poor
woman, was torn between regret at leaving her best
friends here and joy at seeing her children again, who
have been living in America since the beginning of the
war.   Mr. Grew, in spite of his pronounced sympathy
for England, never betrayed his political feelings by word
or deed, and with his really gentlemanly instincts bore
the brunt of all the diplomatic affairs.   Without him the
Embassy would have smashed up long ago.

Mr. Dresel and Mr. Osborne will also be missed.   So
will Mr. and Mrs. Jackson, as they have lived in Europe
for twenty-seven years and have all their personal friends
here, so that the present rupture means a decided crisis
in their life   As they are not in with the present Government they are quietly returning to Switzerland, the work
of their life being over.

The Prisoners' Department was entirely organized by
Mr. Jackson, and the welfare of the prisoners was much
improved by his efforts.   Now, with one stroke, his work
has come to a close, and his business has been transferred

to the Dutch Legation. But no one can manage the intricate workings of the organization as well as Mr. Jackson did, and although we sometimes criticized his apparent want of feeling for the sufferings of the prisoners, he has since assured us that this hardness of heart was only assumed so as to appear absolutely just and unbiassed.

BERLIN, *April* 1917.—It is April again, and, looking through my window on to the Tiergarten, I can see the snow falling incessantly, whirled past by those awful east winds which torment us this year and bring all sorts of disagreeable reminders of the long Russian winter and the revolution which is running its bloody course there.

We have just passed through some chaotic weeks, getting settled down in our apartment in the Blücher Palace, no light task nowadays.

.   .   .   .   .   .

The chief subject of interest is, of course, the great spring offensive on the West Front, and I hear exciting details from acquaintances now and then passing through Berlin. The English are said to have broken through the third German line, but the general impression here is one of confidence in Hindenburg's leadership and the strength of their own iron wall, which they say no human power can ever overcome.

Count Radolin gave us a graphic account of the storming of Arras. He said it was the 1st Garde regiment which saved the situation, but not a single officer survived it. The Bavarians gave way, it seems, before the furious attack.

Ammunition seems to be running short, and trains filled with wounded arrive at the towns in the south and west of Germany every ten minutes. None, however, are sent to Berlin. Bissing, the Belgian Governor, has just been buried, and we have heard that by some strange hazard the same chaplain who officiated at Miss

Cavell's execution attended the last moments of the inexorable old Prussian general.

Young Count Schaffgotsch told us that he ran forward to pick up an English wounded officer, and doing so recognized an Oxford friend of his. He accompanied him to hospital and did everything he could to alleviate his lot.

To-day I got a letter from Captain E. Trafford in which he mentioned how pleased the imprisoned officers at Crefeld are, as the camp is henceforth to become an all-British one, and the prisoners of other nationalities are being sent away, and English officers from all parts of Germany are arriving every day. There are about 400 of them there now. It means a tremendous change to them all, and many old friends meet again who knew nothing of one another's imprisonment until now.

Another piece of news is that Princess Braganza, who has just returned from Vienna, met Mr. D—— there a few days before the declaration of war with America. He was on his way home to America when he left here, but on his arrival in England was asked to go to Vienna to negotiate about English prisoners there.

He gave some interesting details as to the general feeling in England now. The former intense hatred has taken on a more subdued character, and one even hears occasional praise of the enemy. The hatred still existing seems to be more or less concentrated on one person, and they are emphatic in declaring that peace must never be made with a Hohenzollern.

The submarine war, he says, is accepted with calm fatalism, and in spite of its causing some inconveniences and lessening imported wares, they maintain that 20 per cent of the ships still get through, and the U-boats can do no really grave damage to the mercantile shipping.

I heard likewise, from some one else who is in touch with England, that there is now a great peace party existing there, led by such men as Haldane, Lord Robert Cecil (in fact all the Cecils), as well as Lord Ampthill and the Russell family, and other unexpected and well-known personalities.

I heard further that Sir Edward Grey has been working for peace for the last year, and that Wilson's peace proposal was in reality due to Sir Edward's influence. This, they say, is probably the reason why Lloyd George got him turned out; but Lloyd George, they say, will not last much longer himself.

People blame the German Chancellor for not meeting Sir Edward Grey half-way when he put out very decided feelers for peace, some six months before the German peace proposals were ever dreamt of   Here the popular idea is that unless the Russian episode (which many people think will unhinge the earth from its axis) be imitated in a country that shall be nameless, there will be no more question of peace propositions at all.

.   .   .   .   .   .

The other day Dr. Solf, the Colonial Minister, dined here. He was interesting and clever as usual, and wanted to know my opinion of the submarine war. A lady who was dining here too asked him point-blank what he thought on the subject, and he admitted frankly that Prussia had played her trump card and it was doomed to be a failure

The war, he said, was a minor evil compared to the internal evil. Fresh disturbances are expected, and troops of mounted policemen patrol daily through the streets of Moabit. On the eve of an expected riot the Kaiserin hurried personally to one of the chief factories here, and hastily presented one of the leaders of the workmen's party with decorations, which, as evil tongues affirm, he promptly hung round his dog's neck which accompanied one of the processions next day. The whole revolt, however, ended in a few harmless demonstrations.

My husband yesterday had a private audience with the Emperor at the Bellevue Palace. On his return he told me that for the first time in his life, after such an interview, he came away with a sort of feeling of pity in his heart for the loneliness of a monarch. The Kaiser struck him as being so helpless and alone, though at the same time surrounded by cringing, obsequious courtiers. He told me that the Kaiser and he had discussed for some time the present outlook of affairs, and although the Emperor's words sounded hopeful his general bearing was not so, and gave the impression that he was repeating a lesson.

BERLIN, *May* 1917.—Here we are right in the heart of May, and the long arctic winter has given place to blue skies and a more hopeful view in the aspect of affairs. Every one goes about with a brighter face, and a more patriotic optimism prophesies the end of the war in July or August.

The interest awakened by hopes of the Chancellor's speech was somewhat disappointed. He was so excessively cautious No new disclosures were made, no declarations offered as to the German war aims, and no new loopholes opened out for peace feelers, excepting the reserved hint of a possible separate understanding with Russia, which however cheers some people up wonderfully.

Scheidemann's challenge, dashed into the midst of the assembled Reichstag in the shape of a threatened revolution, drew blood, as he hoped, and the Pan-Germans instantly filled their papers with columns of righteous indignation at this open menace to the nation, whereupon the Socialists immediately replied with a corresponding threat, which had been made personally to no less a personage than Bethmann-Hollweg himself by General von Gröning some two years ago.

Amongst the many wandering rumours which reach our ears we heard that the Wittelsbachs and Hohenzollerns are planning the cutting of the Gordian knot of Alsace-Lorraine by dividing it up between them. Scheidemann himself publicly accuses the Pan-Germans of being the cause of the Kaiser's unpopularity with the

Entente nations by always dragging his name into their private plans of annexation.

. . . . .

The sad news of Prince Friedrich Karl's death is deeply commiserated here. He was trained as a flyer in Breslau, and we often saw his aeroplane flying over Krieblowitz. He had only been in the West ten days when he was killed. It is said his death was prophesied through the medium of "Planchette," that it would take place so many days after his arrival at the front, and that it actually took place to the very day.

He was the Emperor's nephew and was one of those attractive youths beloved in both countries, having spent much of his time in England (where he once played in the tennis championship at Wimbledon under the name of Mr. Karl Frederick). There was much criticism here when his death was announced, a few days after he was reported wounded; and it was, needless to say, put down to neglect on the part of the English doctors and nurses. But I have learnt to bide my time and keep silent when I hear such things discussed, knowing that truth will out sooner or later. And a few days after a letter came from the boy himself, written the day he died, saying how kind the English had been to him, what intense care the doctors and nurses had expended on him, and his relief to find himself in a bright cheerful English hospital after his experiences at the front. He said they had moved him from the dressing-station, as it was being shelled incessantly, and went on to say that his uncle, the Duke of Connaught, had instantly sent out the best surgeon from London to attend him, and had telegraphed repeatedly to inquire for him. Much more was in the letter which at present is not allowed to be repeated, in case it might disillusion those who wish to criticize the English treatment of wounded prisoners.

Count Bernstorff, the late German Ambassador in Washington, with his staff have arrived from America, and bitter complaints are being poured forth as to the behaviour of the Canadian officers who examined the Embassy luggage.

Count Bernstorff and his wife are now staying at this hotel. Every one is commenting on the fact that he was not received at Headquarters on his arrival, and it is rumoured that it may be owing to the fact that he was known to be very much opposed to the unrestricted U-boat war, and could have prevented American intervention if he had been given a free hand, and if the unremitting antagonism between the Reichsmarine Amt and the Foreign Office had not precipitated matters. The Mexican blunder cannot be laid at Count Bernstorff's door.

     .   .   .   .   .   .

We hear that a climax has come for Greece, and the monarchy is played out German influence has come to an end and Venizelos has won the day. King Constantine has abdicated, and the German Minister (our friend Count Mirbach) is returning with his staff. My husband came across a publication regarding some of the members of the so-called German propaganda staff, including one who is styled as Count Blücher, and who is mentioned as being implicated in secret service operations against the Entente. Believing there must be some mistake in the name, he has made inquiries, and has found out that the gentleman in question is a member of the distant branch of the Mecklenburg "von Blüchers."

     .   .   .   .   .   .

Great discussion over the torpedoing of hospital ships, the German view being that they were bogus ones, carrying ammunition and troops hidden on board. Even if this were true it would be no excuse, for they ought to give warning to enable the sick and wounded, nurses and doctors, to get off. The naval authorities, indeed, declare that orders have never been issued for such wholesale destruction. But I have heard from some one, who is in a position to know, that the orders were so

worded as to leave too much to the discretion of the
commanders, who, in cases where it was impossible to
identify the real character of the ship in question, took
the benefit of the doubt and acted as their feelings or
ambition prompted them. So far as the German nation
as a whole is concerned, half of it does not believe or
realize that any hospital ships have been sunk; a
quarter regret it intensely; and the rest try to prove
beyond doubt that the ships were camouflaged 'and
really contained troops. Some women, especially, are
horrified at the stories told. My sister, Freda Charlton,
on her long dangerous journey to the Cape, took seven
small children with her, and made them wear life-
belts the whole time. When I showed some German
ladies of my acquaintance the photograph of twins of
two years old standing on deck, each girt with a huge
life-belt, tears came into their eyes, and they said: "Do
people really think that the Germans are so cruel as to
want to sink ships with women and children on them!"

.   .   .   .   .   .

I met a lady the other day who was actually on board
one of the torpedoed hospital ships, and was saved by
clinging to a plank. She described something of the
ghastly experience, and says she will be haunted to her
dying day by the expression of agony on the faces of the
helpless wounded men, unable to make the slightest
effort to save themselves in their tight bandages, as the
waves closed over them. Whilst shuddering with pity
at the picture she drew, I could not at the same time
help recalling the face of a poor German mother bidding
farewell to her second son, who was starting for the
front only a few days after receiving details of the
death of her other son, who had been fearfully mutilated
by black troops.

BERLIN, *June-July* 1917.—How quickly the English
are advancing! I wonder if this last victory will
prove a **turning-point in the war, as it** seems to be

a well-known fact that the English did break through
the German lines, although they themselves were not
aware of the fact until they had retired again.   But the
capture of the Ypres salient is no unimportant factor
and may possibly mean the final road to peace.

Here the military authorities, as they are bound
to do, characterize every advance of the enemy as an
elastic bend in the German line; or if it is reluctantly
admitted that the first German line has been broken
through, the English attack must always waver and fail
on the ever-renewed defence of the German reserves.

Harden's weekly periodical *Zukunft* has been suppressed until the end of the war, as he is one of the few
men who dared to say what he thought, and perfectly
openly argued the necessity of handing over Alsace-
Lorraine whilst there was still time to do it with the grand
air.   Later on, he argues, it will simply mean a matter of
compulsion.   This view is shared by many others.   My
husband is emphatic in his advice to agree to it in
time.   Why continue jeopardizing the whole empire for
a province which, as Bismarck said, will always be a
heritage of woe to whoever possesses it.

We get all our news through the carefully prepared
communiqués let loose on the credulous public every
Saturday and Sunday by the Wolff Bureau, and this
time they mentioned the retreat as a single insignificant
episode in the great general offensive of the Entente.
The retreat is described as a systematic and voluntary
retirement in order to hinder any unnecessary loss of life.

I heard gruesome stories about the German infantry
complaining that they were deliberately sacrificed to
save the German guns, and that out of some 3000 men
in the northern battle of Messines, over 2000 were taken
prisoners by reason of the artillery failing to support
them.

Hindenburg's retreat tactics seem to be formed on
those used alone by the Russians until now, namely,

that of devastating every inch of land left between themselves and the enemy.

.   .   .   .   .

And so another king has been shaken from his throne by the great earthquake, and poor King Constantine has had to abdicate and give way to forces stronger than his own. He was a good man and worthy of a better fate than an inglorious exile in a strange land. He used all the powers God had given him to keep his country from bloodshed, and his political crime was that he refused to sanction the Entent policy of his minister who had a majority to back him.

The Greek minister and his wife, the Theotokys, are hurrying away from Berlin to join the exiled monarch in Switzerland, and we have to look on and see how one more friend leaves the sinking ship Germania.

One of the strangest signs of the time is, to my thinking, the rapid and insidious way in which the tide of democracy is creeping on and overflooding all Europe. People are beginning to ask whether this is the divine meaning of the great catastrophe. In Russia we have seen the bloody horrors of an Asiatic revolt driving the Czar ignominiously from his high place. In Austria the newly fledged Emperor has seized the bull by the horns, and openly pleaded for democracy in his speech from the throne. Graf Tisza, the most unscrupulous and ruthless autocrat in all Europe, was forced to give up office because he dared to oppose democracy as represented in the Hungarian franchise bill. In Greece King Constantine had to abdicate ostensibly because of his refusing to support the democratic party. In Germany, where democracy was not as yet on the official political programme, it is gaining new adherents every day, and in time the new movement is bound to carry everything before it. It is pretty certain that in the future it will be impossible for any one, Kaiser or minister, to conclude treaties which are capable of leading the nation into war without the consent of the representatives of the people, and the democrats are determined that all important negotiations with other nations must be supported by a vote of confidence, and all internal questions must be settled by the Reichstag.

The Chancellor's position has been growing more and more critical, and his day has come. No one was satisfied with him, and Erzberger's vigorous attack in order to extract some definite proposals of peace have at last tripped him up.

There can be no doubt that Bethmann's hands were tied all along, and that he was not a free man. He is, in fact, the scapegoat for covering the faults of his lord and master. I have heard on pretty certain authority that the Kaiser gave his royal assent to Austria's ultimatum to Serbia in 1914, without even mentioning this small matter to his Chancellor until it was an accomplished fact.

Here the impulsiveness of his nature became a crime, and Bethmann, conscious of the fact that it was this consent which set the machinery of war in motion, has never been able to make the error good again, and has now made a final atonement, as he could not betray his royal master to the world   His is a tragic fate, and the rôle of compromise forced upon him lends him a tragic importance worthy of a central figure in the literature of the war in the days to come.

Helfferich and Zimmermann, they say, must go too, as well as a number of other ministers who are opposed to overtures of peace in any form. There is great excitement everywhere, and the world seems turned topsy-turvy. Hindenburg and Ludendorff in Berlin to offer their opinion on the new terms of peace; men without titles stepping into titled men's shoes; the Crown Prince sucking wisdom from the leaders of the different factions; Socialists visiting the Kaiser to offer him their opinion on a republican form of government, and being indignantly called to order for playing the courtier by their partisans.

The Kaiser is daily growing more and more the shadow of a king, and people talk openly of his abdication as a possibility very much desired. He gives in to all the demands of the Socialists, but at the same time makes so many palpable blunders and mistakes that a man in high office said only the other day, it looked almost as if the Emperor's advisers were in the pay of England, so insane is their advice, and that they seem to be deliberately playing into the hands of the enemy.

One consequence of all the blundering is that there is murmuring everywhere, in the army as well as amongst the civilians. For example, when on the advice of Michaelis the bread allowance was cut down, there was great grumbling amongst the people and a revolt seemed threatening. The food controllers in a panic promised them extra meat at a cheap price, to make up for the curtailed bread rations, and ordered all the milk cows in certain districts to be slaughtered.

This promptly took place, to the great rage of the agriculturists, who indignantly opposed the "madness of the order." But it was too late, the order had been carried out, and for a week or two there was such a surplus of meat that it actually had to be given or thrown away, to prevent its spoiling in the hot weather.

The result is now that milk is running short, and there is renewed grumbling, although the extra supply of cheap meat proved a great boon to the populations in the towns and helped them to tide over hard times.

As an accompaniment to the incessant murmuring and increasing incredulity of the people, there is a decided inclination to a milder form of revolt, and riots and disturbances do now and then take place, though they are hushed up. The Germans are such a patient and long-suffering race that they do not as yet realize their own power, and the Prussian precept, "Es ist ver boten," has been so drummed into them that they accept all regulations and orders without any further demur. I do believe that if they were bidden to go out and eat grass, they would obey in herds, without any further question.

⠀⠀⠀•⠀⠀⠀•⠀⠀⠀•⠀⠀⠀•⠀⠀⠀•⠀⠀⠀•

A common soldier, now working in our harvest, just returned from the front, spoke so nicely of all the hardships they had to endure. He had no bitterness for the enemy. The English, he said, were fine men to fight against, and he personally had never witnessed any of the desperate cruelty and intense hatred he is always told of behind the lines

"We all do our best for our own country, and if we meet as prisoners or otherwise, we are perfectly friendly; but," he added sadly, "there must be something wrong somewhere to make us so hated by all other nations, as well as by our own allies. Who is to blame for it? That is what my comrades and I are always trying to find out."

He went on to say that the English army is in splendid condition, and always being reinforced by fresh and perfectly equipped troops, whilst the Germans have only a tired and worn-out army to meet them. Many of the men in the trenches, having been wounded three or four times, are now so exhausted that they can hardly lift a rifle.

Here is another criticism, this time from an officer. He says : "England is more practical in her organization, and is not so hemmed in by red tape as we are. She selects the best men to command, irrespective of rank and age, and only according to their efficiency."

In Germany a strict order of routine and promotion is followed, hence the continual spectacle of the wrong man in the wrong place.

Another cause of discontent in the army is that no officer can be promoted before having served a certain number of years, however many vacancies may occur. Many hundreds of lieutenants are doing the work of captains and majors, but they must retain the rank of a lieutenant in order to avoid the extra pay. This causes much murmuring, which is obviously dangerous, as the Emperor should do everything to keep the army on his side.

BERLIN, *August* 1917.—I have been passing an unspeakably mournful morning at the "Nachlass Bureau," where any small articles picked up upon the battlefield are kept for identification. A feeling of hopeless sadness crept over me as I saw these trays of things, the only mementoes left of men who had such a short time ago been alive in the full flush of manhood. There was a whole stack of battered and blood-stained cigarette-cases, some with inscriptions or monograms engraved on them, many containing small photos or a few written words by the giver. Then there were all the other various small articles generally to be found in a man's pocket —fountain-pens, handkerchiefs, torn letters, purses, coins, etc.; and I felt the tears come into my eyes when I thought of what value they would be to some in England now, and how almost impossible it is to identify even a small number of them. I had a long list of missing articles with me, sent by sorrowful or (worse still) hopeful women in England; and with the sympathetic help of the two Red Cross officers in charge, and by dint of arduous and painful work, at the end of the morning I had managed to identify one or two cigarette cases and a few other small articles, which we had forwarded through the Red Cross to the expectant owners in England But how few they were, and alas! how few ever will be claimed. Time will gradually thrust them aside to the other inevitable lumber of the war, and they will never come into the hands of those to whom they would be relics of great worth.

KRIEBLOWITZ, *October* 1917.—Yesterday I got a letter from my husband, who has gone up to town for the opening of the Herrenhaus, with an interesting piece of news in it. He writes: "I learnt from L. that my former chief (Erzberger) was actually abroad, trying to

establish peace negotiations on a financial basis, namely
an International Financial and Economic Trust; which,
however, is said to have failed on account of the joint
capital of the other side (meaning the two biggest
financial Powers) always being able to overrule us."

This failure, were it generally known, would meet with
a triumphant howl of applause from the "Vaterlandspartei," who are doing all they can to oppose any move-
ments made by the Catholic and pacific elements.

Strange to say, the clergy of the Protestant Church
are also in favour of the continuation of the war, and
only lately have a small party of Protestant pastors in
Berlin had the courage to make a move towards peace
by collecting signatures for a Peace Protest. They are
as a matter of fact State officials, and more or less bound
to think as they are told in State affairs, which may
explain the phenomenon of men of God urging their
flocks on to kill one another. Perhaps, too, a feeling of
hostility prevents their following any lead headed by
the Pope "We hope for a good German peace from
God, and not a bad international one from the Pope,"
is their war-cry at present.

    .   .   .   .   .   .

I hear that the English are daily gaining ground, and
are slowly but surely approaching the object of their
aim, the U-boat base of operations. A letter I received
a short time ago confirms me in my opinion that the
English are not merely fighting to pass away the time.
G. wrote to me to-day that they are now quite near to
the commanding heights near the coast. "If this is
the case, then the Marine Corps and the coast in Flanders,
which is all-important to us, might get endangered."

I see that the English view of operations on the West
is that the Germans have been retiring for a whole year,
and that Verdun, Champagne, Vimy, Arras, Messines,
Langemarck, Westhoek, and Zonnebeke are but stages
in an uninterrupted retreat. For us civilians looking
on, the whole campaign seems to be more or less a useless

slaughter, and one is only able to bear the horror of it by hearing and reading stories of the heroism and self-sacrifice of individual man towards man.

The story of the German soldier who the other day was buried in a shell-hole together with an English officer, badly wounded in the thigh, and whose life he managed to save by stopping the bleeding artery with his two thumbs, himself weak and ill, and in a crouched position, is a deed not quite in character with that of a "Hun."

.   .   .   .   .   .

The regulations as to smuggling provisions are very strict, and a funny scene took place at the station in Breslau the other day. A well-dressed, dignified-looking lady appeared at the luggage-room with the object of checking her trunk. Her flurried mien, and the obvious nervousness with which she hurried on the porter to weigh her trunk, aroused the suspicions of the station-master. The trunk was promptly opened, and to the surprise of the amused onlookers a whole pig was discovered in it. It was confiscated and sold in the town at the official price, to the great discomfiture of the stately lady.

Things of this sort are of daily occurrence, and yet people go on trying them over and over again. The strict regulations seem very superfluous, and are causing much bad blood amongst the people in the towns. We in the country could, in fact, help them very often in many ways if we were allowed to do so.

As it is, people try to obtain by force or stealth what they cannot get in a legal way. The following incident gives an idea of what is being attempted in some way or other daily.

The other day a very fine field-grey military motor-car appeared on our place, and its four occupants began shooting to their hearts' content. Nobody disturbed them, or asked them on what authority they were there, for people took it for granted that they had been sent by the Government. After having satisfied their needs they departed, and it was only discovered a day afterwards that they were poachers pure and simple, who certainly had a glorious time   How they managed to get hold of a military auto no one can imagine.

.   .   .   .   .   .

Last week we spent a day at Fürstenstein with Prince and Princess Pless   Prince and Princess Biron, Countess Saurma and her daughters were there too.   Princess Pless and I being English, Princess Biron French, and Countess Saurma Polish, our conversation was at times what our husbands describe as "dangerous," which, being translated, means, we criticize the German Government and methods too loudly.   In one thing, however, we all agree, and that is that our husbands are very lenient with us; and that it is owing to their consideration and thoughtfulness towards us, and the loyal way in which they have stood by us, that life in a hostile country has been endurable.   And without being over-duly proud, I may confess that my husband is the one who has the best reputation of being clever enough to fight my battles without being disloyal to his Emperor and country.   At Fürstenstein we talked "England" until the walls of the old castle must have wearied of the word.

Prince Pless, who is always with the Emperor at Head-quarters, described to us his life there, and the Emperor's triumphant entry into Riga, at which he assisted.

And now for a description of the state of politics here. Everything is very unsettled.   Michaelis has proved quite unsatisfactory and has given place to a better man. They say some sixteen candidates are on the list, Bülow being first in the running in the minds of many.   Solf has been proposed, and Erzberger, as the strong man, would not be unpopular to the democrats, although I see the *Times* calls his policy "murky and deceitful at the best."

Kühlmann, they say, was offered the Chancellorship too, but very wisely refused, knowing his own limitations. "I know I am suitable for my present position as Foreign Secretary, but I am unsuitable to be Reichskanzler, as I am utterly ignorant of inner politics." People have a good deal of confidence in him here, and feel that he is the right man in the right place. He, as well as the new Kanzler, certainly have their work cut out for them when one thinks that Germany is at present ostracized and alienated from three-quarters of the human race.

.   .   .   .   .

We hear that aeroplanes (either English or French) have done enormous damage to Frankfort and other towns in the south, 50 to 60 people being killed during a raid on Frankfort in one afternoon. And Princess Metternich, who has a large castle outside Wiesbaden, had to leave her bed three times in one night and take refuge in the cellar, English shrapnel being found in the courtyard next morning.

All internal disputes and disagreements are disappearing for the moment, being swallowed up in the vital conflict of the two great parties, the democrats and the "Vaterlandspartei," which is daily increasing in vehemence.

People are devoured with anxiety as to the food resources for the coming winter, whilst the Government has to cope with much more serious questions, were it only known—namely, the increasing shortage of raw stuff and material for ammunition.

Has the "enemy" already noticed, I wonder, that the German ammunition is not as good as it was? Thank God, it only inflicts slight wounds now, and if they search the "Casualty List" in the *Times* with the same throbbing heart as I do, they will notice that the list of wounded is now much longer than that terrible heart-breaking list of dead and missing that used to appear during the first eighteen months of the war,

.   .   .   .   .   .

There are other signs, too, pathetic in their way, of the increasing scarcity of metal, for everywhere the old church bells and even the organ-pipes are being dragged from the churches and turned into ammunition; whilst

owing to the scarcity of oil the Sanctuary lamp, such a
dear familiar sight in Catholic churches, may no longer
shed its tender light before the Tabernacle.

In L., a small town near here, a sad little ceremony
took place the other day. The ancient church bell, which
had rung the people from the cradle to the grave for
300 years and more, was requisitioned by the military
authorities   The grief felt by the inhabitants was so
great that they determined to do their ancient friend
all the honour that they could; and after having performed the regular funeral service for the dead over it,
a procession was formed, headed by the priest in his
vestments, with his acolytes swinging their incense, and
the inhabitants following the bell, which was covered
with wreaths and flowers and handed over to the military
authorities under tears and protestations.

As coffee and tea have entirely run out, all sorts of
berries and leaves are being used as a surrogate   Chest-
nuts are used for feeding the deer, and it is interesting to
see the children, who are not old enough to work otherwise, busy plucking and collecting the different things.

Nothing seems to be left unused—salad-oil being extracted from every kind of fruit-stone, and an excellent
oil for greasing machinery is being pressed from the seeds
of sunflowers. It is marvellous how much has been
produced in this way, and it is only a pity we cannot
use the latter for cooking and eating purposes too.

The difficulty of getting butter is increasing daily, and
one has to use all one's power of persuasion to be able to
entice a miserable quarter of a pound of it, after having
begged in vain at quite a number of small peasants' houses.

The fact is, the peasants have to hand over a certain
amount of butter to the military authorities, who, if they
do not get the proper quantity, keep back the peasant's
monthly supply of sugar. And as every one is longing
for their sugar, and jam cannot be made without it. no
one will sell their butter even for very high prices. For
the fortunate people who grow sugar-beet there can, of

course, never be any dearth of sweet-stuffs, for the beet pressed produces a most delicious syrup which can easily be eaten for honey. But if it is difficult to sweeten one's lot at present, it is just as difficult to season one's cooking, for the prices of pepper, cinnamon, and nutmeg are enormous. These spices are almost worth their weight in gold.

Lighting will prove a great problem this winter, as there is almost no petroleum or methylated spirits to be had; gas-light is next to impossible, on account of the small quantity allowed, and electric-light is also limited. I am surprised that people in the country do not attempt the old way of lighting by means of pine torches. True, they give more smoke than light, but it would be preferable to the gloom of the unlighted houses in the country.

This darkness is especially unpleasant for the people in the town who have to wait for the vegetables and fruit coming in from the country. Our gardener, who goes in daily, tells me that they stand for hours and hours patiently waiting to get but a pound of cabbage, onions, etc., which are all very scarce indeed. Luckily for the purchasers, maximum prices have been settled on all eatables, or it would be impossible for the poorer classes to get anything at all. And still the small peasants, landowners, and gardeners are all growing very prosperous, and our gardener, who only has about two acres of land at his disposal, made 10,000 marks last year.

In addition to the "card" plague, which is bringing every one to the verge of the lunatic asylum, we have the "Bezugschein" (official voucher), which is now necessary for almost every scrap of clothing needed by poor shivering humanity to cover themselves. Everything is on the list, dresses, mantles, coats, stockings, shoes, gloves, washing; and you have to give a list of everything you possess before getting the precious "Schein" handed out to you.

BERLIN, *January* 1918.—The days come and go, and

we have already crossed the borderland and have left the gloom of the old year, only to enter the darkness of a new one. Every hour brings its fears, disappointments, and vague hopes, so that there is but little time for collecting one's scattered ideas.

Christmas was, of course, but a sorry season, although the unexpected and seemingly successful peace movement in Russia undoubtedly created a brighter atmosphere for people here than they have known since the war began. Brest-Litovsk, mingled with the divine proclamation of "Peace upon earth and goodwill amongst men," moved our hearts to a new throb of hope. It remains to be seen how far people are justified in believing this to be the first weak wavelet of the great peace-tide which is gradually but surely going to inundate Europe.

The military party, the "raving Rolands," are doing all they can to obstruct the peace movement, and Ludendorff and Kühlmann have almost come to blows. There were some exciting scenes between the two last week, and people have told me that the cold-blooded, strong-nerved, impassive Kühlmann was almost on the verge of a breakdown. More and more he and his adherents are perceiving the fatal mistakes of the U-boat war, and the madness of ever allowing things to go so far that America should enter the war. But, of course, Kühlmann has a great many enemies, as he has already turned out all the old Excellencies who were having such an easy time in the Foreign Office here, and publicly makes it known that his diplomatic creed discredits the arts and tricks of the old school At any rate there is a breathless tussle going on, and things are being hurried along, I suppose, to avoid the American reinforcements in the spring, although the Germans are still inclined to scoff and jeer at the American soldiers.

I myself wait and watch, firm in the belief that England knows what she is about, even though it looks as if she were losing touch with her old allies at present. In fact,

I feel like the English prisoner whom a friend met in some obscure country place a short time ago. He was sitting by the roadside breaking stones, and when she asked how long he had been a prisoner, and if he ever saw any newspapers, and who he thought would win the war, he answered that he had been there for three years, that he had never seen any paper of any kind, but that he never doubted for a moment that England would be victorious in the end He could not explain why, but something told him "there," and he touched his forehead.

.   .   .   .   .   .

Lloyd George's Paris speech made a great impression on us, and M., as well as myself, thought it was quite right of him to try and wake people up to the fact that strategic blunders have been caused by the military authorities of the Entente not all acting together. Whatever one may think of the grave errors he committed in his abusive speeches against Germany, he certainly has the courage of his opinion, and is not afraid of making himself unpopular.

The other evening at a reception at the Solfs' we met a rather interesting man, a certain Herr Hahn, whom they have just got over from England to inform them as to the state of political feeling there. From him we learnt that Sir W. Tyrrell, whose health had broken down after the loss of his son at the beginning of the war, was no longer in office, but is working behind the scenes for Sir Edward Grey, whose party, including Lord Lansdowne, Balfour, Lord Loreburn, Lord Courtney, and Noel Buxton, are working openly for peace, and doing all they can to oppose Lord Northcliffe's war policy, especially Sir W. Tyrrell.

He asserts, too, that if the nation does not support Lansdowne's policy there will be a Labour Government in England, and that in any case Lloyd George's days are numbered. He seems to think that the Labour Party will gradually gain the ascendancy in all countries throughout Europe, which may lead to civil war here as well as in England. This, I think myself, is not improbable. If the war continues much longer the people will follow Russia's example and take the matter into their own hands

The Hohenzollerns, they say, are perfectly aware of their own uncertain position, and a remark said to have been made by the Crown Prince is being repeated everywhere: "I'm young enough to find another job, but what will happen to the old man if we have to go?"

. . . . . .

As concerns matters here there is a never-ending crisis in Government affairs going on. Hindenburg and Ludendorff, as well as the Crown Prince, are in Berlin, and important conferences are always taking place, the Lithuanian and Polish question being the most difficult to decide. Kuhlmann's position is more shaky than ever, and Hertling is reported to have been "ill" for some days past.

They say the scene between Ludendorff and Kühlmann the other day was indescribable. They shouted at one another so loudly that their voices were heard some three or four stories above. Ludendorff appears bent on becoming military dictator, and his opponents will be done for if that comes about

. . . . . .

"Talk of an angel and you will hear his wings." Ludendorff is so often in my thoughts that I was not surprised this morning at breakfast when, happening to look out of the window, I saw both him and Hindenburg pass by on their early morning stroll into the Tiergarten, as they are in the habit of doing when they are in Berlin for a few days. They were greeted with great enthusiasm by the passers-by, and a respectful crowd followed them at a short distance.

. . . . . .

It has become almost impossible to get out of Germany now, however urgent the need may be, if one is of alien birth. Only a short time ago my friend Baroness

Sternburg, the American wife of the former Ambassador in Constantinople, who had a passport to visit her sister-in-law in Stockholm, was at the last moment forbidden to go without being told the reason why. Imagine her position: an empty flat, no servants, and nothing to eat.

The same thing happened to Frau von M., an Italian by birth, and the widow of one of the most influential bankers in Berlin. She had been advised by her doctors to visit a sanatorium in Switzerland; a passport had been granted and the day fixed for her departure, when she was suddenly informed that the permit had been cancelled. Of course there is always some woman in the background who, from petty spite, has denounced the victims as "deutschfeindlich" to the police authorities.

   .   .   .   .   .   .

My eldest brother has been lying very ill in a hospital, which to me seems providential, or he would have been in the fierce fight.

My other two brothers and my brother-in-law are still in the thick of the fighting, and my nephew, whom I left a boy at school, is now a cavalry officer in one of the most dangerous and exposed positions. How odd it is to see the next generation cropping up and already responsible for the life and death of so many of their fellow-creatures, whilst we passively look on, superfluous units in the great struggle of the world.

   .   .   .   .   .   .

I have received a letter from my sister, Lady Charlton, from Cape Town, dated November 28, in which she mentions a curious coincidence. The officers under her husband's command were ordered to bring in all the foreign rifles found in South Africa, and amongst others one was brought in with my husband's monogram engraved on it. It was the one which he had used out there fourteen years ago. I am glad to hear that she says he has still many friends out there.

   .   .   .   .   .   .

Outside the snow is falling thicker and thicker, and

the trees are covered with soft glittering layers of frozen snow. It is almost impossible to clear the tracks of the tramways, and the traffic is being obstructed all over the town. Crowds of people are waiting at every stopping-place to force an entrance into the over-filled cars; most of them, of course, have to reach their destination on foot. Berlin will soon be cut off from the rest of the world if the snow continues much longer, and the white-carpeted streets will be given over to an unknown silence and loneliness

Yesterday was quite a great day, as the Herrenhaus met after a long pause, and Graf Hertling made his appearance for the first time as Kanzler. As he is a Bavarian and a Catholic, his début was looked upon with very mixed feelings, as it is a long time since a Roman Catholic was Chancellor of Germany. The House was packed with members ready to tear his speech to rags. He has a great party against him, and there are all sorts of underhand intrigues going on. His speech was rather disappointing, as people had been expecting a detailed discussion of the "peace" question and a criticism of Lloyd George's policy, but it seems at the last moment that he was obliged to change his tactics owing to new developments in the policy of the Entente.

His short simple speech met with a good deal of malicious criticism, and we heard afterwards from Prince Munster, who joined us with Graf Magnis in the gallery, that Prince Bulow had been loud in his disdainful comments on what Graf Hertling said.

It was very interesting to see all these ex-Ministers, ex-Kanzlers, and ambitious nobles who, like the robber-barons of mediaeval times, are quite ready to rebel and turn the Kaiser off the throne if he does not fall in with their wishes. Bülow and Tirpitz especially wore an expression on their faces which boded no good for Graf Hertling. But Graf Hertling is an old statesman, well versed in the devious struggles of modern politics, and will be able to hold his own, in spite of its being said that he is too much of a diplomat and not enough of a statesman.

Besides Graf Hertling, the Vice-Chancellor von Payer is also a Bavarian, and one can judge from this fact what strong motives there must be for allowing the Bavarians to take such a prominent part in the government of the Empire. It seems to be necessary, for the war has so intensified the antagonism already existing between the Bavarians and the Prussians that they say the hatred of the former for the "Sau-Preussen" (Pigs of Prussians) knows no bounds, and they allow no food to be sent to Prussia, although there is a superabundance in some parts of Bavaria.

The feeling towards the Kaiser is steadily diminishing in loyalty and respect, and the same people who greeted him so warmly a short time ago with "Ave, Caesar!" are now distributing leaflets in the back streets of Berlin proclaiming, "Down with the Kaiser, down with the Government," and the police, when called upon to suppress the evil-doers, refuse to act, and are more than suspected of being behind the movement themselves.

From Herr Hahn, whom my husband met at the Solfs' last week, he heard that he had just been to The Hague and had spoken with an English delegate who informed him that England would only agree to negotiate with Germany if she consented to withdraw from Belgium, but not otherwise. And as the military party here will in no wise consent to this, I suppose things will go on indefinitely as they are.

.   .   .   .

The Brest-Litovsk negotiations seem likely to come to nothing, as Trotsky seems to be playing a double part, and people say he is only toying with the Central Powers to be better able to sow the seeds of sedition and rebellion among the West-European peoples. They say that already the German prisoners have been set free in Russia, and that common soldiers are being placed in command over their former officers.

There are many different opinions about Trotsky here, some calling him a dreamer and idealist, others abusing him as a bloodthirsty tyrant; whilst there is a whole class of admirers who declare him to be the greatest man since Christ lived upon earth, and the prophet of a new religion which is to regenerate mankind and create a new paradise after the deluge of the war.

Who knows what part this man may be going to play in the future fates of Europe? Some 120 years ago people were saying almost the same things of a certain unknown little officer who out of the reign of terror and bloodshed developed into the vampire-emperor, who almost succeeded in draining the blood of all Europe.

BERLIN, *January* 1918 —A more cheerful note in the gloom of universal antagonism is the news of the accomplished exchange of wounded officers and soldiers, and the repatriation of the interned British in Ruhleben over 45 years of age. I see that one party of men who were captured at Mons on August 24, 1914, arrived at The Hague December 30, whilst another party of 412 men have been distributed in various camps in Switzerland One can imagine their feelings at again being free to come and go as they like. The hideous nightmare of barbed wire fences which has so often called forth a passing form of neurasthenia amongst the prisoners is a thing of the past.

It has been a relief to us, and at the same time a cause of sadness, as our work is done. We had watched and worked for these countrymen of ours against so many odds, and as if in the dark, never having the satisfaction of knowing the result of our efforts; and now they are leaving, and our self-formed band of helpers will automatically be dissolved. A "left behind" feeling comes over us, the same as we used to experience when one by one the Embassies left as their various countries declared war.

We had divided ourselves methodically into branches.

Princess Münster, Princess Pless, and I, all being English, had undertaken the correspondence as regards wounded and missing English, and the supply, as far as we were allowed, to officers and men of extras in the way of "unobtainable necessaries." Princess Biron being French had done the same for the French, and Princess Isenburg and the Duchess of Croy, both being American by birth, had undertaken the French and Belgians as well, the latter principally helping the Belgians, as, her husband being partly Belgian, their sympathies were much with that country. She had even obtained permission to visit their cousin Princess Marie of Croy when she was imprisoned after her trial at the same time as Miss Cavell.

I wish I could add here a few of the letters we have received from and about the wounded and missing and prisoners of war. In this work all my family have helped incessantly, especially my sisters Edith and Monica, whose weekly letters have enabled us to glean an enormous amount of information for anxious relatives at home. Cecil Tempest, too, my great friend, has been an invaluable assistant. Their correspondence would almost form a book of its own. I must have received over a thousand letters from all parts of the world, and in this way one has learned so much of the sorrow and anxiety that war has brought about. One got to know the position of regiments, the districts where peasants could be depended on for information, or where doctors of the Lazaretts were humane and ready to help, or *vice versa;* and, last but not least, we were sometimes the sole possessors of information as to the whereabouts of some lonely English grave, which, if it had not been for the kindliness of some German officer acquaintance of ours, who went out of his way to obtain the name and particulars for us, would, maybe, have remained for ever unclaimed and unidentified.

All this will one day be published by some one, **or**

some society whose object will be to improve the treatment and conditions of prisoners of war in all countries before the next war. I sincerely hope that one great and important change in this branch of warfare will be that all prisoners may be held on parole.

BERLIN, *February* 1918.—Strikes are breaking out in different parts, leading to disturbances which have already caused the deaths of a few unfortunate policemen. They are at present only sporadic, and are hushed up as much as possible, every one, even the Socialists, dreading the responsibility of civil war. But I have the feeling myself that they are growing and uniting like an elastic belt which may tighten any day and make itself very disagreeably felt.

Next to us, in Tattersall's, there are fifty policemen stationed night and day, which I can't say makes one feel safer, for it rather looks as if some special demonstration were being planned for the front-door of Berlin, the Brandenburger Tor, which means our front-door too.

My old friend the Commandant of Berlin, General Kessel, is doing his best to stir up the troubled waters by stamping with his heavy foot and rattling with his iron fist.

We are now entirely at the mercy of the military courts of justice, and after sentence has been pronounced there is no further court of appeal possible for the delinquent; and any one who strikes is being sent off to the front at once. In the darkest days of serfdom men could not have been more in a state of slavery than we are in these days of militarism.

The Kaiser himself lives in a constant state of fear, anonymous letters being often sent to the gentlemen-in-waiting, threatening that he will be shot. The other day there was some special service in the Dom, and we saw the motors of the Emperor and Empress flying by like lightning as they went there. A public ovation was given him when he quitted the church, but they say he

only answered with a curt grim greeting and drove away
with the same speed he had come.

.   .   .   .   .   .

Things are not cheerful, it must be owned, and yet
there is an almost insatiable craving for pleasure of any
kind amongst every class of society. It is as if the long-
repressed desire for amusement innate in human nature
is now breaking forth stronger than ever, and as there is
money enough in circulation, the theatres, cinemas, and
concert halls are crowded to overflowing, utterly unlike
the preceding years when tickets had to be given away
to get any audience at all Every one is anxious to forget the depression of the times and get rid of the heavy
burden of sorrow and care which has so long been clog-
ging and depressing public and private life, and "Merry
Evenings" and dancing matinées are being organized
everywhere, assisted by the greatest artistes of the day,
to try and raise the flagging spirits of the nation.

Private dances and balls, which were so long forbidden,
are again coming into fashion, and the concert-teas at the
great hotels are increasing in price as the food offered
decreases in quality

Our social gatherings are somewhat monotonous, the
circle of our personal acquaintances being so limited in
comparison with two years ago   The American and
Greek Embassies were then here; but in consequence of
Germany's "splendid isolation" of to-day we now have
to depend chiefly on the representatives of the few
countries which still keep up diplomatic relations. Here
is a programme of our festivities last week. We had a
dinner-party at the Dutch Minister's, Baron Gevers, who
is looking after the interests of the British prisoners of
war. Then there was luncheon at the Spanish Embassy,
where the Spanish Ambassador, Ex. Polo, confided to
me that they are practically living on their trunks, as any
day may bring notice to leave Berlin, as America and
England are doing all they can to force Spain to side with
the Entente and take part in the war.

Then there was a dinner at the Rizoffs', the Bulgarian Minister and his wife, which was rather interesting, she being rather a lovely woman, the acknowledged beauty of the diplomatic corps, and he a clever man, with an unlimited faith in Bulgaria and the Bulgarians, not to forget himself. He has just written a book in the one language he knows. It concerns the future of Europe, and he has had it translated into four languages for the benefit of "the other world" which does not speak his own. He is to a certain degree modest in his views, and is just in his partition of Europe, for he leaves Berlin to the Austrians, and only appropriates the rest for Bulgaria.

Besides the aforementioned there are of course the Austrian Embassy, with Prince Hohenlohe as Ambassador, and his wife, the Archduchess; Count and Countess Moltke of the Danish Embassy; and Baron Essen, the Swedish Ambassador, with his newly married wife. Then there are Princess Taxis, Count and Countess Larisch, Baroness Sternburg, Count and Countess Henckel, Prince and Princess Löwenstein, and the young diplomats and secretaries of the diplomatic corps.

The great problem is how to provide for our guests, and each course is duly commented on and discussed, the origin and adventures connected with it forming the chief topic of conversation

I may add that England is unconsciously bearing the burden of our dinners, for the food which we manage to get generally comes from Belgium, and has been sent over for the Belgians

Herr von Jagow was here for a week, and as he was ill, he held a sort of levée in his room every evening, where my husband, Kühlmann, and others met to discuss affairs. They all agree that Germany is in a terrible plight and, as the Empress' brother, Prince Ernst Günther, said at a dinner the other evening, "Germany is going to the devil."

And yet the militarists continue babbling about the

great victory that is to mean the final triumph of the
Central Powers and the speedy entry into Paris and the
taking of Calais by means of the new big guns. Why
this must mean the end of the war I cannot comprehend,
for it has proved the tragical destiny of Germany until
now, that the greater her success on the field of battle
the more complicated does her political and economical
position become.

The chief theme of conversation with American friends
is their ever-increasing scarcity of money, as they cannot
get any from America. They tell me that if Germany
cannot or will not pay the indemnity demanded of her
at the end of the war, the private fortunes of German-
Americans will be seized upon to pay it, and are accordingly in a great fright. In their letters from America
they say they are being constantly advised to leave
Germany as soon as possible, to take all their money
from the banks, and on no account to deposit it in Swiss
banks, but to hoard it up in the good old-fashioned
stocking.

The unfortunate part of the matter for them is that
no one may now leave Germany or go to Switzerland,
with the exception of theatrical troupes, etc., so that if
one wants to get out of the mouse-trap the only way left
is to become a ballet-girl or wandering musician.

This severity about granting passports is carried to
such lengths as to become ridiculous very often, and
Princess Lowenstein told me that so many difficulties
were being made about her getting her six-weeks'-old
twins to Austria that they might be the most dangerous
political suspects.

The atmosphere here is growing more and more democratic, and one is forcibly reminded sometimes of Paris
in the early days of the Revolution, when the people
became more and more conscious of their terrible power.
All outward distinctions of class and rank have to be

avoided as much as possible, and even the few sorry carriage-horses still permitted may not show any silver on their harness.

The proletariat are daily growing more touchy and jealous of their rights, and the numerous parvenus who have grown rich through the war are especially detested Finer distinctions are not always made, of course, and any one wearing a fur mantle or a specially well-made pair of boots is suspected of being a "Kriegs-Gewinner." It is no uncommon occurrence in these days of gloom and fog that the happy possessors of such things are spied out and followed, robbed of boots and furs, and forced to walk home in their stockings.

Travelling is one of the most difficult problems of the day, the trains being all over-filled, and such delays take place that one can imagine oneself back in the good old days of mail-coaches   Princess Isenburg told me that the other day she had places reserved for her in Munich for the train to Berlin, and on arriving at the station a whole hour beforehand, she found not only her own places already taken, but the whole train so overcrowded that the guard told her there was no room for her at all, and no fuss might be made as the people would make a disturbance.   After a great many useless remonstrances she was able at last to persuade the station-master to help her, and he actually had to lead her through the whole station, cross the goods-yard, pass through five intervening trains, and thus ignominiously enter the train from the other side, so as not to be seen by the people.

Another example of the spirit of the times.—Countess H—— told me she was travelling the other day with her three daughters from Leipzig to Berlin. They had taken first-class tickets, but found their compartment overcrowded, as usual.   One of their neighbours, a stout gentleman looking like a "Kriegs-Gewinner" of the worst kind, seems to have been especially objectionable to her eighteen-years-old daughter, who whispered incautiously in her mother's ear, "If we had known we had to travel with the Plebs we might just as well have gone third class." Unfortunately the stout man heard this remark, and made the most dreadful scene imaginable. He stopped the train, called in the guard, and complained. Countess H—— insisted on her daughter apologizing, which, however, did not appease the good man's wrath, for the whole way he continued fuming at the bad manners of the aristocracy, and not content with this he has actually brought a suit against the girl for abuse in public.

Another incident which occurred but a short time ago was that of one of the Empress' ladies-in-waiting, who was forced to take a tram, the roads being too bad for the horses. The tram was full of working-men, who began abusing the Kaiser so violently that she felt herself called upon to defend him She assured them that he was a very kind man, filled with the feeling of his great responsibility. This, however, only increased their anger, which was now turned on her, so that she had to get out of the tram to escape further abuse.

BERLIN, *March* 1918.—I have lately been boiling with resentment against the whole German nation, owing to their official red tape which refused to allow me to go and see my cousin Captain Trafford, *en route* for Holland, when he has now gone with the rest of the repatriated officers from Germany.

For the last three years I have been periodically sending in an official application to be allowed to go and visit him, as, after all, he is my first cousin and is like a brother to me. The authorities never refused me outright, always putting me off with answers either that I may see him in a few months' time, or when he goes to another camp, or when he passes through Berlin; and getting a bit tired of these evasive answers, I began asking for a more decided date to be fixed, and the answer was that they promised me he should not leave the country without my seeing him. One day in February I got a telegram saying that in three days' time he would be passing through Aachen station *en route* for Holland, and that I might go and see him at the station. I obtained a travelling permit, secured reserved seats for myself and maid, and filled in all sorts of forms, when an hour or so before starting I received another notice to say that the commander of the camp had exceeded his rights in giving me permission and that the military station-master would not allow me to go on the platform, as owing to the coming offensive the place was reserved for troops alone.

I was dumb with disappointment and rage, and my friend Baroness S—— came in that evening, also laden with a grievance, as she had just had a passport given her to go and visit her sister in Copenhagen, and within twenty-four hours of starting it was taken away. So we were suitable companions in our mutual grievances, and consoled ourselves by giving free vent to our feelings on the subject   It was one more example of over-organization; give with one hand and take away with the other. The disappointment brought on such an attack of home-sickness that I took a long time getting over it; and as my husband was absent in Vienna for a month it made it still harder. I consoled myself by picturing the relief and joy it must have been to my cousin to be "on his own" once more, able to shake off the dust of the German prison camps from his feet for ever

My cousin in his first letter from Holland told me that the officials at Aachen station had told him I had telegraphed to say "that I was too busy to come and see him."

.   .   .   .   .   .

From all the letters I get from home I can read between the lines that a great offensive is pending in the West, but that the Entente are perfectly prepared for any emergency. So minute is their knowledge of the preparations on the German front, that the French papers are full of surprise that the enemy let week after week of the splendid March weather go by without making a move. The fact is probably that Ludendorff has to be perfectly certain of how many fresh divisions he can count on from Russia before beginning the most dangerous and uncertain adventure of the whole war. As most people say here, it is a case of "to be or not to be," and the militarists are throwing the gauntlet to fate in their own way.

The Russian Peace, although greeted with a great show of flags and ringing of bells and universal holidays for the school-children, has on the whole been received with shakes of the head and disbelief in the duration of such a treaty. Fighting still continues between the German troops and the Red Guards, and one hears horrible stories of bloodshed and anarchy. Not only are German officers and soldiers being murdered in their beds and their houses set on fire over their heads, but many great Russian magnates are being treated in the same way. The Germans here are all boasting of the future happy state of the country when it has come to know the blessings of Prussian law and order, whilst the Annexationists and Imperialists are pluming their feathers in great style, under the pretext of re-establishing public order. A German armed force now occupies territories whose populations are pre-eminently Russian, and the Commercial Treaty of 1904 has been renewed in favour of the German agrarians.

.   .   .   .   .   .

At a luncheon party the other day I sat next to Dr. Solf, who gave me much interesting information. He said that half an hour before the Kanzler's speech he had gone to see him and had clearly and concisely begged him to declare *the disannexation of Belgium without any conditions whatever.* Hertling promised to do so, but when the moment came he limited his statement to "we will withdraw from Belgium under the condition that we receive compensation," etc., etc. He confided to me that at the last moment the military authorities had insisted on his adding this limitation.

Solf further told me that Bethmann-Hollweg's political outlook was broader than Hertling's, but that he had not the courage of his convictions. For instance, last year, during the American crisis, the Emperor, Bethmann-Hollweg, Helfferich, and himself had been dead against the wholesale submarine warfare. They foresaw that it would eventually mean Germany's ruin Solf's own words to Bethmann-Hollweg had been, "You disapprove of the increased submarines; Helfferich and I do so too; let us all go to the Kaiser and beg him to stand by us in this or we will all three resign." Bethmann had agreed that he was right, but had not dared to take such a step himself.

.   .   .   .   .   .

The "Lichnowsky Revelations" are in every one's mouth. He is being condemned by most people, and even such partisans as recognize the truth of his statements agree in condemning him for disclosing State secrets in his own personal interest. It is believed that he will probably be tried for high treason, and that he will be impeached by the Herrenhaus and probably turned out of his regiment.

Of course, every one's question is how the document got out. Lichnowsky himself will be more surprised than any one at the publicity of a manuscript which he had only written for his family archives. It is said that he sent it to several private friends, amongst others to a certain Herr Wittenberg, a director of the National Bank, and brother-in-law to Harden, to quote from in a lecture he was going to give Wittenberg seems to have indiscreetly shown it to an officer working on the General Staff, who was at the same time an extreme religious pacifist, and who was so horrified by the information revealed, showing the deception of Bethmann-Hollweg's Government, that he thought it an act of duty to hand it over to the Press. As this man has been staying in Switzerland people are suggesting that he has been caught in Northcliffe's nets, and that this is one of that minister's first steps for promoting the truth in the enemy's country. If it is, he has certainly been very successful.

As a matter of fact, these so-called "revelations" are exactly the facts that Lichnowsky told us on our journey out from England at the outbreak of the war. He also showed the pamphlet to my husband and Prince Münster in 1916, and although it has been corrected and added to, it is by no means all news to us, and for me certainly is not the meaningless raving of a madman, as many people here would have us think.

.   .   .   .   .

Lately Princess M and I have received letters from our cousins who have just been freed from their long imprisonment in Germany and sent back to England. These letters confirm my belief that there is still a great deal of unnecessary bullying and ill-treatment of imprisoned British officers going on, and that too much personal authority is accorded to the officer in command of the camp. Whilst one commander is tyrannical and incompetent in his methods, and bullies his unhappy prisoners by issuing all manner of petty irritating regulations and limitations to their manner of living, others can show tact and sympathy with the unenviable lot of the men placed under his command for the time being. One man only sees a chance for humiliating and humbling men whom he hates simply for being the enemy, whilst the others use the occasion for doing unto others as they would be done by in the same case. But one realizes how unconscious some of these bullies are at the contempt they have aroused, as we are told that during the few weeks previous to the order for exchange being issued they tried all the means in their power to be friendly and considerate towards those whom they had so grossly misused.

On receipt of the above-mentioned letters we both set our usual wheels in motion. Princess Münster has written on the subject to Prince Max of Baden, whilst I went straight to General Friederich and asked him to investi-

gate the matter. Prince Max was very sympathetic; but
with regard to others, if the matter was not so serious one
would feel inclined to smile at their naïve surprise on
reading the letters, and their remarks that such things
cannot be going on in a *German* camp. Last, but not
least, I then made my way to the Dutch Legation and
saw one of the staff who represents the interests of the
British prisoners of war. In society we are great friends
with them all, but on occasions of this sort they are apt
to assume the defensive, and imply that I am criticizing
their management. But by now I am hardened against
snubs of this kind, and peg away at my complaints until
I manage to extract a reluctant promise to send some
one down to inspect and report on the particular camp in
question. Of course, I rarely hear the result of the inspection; that would be too considerate an act to expect at
such times; and I am only greeted the next time we meet
by a look that means, "Do leave off interfering"

This treatment of the English in certain camps makes
my blood burn, and I feel especially galled when I talk
to men like Captain Rauch, who has just returned from
a three years' imprisonment in England, where, as he
tells me, he met with much kindness. He related how
he was allowed to see friends for an hour whenever he
liked, in the presence of an English officer, and that
when they were first captured General French came and
addressed him and his men personally, telling them they
were a gallant foe and had defended themselves bravely
to the last.

BERLIN, *March* 1918 —Do you remember the words of
Byron's stanza describing the ball on the eve of the battle
of Waterloo?

There was a sound of revelry by night,

The lamps shone o'er fair women and brave men;

And all went merry as a marriage-bell;
But hush! hark! a deep sound strikes like a rising knell!

They well describe the atmosphere of our first great reception in Berlin last night.

The scene was as brilliant as one could wish for, and gained in historical depth and meaning by the tragedies underlying the surface. Although there were 150 people present (of various nationalities), our large rooms were by no means overcrowded and looked charming. There was a wonderful display of jewels, and the ropes of pearls and brilliant diadems seemed to gleam with double lustre over the forced simplicity of the dresses, which certainly bear the sign of the times, thin flimsy muslins and silks being almost the only stuffs to be had. Of course, there were some magnificent robes, but they were evidently reminiscences of other times.

We began the evening with a dinner-party of twelve, our guests being the Duke and Duchess of Schleswig-Holstein, the Rizoffs, Count and Countess Oppersdorff and Count and Countess Larisch, Countess Götzen and Count George Wedel.

As it is not etiquette to talk politics on such occasions, we mutually avoided touching on the subjects most occupying our minds, and the Duke, who took me in to dinner as his hostess, talked English the whole evening, discussing English friends, shooting in Scotland, the Kiel-week, in fact everything but the war. My husband in the meantime talked Austria to the Duchess, and Bulgaria and Montenegro to Madame Rizoff, until the other guests began to arrive.

By the Duke's permission we were allowed to have English and French songs sung, which were a great success, but the chief musical attraction of the evening was a Dutch singer from the Royal Opera, Herr van de Sanden. He is a new comet in the world of music here, only having been discovered in Holland a short time ago, and so he was a revelation to us all. His rich full baritone, of immense volume and strength, enchanted every one. Baroness Sternburg was also persuaded to sing for us, and won enthusiastic applause. It is the first time she has sung before such a large gathering.

As for the food question, which is generally a vexed one, the supper-table certainly looked very opulent with its dainty dishes and masses of blood-red tulips; but everything was raised on our own estate, and the geese, ducks, pheasants, ham, fowls, salads, etc., could all be offered with a good conscience, and there was nothing "forbidden" on the menu. The Spanish Ambassador whispered in my ear that he only regretted one particular guest not being present at the scene. On my asking whom he meant, he replied: "Lloyd George; for if he could see that supper-table he would know how nonsensical it is to talk of Germany being starved out."

The great man of the evening, as far as rank goes, was the Duke of Schleswig-Holstein. He is brother to the Empress, and I suppose still holds a secret grudge against the Prussians for having annexed his land; but *cela va sans dire,* he is very loyal now.

Of the women, Countess Oppersdorff looked handsomely striking in her tall fair decorative style. There is "race" written in every line of her, and she looks what she is in reality, the descendant of an ancient line of kings. Her forefathers had the somewhat dubious pleasure of reigning over the Poles in the good old days, when they were continually quarrelling as to who was the reigning monarch, and she holds the Prussian Court a little cheaply, maintaining that the Hohenzollerns are parvenus, and their ancestors nothing better than knights-errant when hers were reigning over a nation of great culture and learning.

Madame Rizoff, who is one of the undisputed beauties of this winter, hovered like a butterfly over a flower-garden, graceful, vivacious, and amiable. Her husband, the minister, looks what he probably is in his own country, a good-natured bourgeois with a slight French polish. But his young wife is surrounded by quite a nimbus of romance. She is said to be closely related by blood to King Nikita, and has all the charm of a nymph who has lost her way in this prosaic old world of ours. She is certainly good to look at, this dainty daughter of the gods, with the wonderful sweep of neck and shoulders; and the play of her delicate muscles when she moves her head is a thing for a sculptor to dream of, whilst her big dark, astonished-looking eyes, and black hair bound by a simple blue ribbon, suggest to you a pretty Bo-peep who is looking for her sheep in the wrong place.

The Dutch Ambassador and his wife were the centre of all eyes, for every one was trying to make out from their manner what the answer to the Dutch ultimatum was going to be. Of course, we did not touch on politics last night, but they had laughed at my anxiety the day before when, making out the programme for our Dutch singer, I had jokingly remarked that I hoped the answer to the ultimatum would at least be postponed until the following evening, as it would be so inconvenient if my Dutch friends all left before the soirée.

The Spanish Ambassador and his wife were there too, both of them vaguely wondering how many more Spanish ships Germany was going to sink by mistake, before they, too, "must fold up their tents like the Arabs and noiselessly steal away"

Looking like a vizir from the court of Haroun al Raschid masquerading in European clothes, the Turkish Ambassador wandered about from room to room, carefully steering his formidable double chin and the rest of his *embonpoint* through the gay throng He is said to be very wise, and as somebody said of him, he looks as if he kept all his wisdom packed up in his inside.

The Bavarian Minister and diplomats were all present, in fact the rooms were thronged with ministers, high officials, and military potentates, with their wives. Some members of the "haute finance" were present also, the ladies rather overdoing it in the way of jewels; one of them almost looked as if she were wearing a diamond cuirass.

At the last moment several people had been forced to telephone their apologies owing to the military situation, and I think there cannot have been any one who was not conscious of the importance of the hour. At any moment the long-expected offensive may take place, and it almost seems as if some great decision were imminent, to judge by the number of officers who have suddenly had to hurry off to their regiments at a moment's notice. And yet there we were, all apparently gay and careless, chattering away to one another as if we had not a single fear beyond how our guests were to get home again

The evening passed very quickly, and although the music went on till after midnight, most of our guests began to disperse at about 11.30, for the electric trams and underground wait for no man, and droshkies and motors are very few and far between, and the dangers of a solitary midnight walk in Berlin are not to be underrated in these days of universal theft and robbery.

As for myself, I still feel in the Byronic mood, and wonder how many of the men who were my guests last evening I shall ever see again. There are reports circulating of the great offensive beginning already. Here is the last verse of Byron's canto, which might have been a prophecy of to-day:

Last noon beheld them full of lusty life,
Last eve in Beauty's circle proudly gay,
The midnight brought the signal-sound of strife,
The morn the marshalling in arms,—the day
Battle's magnificently fierce array!
The thunder-clouds close o'er it, which when rent
The earth is cover'd thick with other clay,
Which her own clay shall cover, heap'd and pent,
Rider and horse,—friend, foe,—in one red burial blent!

BERLIN, *March* 1918.—The great offensive has begun, and the newspaper headings all speak of a great German victory. The whole town is being flagged and the bells are ringing. Standing at my own window, gazing sorrowfully out at the Tiergarten, which is already showing a thin veil of green in the brilliant March sunshine, I can hear some of the remarks made by passers-by, and, shall I confess it, for the first time since the outbreak of the war I am beginning to doubt, and wonder if it is in any degree possible that the Germans can reach Calais!

My soul grows sick when I read or hear the particulars of these first victorious days; of the new long guns that are being used for the first time, and that are now bombarding Paris from the incredible distance of 150 kilometres; of the awful effect of the devilish new gases, of whole batteries of Englishmen found dead over their guns, of the 25,000 prisoners captured and 400 guns taken, together with great stores of food and ammunition

We hear that the English say they were taken by surprise, and that the prisoners blame their generals and complain of Haig being in England just at the critical moment.

It is a beautiful morning, one of those spring days when the world seems to have grown young and strong and full of hope in the night. Everything is brisk and vigorous and full of movement as if hurrying on to some new era of history. The flags are flying from the housetops, the branches of the trees are waving in the wind, and the high white clouds hurrying by, as if carrying the news of the great battles to other lands. The day looks as if it were rejoicing, but Nature is always callous to human suffering, and who can think of rejoicing, whether friend or foe, when such horrible suffering is being inflicted on mankind?

Our house stands in a very central position, being in the main thoroughfare connecting the two big stations, the Friedrich Strasse and the Potsdamer Bahnhof; and there is always a great deal of traffic passing our windows. This morning I feel fascinated by the seemingly cheery life going on out there, and stand rooted to the window, trying to escape my own sad thoughts. There are the freshly equipped troops marching away staidly and soberly enough, with the small pathetic following of white-faced women trying to keep pace with their swift march. How many of them will ever see the Brandenburger Tor and the victorious figures on it again?

There is the newspaper-man shouting out the news in a voice that almost makes one believe that the Germans have crossed the Channel. There is the flower-girl offering her small first bunches of violets and snowdrops to women who have no thoughts of flowers, but hurry by with anxious pale faces all in one direction, and I know where, to the Kriegsministerium in the Dorotheen Strasse, where the fresh lists of casualties appear daily.

Carts filled with enormous bottles, each six in its big basket-packing, rattle by. I hate the sight of them, I know them too well; they are filled with those abominable gas-stuffs which are made in Moabit, and are now being dispatched to destroy more victims. There, too, a whole waggon-load of empty stretchers passes by, new and unstained as yet. How long before they will each be filled with some poor bleeding remnant of humanity?

There comes a troop of men in various uniforms, and bearing no weapons. They are English and French prisoners, and I feel glad inwardly, for I know that at least these mothers' sons have escaped from the further horrors of the war.

I feel a great wave of bitterness and hatred overflowing my heart, hatred for all those in this and in other countries who were the cause of this hell-being-let-loose on the earth, and I turn away from the window with an indignant sob in my throat as I hear the sound of church bells imperatively summoning the nation to rejoice, but the sound of approaching music forces me back to the window, just in time to see the returned crew of the cruiser *Wolf* passing by in gala procession, accompanied by a scanty but admiring escort of men and boys. At the sight of these my thoughts veer round to the naval side of the situation, and I wonder vaguely if the report that I heard yesterday is true, that England is going to make a naval attack on the sea-coast.

My husband enters the room full of the latest news just received straight from the General Staff. They have informed him that a success is certain, but that it seems to be of a local nature, and not so great as the papers make it out to be, and by no means important enough to make those in authority confident of a great ultimate victory. It seems to be true that the guns are really bombarding Paris from a distance of 120 kilometres, and that the Opera-house is partially destroyed, but this does not mean anything of a decisive nature.

A member of the General Staff here has also told him that his office in Berlin is in direct telephone connection with the General Staff at the front, and that he can hear the sound of the shooting going on through his telephone, and can also telephone personally to an aeronaut who is at that moment suspended high up in the air over the enemy's lines.

Names of the fallen keep coming in at every moment, and Princess Reuss has just had a telegram to say that her second and much beloved son has fallen in the victory.

BERLIN, *April* 9, 1918.—The terrible offensive is still raging, and although the quick onpush of the Germans in those first harrowing days has been checked, we still hear of the steady if slow advance of the German troops.

All these two weeks I went nowhere and would see no one. I could only sit at home wondering which member of my family would fall first, and when I should receive news of it   The anguish and suspense of waiting, knowing nothing of what is happening to one's nearest and dearest, is terrible.

I have newspapers containing the casualty lists up to March 30, and until now I have seen no names I know; so I must take hope and pick up the threads of everyday life again and quietly visit my friends once more. Through news gleaned from them and from my husband, who is continually meeting military men, I learn that the offensive has not been successful enough to justify the confidence proclaimed in all the newspapers Everything had been staked on their breaking through the enemy's lines, and they have not done so, although they have driven the enemy back. Indeed, I hear the German troops are even being scattered and separated, owing to the French offensive at Verdun and the renewed trouble in Italy, where the Czechs have gone over wholesale to the enemy, forcing Germany to send eight army corps from the West Front to the Italian to replace them.

The so-called victories have been painted in glowing colours, for "dressing up" the war loan. Morally, too, the offensive has not made the wished-for impression on the enemy, but if anything has put new courage into them. The pacifists in England and France are fewer and have retired into the background.

We hear universally that the pluck shown by the English was almost superhuman when they were taken by surprise, and when through the failure of the Portuguese they were left to face such great odds alone. Even Ludendorff, hard stern man that he is, confessed that he would take off his hat to the English for their absolutely undaunted bravery. He said they never lose their heads, and never appear desperate; they are always cool and courageous until the very moment of death and capture. I will put it exactly as I heard it straight from the Grosse Hauptquartier: "The English Generals are wanting in strategy. We should have no chance if they possessed as much science as their officers and men had of courage and bravery. They are lions led by donkeys "

I wonder how much of this criticism is true. It is, of course, difficult for me to judge, but it is nevertheless interesting to hear, coming from such a quarter.

Yesterday I went to the first really smart wedding which I have seen since the beginning of the war; all the others being "Kriegstrauung." It was the Henckel-

Schaffgotsch wedding and was very beautiful. The union was such a happy one that the parents had determined to make it a scene of rejoicing for once; and the young couple certainly deserved it, for the bridegroom has been continually in action for three and a half years, and the bride's father has served in the ammunition columns since the beginning.

The ten bridesmaids at the wedding were all decked out in dresses of pink chiffon and carried bouquets of spring flowers, and each was attended (as is the custom here) by a young officer in uniform; and only that morning each of these youths had received notice that he was to hurry back to the front to-morrow.

.   .   .   .   .   .

I felt a little relieved the other day when a lady in an important official position came up to me and gave me some secret information. "I may be committing a patriotic crime," she said, "but I feel so much with you in your anxiety about your relations 'over there,' that I mean to risk it. The reverses and losses last week were not so much amongst the English as amongst the French and Americans. The Germans wish the people to believe the contrary, but the real fact is that although some English regiments were obliged to retreat, they are not the ones who made the mistakes or who have suffered most."

.   .   .   .   .   .

Last night Prince Max Taxis dined with us; he had arrived only a few hours before from St Quentin. He was greatly affected by the remembrance of it. Last year, he said, it had been a flourishing town, and now it was a deserted ruin, most of the houses being absolutely razed to the ground and nothing to be seen in it but streams of prisoners passing through.

I heard to-day from Princess Munster, who sent an extract from a letter from her husband. She writes: "He says he is back in Alsace now with the Xth army corps. He has had a most interesting time for the last

ten days. He dined with the Crown Prince at his headquarters, and spent half a day with him, besides being
shown round everywhere. He says: 'Your heart would
have warmed with pride at the way he speaks of the
English prisoners (officers and soldiers), and he never
misses an opportunity of visiting the English wounded,
giving them cigarettes and cheering them up.' "

     .   .   .   .   .   .

The Lichnowsky affair continues to excite the greatest
interest.

Herr von Jagow has been dining and lunching with
us often lately, and has explained his (Lichnowsky's)
position very clearly to my husband, who has in fact
been helping him to write his "Explanation" which appeared in the German papers last week and is being
reproduced in the English papers this week.

Yesterday the case was brought before the Herrenhaus. It will be tried by his peers, and they will decide
his fate. As G. tells me, the scene was most impressive.
The House had been packed the whole morning for the
Polish debates, but when this great "case" came on,
the House was cleared and the whole affair thrashed out
in camera. As most of the nobility present were either
his friends or relations, it was a painful moment for them
all. It seems the question to be decided is whether he
will lose his seat in the Herrenhaus and be expelled from
his regiment, etc , etc. He will be allowed to appeal,
so the case may last another six months.

Although Lichnowsky has been trying to show the
world a bold face up to now, and might have been seen
walking in the Tiergarten in front of our windows every
morning lately, he left Berlin the day before the opening
of the Herrenhaus, and is now at his Silesian seat. I
hear that he is very depressed and surprised at the turn
affairs have taken.

     .   .   .   .   .   .

The other great topic of conversation in the salons
of Berlin is the "peace movement" going on under

the surface between France and Austria, for all the "démentis" in the world cannot alter the fact that the royal pair in Austria have been trying to negotiate quietly with France. It has, of course, been absolutely denied officially, as such a move would be considered "disloyalty to their ally."

The story runs here that it was not the Austrian Emperor but his young wife who wrote to Clémenceau, suggesting an opening of peace negotiations, and that it was quite unofficial and, so to say, without the Emperor's cognizance; but it is really just the sort of impulsive thing that a young impatient couple would do, so that I admire the effort even if it has failed to succeed.

I have been told another little interesting episode to-day, coming in fact from some of the Austrian relations themselves. The Austrian Empress has two younger brothers (Dukes of Parma) on the other side, as so many of us have. They are attached to the Belgian Red Cross, and, filled with an intense longing to see them, besides being probably moved by political reasons as well, she planned a little scheme for this purpose which came off most successfully and is still absolutely unknown to any one outside her own family. The two Princes actually visited her in Austria. They entered a train in Belgium in the uniform of Belgian officers, and left it in Vienna in the costume of Austrian sportsmen, and were quite unrecognized. They spent some three days in one of the royal shooting residences, and were again smuggled back to Belgium in the same manner, where they have rejoined the Belgian army.

. . . . . .

Running through the more important subjects of the day there is always a red thread of gossip and criticism on the poor old Reichskanzler and Herr von Kühlmann. The "Vaterlandspartei" are always at work, and do not shrink from any methods to unhorse the latter. Now they are trying an attack on his private life. It is very despicable, and one cannot help agreeing with Kühlmann who, a few days ago on his return from Bukarest, where he had been working at the peace negotiations, complained bitterly of the treatment he was exposed to. As he said, although he had trained himself to have the hide of a rhinoceros and to be absolutely indifferent to criticism, yet it is cutting even to the most hardened to return from such a difficult mission, where he had been doing his utmost for his country, to find that in the meantime he had become the victim of a low intrigue got up by his political antagonists to ruin him. He was alluding to reports which have been circulating here to the effect that while in Bukarest he had inaugurated "wild orgies" with smart Roumanian ladies who were trying to influence him to make a weak peace for Germany.

Ridiculous as these reports may seem, they were so skilfully set in motion that they grew in interest from month to month and were believed by nearly every one before the source of the calumny was exposed. The alleged weakness of the peace with Roumania is that she is to be allowed to keep her guns and weapons. Germany's ally, Bulgaria, particularly resents these terms, as she says the guns will inevitably one day be directed against her.

BERLIN, *April* 1918.—I suppose that I was feeling more than usually anxious about my family just now, and as I am a great believer in telepathy, the following is a curious instance of it. I have been undergoing a course of massage lately, and the lady who gives me the treatment, although not professing to be a clairvoyante, has at times an extraordinary gift of second sight. In the course of conversation during my treatment she said, "You are terribly worried about something, aren't you?" "Yes," I said, "I am anxious about my brothers and brother-in-law, owing to this last offensive." Looking round the room and seeing their photographs all about, she begged me not to worry, and taking up each photograph in turn she told me the following, which I noted down as she said it. Holding up the photo of my eldest brother, she said he was in a distant land and had been in a hospital there, ill but not wounded. "This one," and she took up the photo of my brother Edmund, "has a scar or sore all along one side of his face."

I knew nothing about them at the time, but about ten days after I received a letter from my mother, saying that my eldest brother was in Palestine, and had been very ill in hospital; and that Edmund, my second brother, was home on sick leave owing to an abscess on his chin and jaw caused by the unhealthy food and water in the place he had been at!

"These two," taking up the photos of my brother-in-law, Colonel Rowland Feilding, and of my brother Vincent, "have been for the last few days in terrible danger, but it is over for them at present." Then, singling out the one of my brother, "He is lying at this moment in hospital with a broken leg. I see him fall," she continued, "with a wound or accident to his leg; I see two soldiers coming on either side of him and picking him up and supporting him under the shoulders; they half drag and half carry him across a temporary bridge, made of rafters, across a canal.[1] He is now in a hospital, where he will remain for about six weeks and then will be sent home, where he will remain in hospital for many months. He will recover, but he will limp for life"

I must confess I felt partly relieved at the thought that he and Rowland were for the moment out of danger, and just waited patiently for definite news to come. On the evening of this same day I took up a paper and read the description of the fighting that had taken place near Givenchy from the 9th to 14th April, how on the 11th and 12th the West Lancashire Territorials had saved the situation, but that their losses had been so fearful that they had had to fall back on the "engineers of this regi-

[1] These details were proved later to have been correct.

ment" as infantry reserves (Vincent's regiment; and he was, in fact, an engineer).

As I am now, thank God, in constant uncensored communication with my cousin at The Hague, who is my one link with the outer world, I hoped to gain more news through him, and telegraphed to ask if anything had happened to Vincent. On April 28 I received a wire from him saying: "Vincent has a broken leg, and is expected to be well enough to be moved to London from France in six weeks' time." The prophetic words being thus so exactly verified almost terrified me in the contemplation of how ignorant we are of the hidden forces of Nature. Yet how grateful I was for this good news, and I think no one ever before rejoiced more at a broken leg than I did over my brother Vincent's.

At the same time it seems as if our family is not to be spared suffering in any generation, for on April 22 I received a *Times* of the 11th, and in the list of casualties saw the name of my nephew Osmund, the only son of my eldest brother

BERLIN, *April* 1918.—Friends to luncheon and friends to tea; with somehow or other a feeling that perhaps these will be the last meetings of our little "ausländerische" coterie   At luncheon we were only a small party of four—our two selves, Herr von Jagow, who was pessimistic, and Princess Isenburg, who is always cheerful and in good spirits. She, as I omitted to mention before, is the American wife of Prince Karl von Isenburg-Birstein. She and her husband having generally spent a part of the year in Paris before the war, their position was a difficult one.

Princess Isenburg worked in the American Hospital at Munich until it was closed on America coming in. She then lived quietly at her country place, where she had a convalescent home for soldiers, and worked very hard for the French and English prisoners of war. Her work was much criticized, and she was twice denounced and had to pay a fine of 50 Mk. for her too zealous interest in the enemy. Princess I. always answers laughingly when asked her opinion of the warring countries: "I have to love them all, because I was born in America, educated and lived most of my life in France, am married to a German, and have two charming English brothers-in-law!" Her husband was less diplomatic in speaking his opinions, and was consequently considered too international and cosmopolitan in his ideas to suit the taste of the German Staff. He went out as a voluntary automobilist, not having been in the army.

The Prince is often taken for one or other of his two political brothers. The younger one, Prince Victor von Isenburg, worked for a couple of war years in the Foreign Office under Herr von Jagow. His elder, and politically better-known brother, is Prince Joseph von Isenburg, who was Military Governor of Lithuania. He has been much criticized, and succeeded in making many enemies in that country and in Poland. During luncheon this subject was discussed, and Bertha I. defended her brother-in-law, saying that as an officer he had had to fulfil the orders given him by his superiors, General von Ludendorff and General von Eichorn. He had 800 officers under him, and could not be held responsible for the foolish way some of those under him carried these orders out. There was continual strife among the Lithuanians and Poles, hardly a Sunday passing without fights and even bloodshed in the churches. This was because the sermon was either in Polish or Lithuanian, and the people whose language was not used protested violently.

In the afternoon I had as large a tea-party as I could collect from the remnants of our now disbanded set, most of them, in fact all but myself, the American wives of German husbands, and all, needless to say, somewhat anxious and worried as to the fate of their fortunes in America Countess Matuschka, being one of the well-known heiresses, had no very hopeful news to give, and Princess Miguel of Braganza was much in the same position; but as her husband is in the succession for the Portuguese throne, we laughingly told her that when everything else fails, she can persuade him to start a royalist revolution on their own in that country.

Baroness Stumm (the beautiful Constance) also came in for a moment, on her way to The Hague, where her husband has been a member of the Legation for some years. "Why live in misery here when there is so much peace and luxury to be had elsewhere" is the impression she gave us of life in a neutral country. Countess Götzen was the last of our guests to come. She is the widow of the late Governor of East Africa and late Ambassador in Washington, and a feeling of mixed anxiety and sadness came over me as I bade her farewell; sadness, as she was leaving Berlin for good and all shortly, and anxiety, because our present apartment here is partly furnished with some of her beautiful furniture, and in these times of threatened plunder and Bolshevism one does not like the responsibility of other people's valuables. However, she was more optimistic as regards the harmlessness of plunderers than I was. Another American present was Baroness N——, who was depressed by the recent discovery that she was under police supervision. We soon reassured her by telling her that there was nothing exceptional in *that,* and that we had each had our turn; we then proceeded to compare notes on our different experiences, and on the elephantine finesse which German detectives display in what they consider the acme of secret intelligence work.

I remember one day, at luncheon at the "Esplanade," noticing two middle-class men very badly dressed in obviously reach-me-down clothes, who sat at the next table and kept their eyes fixed on me without cessation with the offensive stare of the Berlin official which is so well known to those who have suffered from it   And on inquiring afterwards I learnt that they were two policemen in plain clothes, sent there to watch whether I displayed excessive anti-German views during the said

meal. Their habit is on such occasions to send their card
in beforehand to the restaurant manager, with the words
"Kriminal Detectiv So-and-so" printed on it in large letters, stating the time of arrival, and what particular form
their Sherlock Holmes-like work would probably take.
By this means every one is thoroughly well forewarned
and forearmed, which, from our point of view, certainly
has its advantages.

BERLIN, *May* 3, 1918.—This afternoon, among my
many farewell calls before leaving for the country, I went
to say good-bye to Countess Brockdorff, the dear old
Hofdame of the Empress. She is in fact a typical one,
and, as they say, manages the Empress in quite the historic manner of the Hofdamen of former times, not fearing to tell Her Majesty home-truths, and not permitting
her to be too ultra-Prussian, or anti-Catholic and narrow-
minded in her ideas, as she is inclined to be more and
more each day.

The Countess is very broad-minded, and was most
sympathetic about my anxiety concerning my brothers,
etc. She had just returned from the memorial service
for Herr von Richthofen, the gallant flyer, and mentioned how sad it was to see the grief of the poor parents
All Berlin had assembled to do honour to the dead hero,
but this seemed little compensation to his mother for the
loss of her son

On my way home with Madame Polo, we passed the
Russian Embassy, and for the first time I saw the red
flag of revolution waving over it. It must be a very
unpleasant sight for the Emperor when he passes down
Unter den Linden, and altogether people are inclined to
mistrust these freshly made Russian diplomats, who do
not manage to inspire us with that feeling of security
which one hopes for when a "peace" has been proclaimed
and signed after a great war like this.

There are said to be some forty members of the Embassy all told, most of them being common soldiers or

sailors, the only educated gentleman among them being a Socialist doctor. They refuse to associate with any one in Berlin but the most blatant Socialists, and one hears strange stories of their manners at meals and their habits in private life, which are more or less those that one would expect from the lowest class of Russian peasants. Privately I am inclined to believe that they are a great danger to Germany, and *that they have come for any other reason than peaceful ones.*

The whole of the Russian prisoner affairs have been handed over to them by the Spaniards, and time will show, but I believe that they are arranging a general rising among the prisoners, instead of organizing peaceful work on peaceful terms. I may, of course, be mistaken, but I should be by no means surprised to wake up one morning and find that the signal has been given for a Russian revolution in Germany, and that we are in the midst of a great mutiny. It is an interesting question how many Germans of the lower classes would join them, for even I have noticed a growing intimacy and friendship amongst those who have come under my observation lately, not to mention the rumours one hears of German soldiers rebelling in Russia and compelling their captive officers to assume the same rank as themselves. All this tends to make one believe that there is a systematic undercurrent of action going on. I fervently wish, however, that we poor "Ausländer" could get away to some neutral country before this interesting development takes place. I hear so many strange things said that I often wonder how much more is being kept back from us, and how soon it will be too late to do anything but resign oneself to an irresistible course of events.

On passing out of the dining-room at a dinner-party the other day, I heard one member of the Foreign Office whisper to another, "Well, England seems to have 'caught on.'" "Yes," said the other, "things look pretty bad." Again, at a luncheon-party a few days later I heard some one say: "It is shocking how pro-Entente the young Austrian Empress is, and what an influence she has over her husband." "Yes," was the reply, "all those who have brothers fighting on the other side are 'pro' that side; it is in their blood, it has always been so in all history, and one will never be able to eradicate it. The Empress's idea, of course, is to get one of her brothers made King of France." We can see through such remarks how the feeling is veering round, and how the tension between Austria and Germany is increasing every day.

I was amused at a little story I was told about the Austrian Emperor the other day. He and the Empress are longing for peace almost at any price, not only for reasons of humanity, but because they are both perfectly aware that Austria cannot hold out much longer, and being young and sanguine, they employ every means privately and publicly to bring about an end to the bloody strife; besides which, just because of their youth and inexperience, they are both secretly rather afraid of their ministers, and one day when the young Emperor was having a private interview with a well-known pacifist leader from Switzerland, Czernin was suddenly announced. The Emperor hereupon, feeling like a naughty boy, had to hide the great pacifist in his dressing-room, whilst he interviewed the warlike Czernin.

They are, of course, rather like grown-up children, trying to save the world; but one must admit their good intentions, and admire and love them all the better for their so-called "faults," which spring from such a different source from all the cold-blooded, ruthless, and cruel methods which are lauded up to the skies over here.

When trying to impress on one the perfidiousness and treachery of the young Empress, people always say she is just as pro-Italian as she is pro-French in her feelings; and a turning up of the eyes and a tightening of the lips are meant to emphasize the wickedness of the young Queen's heart at thus following the call of flesh and blood.

I was told by some Germans the other day that the Austrian Generals had at last persuaded the Emperor one day to agree to the use of all the most drastic methods of warfare in order to attain their end on the Italian front, but when the young Empress came to him with tears in her eyes, and begged him not to allow beautiful Venice to be bombarded, he at once gave in and countermanded his orders, much to the rage of some of the most virulent of the Generals.

KRIEBLOWITZ, *May* 1918.—Gebhard's two nephews have just written home. They say that no words can describe the horrors of what they have been through. They write that they are almost dying of starvation. They say they advanced so rapidly that no provisions could reach them, and their division was five days and nights fighting incessantly without food or even sleep at all, and those of their companies who were not killed or wounded died of exhaustion, and it is only by a miracle that they themselves are left to tell the tale. Their letter ends with the significant words: "Send us some food somehow, as quickly as you can, or we also shall die."

Here in Krieblowitz, the peasants and village people receive the news that sometimes one sometimes even two of their sons have been killed on the same day. It has been a wholesale slaughter of late.

My maid's husband writes: "It is indescribably awful here in Laon. We live in the midst of an incessant hail of bullets. The men on each side of me were both killed yesterday, and I expect my turn to come any day. The French are shelling the town from airplanes night and day, as they know that the big gun which is bombarding Paris is near here, and they are trying to destroy that We had been boarding and sleeping since we have been here in a large almshouse, where eighty old French women, all over seventy years of age, lived, and we soldiers had all grown fond of these old ladies. When we came back as usual last evening, we found the place in ruins, and all the old women buried beneath the debris— French flyers had done it!"

From Trier the nuns write that so much damage has been done to their convent that now they live entirely in the cellar, and they have their chapel and have daily mass there.

.   .   .   .   .   .

Yesterday a man lunched with us who had been dining the previous week with Captain Muller of the *Emden,* who had recently returned from his imprisonment in England. Müller confided to him how much annoyed he was at the accounts of his bad treatment in England, printed in the German newspapers. He said they were absolutely untrue, and that he had been treated as a gentleman and sportsman throughout, and had made many friends there.

Instancing the single case of impoliteness he had met with, he had (in joke) related a remark made to him by a common sailor when coming over, and this had been doctored up into "ill-treatment of prisoners in England" by Boy-Ed, who used it as a means for working up the dying feeling of antagonism here. Müller said he was so angry that he was going to insist on a contradiction being published. "What will they think of us in England if he twists the truth, even in a matter like this?" were his words.

.   .   .   .   .   .

I notice a great change in the people here from what they were last year. They are all "tired of suffering," as they express it. "We want our sons and husbands back, and we want food," is all they say. And the priests and clergymen too say how difficult it is to hold them in now. Any moment they fear them breaking all control. A man whose business it is, as he puts it, to go round begging for the new war loan, told us that it is very difficult now to persuade people to subscribe, not that they have not got the money, for they have more than they know what to do with; but "patriotism" is dead, it does not "catch on" any longer, and he can only get them to subscribe by exerting real pressure, and telling them that if they do not do so they will lose everything they have already invested

"What will they say," I asked, "when they realize that all these big 'Kriegsanleihe' figures are in reality bogus, and are only the same numbers re-entered?" "Please God they never may realize it!" was his answer.

Food is growing scarcer from day to day, and we have been reduced to killing and eating our kangaroos. They have been kept here as a great curiosity and rarity for years past. Yesterday my husband received a letter from one of the provision-dealers in Breslau, saying he would give any price my husband liked to mention if he would sell him a kangaroo.

. . . . . .

It is very difficult to turn my thoughts away from my own personal anxieties to things of more universal interest. We are expecting a bloody Whitsuntide, when the German troops will have recovered from the exhaustion following on the forced marches of the past offensive. The silence at present is ominous.

The Austrian Emperor, Kaiser Karl, is visiting the German Emperor at Great Headquarters. It is meant to patch up the inner conflicts which are growing more serious every day between the two countries. The Austrians complain that other nationalities are only entitled to exist in the manner Germany sees fit to allow them.

. . . . . .

Clothes are growing so scarce that the men are being called upon to hand over their superfluous clothes (they are officially allowed two suits). If they do not respond willingly, compulsion will be brought into force, and we shall soon have policemen overhauling our wardrobes to see what is in them. Robbery and plunder are the order of the day, and one is practically surrounded by thieves.

BERLIN, *May* 1918 —Here are some impressions re‐
lated to me by a soldier who took part in the great offen‐
sive near Armentières in April 1918 —After describing
the perfect organization and timing of the attack as the
infantry worked forward, cutting through barbed wire,
overcoming all obstacles, and with breathless haste tum‐
bling into the first line of English trenches, he said, they
found not a soul! They had been evacuated, evidently in
a hurry, for only the men were gone, everything else had
been left. Stacks and stacks of food, cases of biscuits,
jam, tobacco, corned beef, milk—all that a poor starved
German's imagination could desire in his wildest dreams.
Then clothes, mackintoshes, leather waistcoats, silk socks,
books—wonderful waterproof trench boots, depots of
leather goods, saddles, reins, bags; real English compact
army outfit of every kind. One thing that particularly
fascinated this soldier was a perfect little leather case
containing twelve aluminum plates. He had not seen a
plate since he had left the last town of rest! The case
too looked as though a lady of fashion might go to pay
calls with it; a German soldier is not used to dainties.

The second line of trenches proved as interesting as
the first, but the third line was so well defended that the
retreat was sounded and we hear no more, for soon after
this soldier was wounded and helped back along the line
by an English ambulance-man who had been taken pris‐
oner. Other English prisoners were on the road, mostly
swearing at the war, at their bad luck, often enough too
at Lloyd George and the state of affairs at home. The
Germans thought *tout comme chez nous,* because "state
of affairs at home" conjured up the state of affairs in
Germany. But when they remembered those two lines
of trenches and the treasures therein, they began to think
there were different kinds of "states of affairs at home,"
and different degrees of suffering.

On arriving with a Lazarett-train at Essen the relief
was great, for the journey had been long and wearisome.
Hardly any food had there been and hard stretchers

without mattresses. At one station the wounded had even had to change trains, and while standing in a limp line along the platform, an "Unteroffizier" had come along and called to the men to stand at attention. Fortunately there was a "Vizewachtmeister" among them, who is a grade higher, and who gave the tactful "Unteroffizier" a piece of his mind. At Essen they were carted on stretchers to an electric train, and so taken to the hospital. The hospital was full to bursting, and men with bandaged arms and legs had to lie on straw. The men were all very sore about the officers, and there was no pretence at respect or love for them.

One man told a story of a wounded officer who had said to him, "If you don't lift me gently, I'll hit you across the mouth." "I plunged him down then," said the man, "wound or no wound."

The men who are convalescent have to wait on the officers, who send them running for every trifle. One had limped to town to do shopping. On his return deadtired, he was told to go again for one toothbrush! Still, the officer might have been in need of a toothbrush, which I can understand better than the story a common soldier told of having had to scrub out a cupboard with a toothbrush, as a punishment for a small spot of dirt on it!

Imagine what a Russian pupil told me. "Not only do we still have to report ourselves twice a week at the police station, but the people of the Russian Embassy have to go once a week. Think of that, and the red flag outside the Embassy too! This peace is a pure farce."

The Roumanians also have still to report themselves, though the schools have offered to take back the Roumanians they turned out when war with Roumania was declared.

Here is another little tale of a friend of mine, a German. A policeman went up to her studio to make inspection concerning fire-escape, etc. He asked her to show her papers. "No," she said, "you've no right to ask for them. Duplicates are deposited at the police station, as is the case with every Prussian subject." "You've been abroad for a long time, missie," he said. "How do you know?" she asked. "You would never have dared answer up to me like that if you hadn't," he said. That seems to me a characteristic touch.

We have now great queues of people in the street waiting for their one allotment of sewing cotton—forty yards of cotton, to last four months, I have no doubt. Yet they say that things in the Ukraine are much worse. A man's suit of a normal kind costs 1000 roubles there, and stockings are not to be had   For the matter of that, though, all the poorer women walk about the streets stockingless now; I've even seen better-class people adopting the healthy mode of sandals without stockings— "health" being a mere excuse for lack of stocking vouchers!

BERLIN, *May* 1918.—We are gradually beginning to hear details of the naval raid on Ostend and Zeebrugge. Here the newspapers make as little fuss as possible about it, treating it as an episode of minor importance, so that the attention of the nation may not be attracted to the real significance of the attack, which means the restriction of the Flanders flotilla to Ostend, from whence they can be much more easily handled. I must confess the news of this naval success has done my heart good. So many of my people are in the navy, and on the whole I have felt secretly a little disappointed at the slight successes obtained until now   One expected such startling results, grand sweeping victories in the style of the old Nelsonian days; instead of which they seem to have grown so exceedingly careful and cautious in their operations.

The offensive is taking on more and more the character of a race between Hindenburg and America, and people are beginning generally to perceive the terrific consequences of their fatal mistake in allowing America to come in. Every one is forced to admit that it is America now that is keeping on the war. How foolishly they laughed at the idea two years ago! The American methods sound strange to us, and, if one may believe the accounts one reads, they are a little blatant in their appeals to the sentimental side of the nation, and in the means employed to work up their belligerent qualities. What can one say to such a legend as "Come and hiss at the beast of Berlin," stuck over a photograph of the Kaiser in the office of one of the leading New York papers!

BERLIN, *June* 1918.—We have just returned from a visit to Munich—my first; and after having heard so much of its beauty and the charm it possesses for all who have lived there, I was, as is often the case, rather afraid of being disappointed. But it is not so, and I am just as much under its spell as if I had lived there for years, instead of only having been there for some days.

I am afraid, like most people, I am somewhat unfair in my comparison between it and Berlin. The latter seems so ostentatiously clean and parvenu, and its absolute lack of style verges on vulgarity. One is inclined to forget that it has been built up in the midst of a dull sandy plain by a patient hard-working people who have no traditions of culture and style to carry on, but are more or less at the beginning of their history.

In Munich one perceives the centuries of culture of a beauty-loving people who have left their mark on the town for ever. There is dignity and a happy feeling for space and proportion in its wide streets and broad squares, combined with a romantic "Gemutlichkeit" in the alleys and by-streets of the inner part of the town. And there one always feels in touch with Nature, untrammelled and unspoilt.

The green waters of the Isar are so superbly insolent that no boat can breast its rushing waves, only in the early spring-time flocks of white-winged sea-gulls float on its foam-flecked surface. Wild storms tear over suddenly from the mountains, and the grand shining line of the Alps rises fantastically on the horizon, a never-ending source of inspiration for poet and painter.

The people impressed me as being particularly kind and warm-hearted, and even their slow broad dialect struck my ears pleasantly (although I could not understand it), in comparison with the abrupt and slangy speech of the people in Berlin. Those who know the Bavarians well tell me that they are not quite so simple and kind as one might believe at first sight. They are in reality more complicated and more endowed for good and bad than the Prussians, who at present seem to be intensely nervous and irritable compared with the people of Munich. The Bavarians, they say, like all mountainous people, are passionate and violent of temperament, and in spite of a generous breadth of feeling in their character, they are wary and suspicious with strangers under the surface. They have a deep feeling for humour and sarcastic wit, but they are not a talkative race and despise the loud-voiced vulgar garrulity of the Berliner. They are very gifted, most of the German artists of note being Bavarians by birth, and the many schools of art in Munich are all more or less inspired by the grandeur of this most beautiful of all German lands.

My nephew Norbert, who is nineteen years of age, has just been staying with us. He is on leave, after having been through the whole of the Western offensive. His descriptions of it are terrible. For six days and nights, he says, they lay in the front trenches, with nothing to eat but what they found in the English trenches on the first day. From these they obtained a perfect banquet, such food as none in Germany is accustomed to any longer, with cigarettes and other luxuries.

He described to me the friendly manner with which they discussed the war with English officers who were taken prisoners. One Englishman, on being asked when peace would be, answered: "Well, I suppose it will take two years more *before you are really beaten.*"

He told me that the English gas is much more deadly than the German; that French strategy recently has been better than their own; and that the Americans are daily becoming a more serious asset to the enemy, as each day more troops are pouring in, all fresh and well equipped, a contrast to the tired-out troops opposing them.

.   .   .   .   .   .

The food question is always the most important topic of the day. The less there is of it, the more do we talk of it. The Austrians have already eaten up their stores, and are grumbling and turning to Germany for fresh supplies. It is rather like turning from a sandy desert to a rocky mountain for nourishment. And there is unfortunately no Moses to show us the way to a promising future.

We ourselves have little to eat but smoked meat and dried peas and beans, but in the towns they are considerably worse off. The potatoes have come to a premature end, and in Berlin the population have now a portion of 1 lb. per head a week, and these even are bad The cold winds of this wintry June have retarded the growth of vegetables, and there is almost nothing to be had. We are all waiting hungrily for the harvest and the prospect of at least more bread and flour.

.   .   .   .   .   .

Here is an extract from a letter from Berlin:

"What do you say to Kühlmann's speech? The article criticizing it in the *Vossische Zeitung* this morning is about the acme of foolishness. It tries to prove that Napoleon only waged war to break the ambitions of England, just as Germany is doing now. Napoleon's way was rather a round-about one, to say the least of it, with his uncomfortable expedition to Moscow. But then, of course, Russia was polluted by English influence, and Napoleon had to try to crush that too!

"How weak-minded people must be growing through the war to make that article possible; whilst to count on its being believed is almost a sign of something more than weak-mindedness.

"You will probably have heard about the fearful state Cologne was in, on account of the flyers, though it was not allowed to be in the papers. A hundred persons were killed, and the wounded in the hospitals are dying because the exploding powder was poisoned. In the hospital of St. Vincent the people could be heard shrieking with the great pain, and the syren goes continually warning one of the danger."

.   .   .   .   .   .

Kuhlmann's speech has fallen like a bomb, and every one is discussing it. As a political act it invokes criticism, and would have been admirable, in my view, if he had not yielded to pressure and recanted the next day. His action is incomprehensible · he ought to have said his say and abided by it. Now he has lost ground on all sides, and the house in the Budapester Strasse will soon see a new tenant. Every one seems to agree that what he said was the truth, and nothing but the truth, but it was a heinous offence to say it.

.   .   .   .   .   .

The unfortunate "peace" reports, those ghostly birds of despair, are again flitting about amongst us. We hear that a Dutch committee is circulating notices to the effect that the conference in The Hague should be turned into a Peace Congress. This too belongs to the region of Utopia, I am afraid   I have seen one of these notices myself. It pretends that Lloyd George, Wilson, and Asquith are all quite willing to listen to the proposal! Too good to be true, I fear.

I have been much interested in following the negotiations at The Hague regarding the exchange of prisoners of war. My husband and I were pleased to see that men like Prince Hatzfeldt and Baron von der Heydt have been chosen among the envoys on the German side.

They are old acquaintances of ours, and as they have both lived in England and America, they will know how to negotiate with the other side better than many others.

.   .   .   .   .   .

Baron Kühlmann was dining the other evening at the Larisches', and sat next to me. Being a Bavarian, he has much of the genius of that nation, and a great deal of their renowned disregard for convention and fearlessness of public opinion. He made many enemies in the first days of his office in Berlin by turning out all the useless decorative "Hofräte" of the Foreign Office, and nominating men he thought more capable in their place. These were chiefly Bavarians too, so that he caused a good deal of bad blood amongst the Prussians, who are all, of course, now trying to trip him up Argus eyes watch his every movement, and though he is at present too popular with the majority in the Reichstag for them to attack him publicly, they are waiting for a chance to catch him in his private life.

KRIEBLOWITZ, *July* 1918.—The lack of clothes and boots and shoes is growing more and more disastrous. In summer people can manage to scrape along, as every one is more or less shabbily dressed, and people in the country and smaller towns wear wooden sandals in place of shoes, the children either going bare-footed or stocking-less, as a rule. They run about merrily enough with their little bare brown legs In the big towns, of course, more boots and shoes are worn; but here too a virtue is often made of necessity, and wooden sandals are the unwilling fashion of the hour.
It is next to impossible to get new boots and shoes. By bribing a shoemaker who is the lucky possessor of leather with a pound of butter or some bottles of wine, he may promise to make you a pair at the end of six months, for the price of 100 to 150 marks, in the country 80 to 100 marks. The ready-made boots available in Berlin are mostly of an extremely inferior quality, made

of common grey cloth and bad leather; they cost about 50 to 60 marks, and are only to be had by the customer going and standing outside the shop some five or six hours before it is opened. In Berlin the shoe shops are not opened before 10 o'clock in the morning. A friend of mine, after running from one shop to the other for days, at last managed to buy a pair of boots for her little girl eight years old. The first time the child put them on, they cracked and split in a dozen places, and they discovered that the material was not leather but wretched cotton stuff covered over with a thin veneer of varnish. They had cost 27 marks.

A costume, jacket and skirt, of good cloth costs from 400 to 800 marks; formerly it would have cost 80 marks. Very thin cotton stockings of a cobweb fabrication cost from 10 to 20 marks a pair. Calico for underclothes is not to be had.

In the country all the old forgotten arts of hand-spinning and weaving are being cultivated again, and careful housewives are busy preparing flax for spinning in the long winter evenings. Every peasant has now his patch of ground covered with flax, and the women in some places bring to light splendid rolls of strong home-spun linen which have been stored up for years. They have it dyed and made up into practical and tasteful dresses for themselves and their children.

Many people keep two or three sheep for the sake of their wool. Nearly every village possesses some old dame who still understand the art of spinning wool into coarse worsted which is then used for stockings.

Except as regards light, people are better off in the country in every way than in the towns. From other parts of Germany I hear that the peasants have enough to eat, and look in splendid condition. They are gaining more money for their produce than has ever been known before; they have all the necessaries of existence near at hand, and are able to lay by an ever-increasing balance in the bank. On the other hand all farm-buildings are growing dilapidated, and they are not able to mend or replace the necessary implements of work Moreover, the farm-stocks are being so reduced by lack of fodder and the slaughter of milk-cows for food, that farmers tell me the capital necessary for repairing and buying up new stock when the war is over will swallow up all their savings.

At Krieblowitz we ourselves are self-supporters, and live in a patriarchal way, the whole house being dependent on the results of my husband's shooting—at present wild duck and roe-buck. As in the good old days (how good we never knew until now) of the dark ages, he goes out daily with his gun and brings back something for dinner. If he is lucky and has more than we want for our own needs, we exchange the surplus with the tradespeople for butter, eggs, sugar, articles of clothing or anything else that is only to be obtained by bribery of this kind.

It has become a yearly institution to invite a number of town-children from the poorer classes for the summer months. Every country house, castle, and peasant's house is called upon to keep and feed so many They are very interesting little people, and talking to them one can get a deep insight into the privations and sufferings of the people in the big towns. Many of them, too, have already experienced strange adventures and vicissitudes, and three of those here can hardly speak any German at all. Their father had been a civil prisoner in England until last year, and their English mother had had to support the family in a London suburb during the last two years of the war. In England they had been looked at askance for being German, and here they have the greatest difficulties at school, as they are only able to speak English.

    .   .   .   .   .   .

I am glad to say we are at last able to communicate with our own Russian prisoners, from whom we have always been cut off until now by a similar difficulty of language. Madame Rizoff and her two children have been staying here. She is the beautiful young widow of the Bulgarian Minister, who died three months ago in Berlin. She is here for a change of air and scene, and as she speaks Russian perfectly, I got her to talk to the Russians. We are not really allowed to address them, but their fervent gratitude at hearing their mother-tongue was worth the risk of disobeying orders for once.

They told us how happy they were to be here, and that before they came they had been in a prison camp with 13,000 other Russian prisoners who were literally treated like animals, being herded together in a yard, sleeping on straw and fed like swine. Five thousand of them had absolutely died of neglect. It had been like coming to heaven, they said, when they arrived here, where every one had a smile for them and was so friendly.

They knew all about my being English and having brothers fighting on the other side, and of my husband having been to the Caucasus.

They ended by saying they hoped to stay on here until the end of the war, and that they certainly did not wish to return to Russia in its present disturbed state, and that in any case any fate was better than the misery and filth and horrors of the Russian trenches in the first years of the war.

.   .   .   .   .   .

The news of Graf Mirbach's death to-day in the paper, and the cold-blooded way in which he was murdered, has given me a great shock. My husband is especially affected by it, as they were very intimate friends, and Mirbach was such an attractive, quiet personage.

One feels the tragedy of an individual case like this so much more keenly when one has known a man well Count Mirbach dined with us several times in the week before his departure for Moscow in March, and he was then very sad and depressed, assuring us that he did not in the least appreciate the honour done to him by being chosen as Ambassador. He realized the danger of his position even then, and packed his things with a heavy heart, filled with forebodings, and dreading the effect of the parting on his old mother, who perfectly comprehended what such a journey meant.

.   .   .   .   .   .

Amongst the many visitors here this summer one hears a great deal of tittle-tattle about people in high places, and a good many guesses are made as to the way His Majesty would accept a reverse of a very decisive order. People say that, although his attitude has not shown conspicuous moral strength, he is not physically a coward, and would rather die with his troops than return with a vanquished army; whilst others say openly that if he only had the courage to abdicate now, he might save his whole country from the terrible fate impending.

Another discussion touched on the extraordinary way in which Germany has always underrated the importance of the danger coming from America, almost the whole country making fun of and laughing at the idea of an American army. Some one who happened to be present with His Majesty at the time when Roumania declared war, and also when the news of the American declaration became known, assured us that on the first occasion the Kaiser came into the room trembling and white as a sheet, his knees shaking as he said, "All is over; I may as well abdicate at once"; whereas on the second occasion he and those round him were jaunty, laughing, and saying that it made no matter at all, as America could never get an army together, and if it did, they were much too far away and could never possibly get their troops over because of the submarines.

I wonder why they did not listen to the few wise people who perceived the danger of the American intervention in all its sinister meaning, as it is now proving to be the final undoing of Germany.

In the meantime, Kühlmann has succumbed to the attacks of the Pan-German party, and gone the way of

all Ministers for Foreign Affairs in Berlin. No enlight-
ened man can stand up against the dark powers of the
military intrigues, but we feel very little interest in
anything at present but the news coming from the West
Front.

The great French "counter-offensive," as the new
term goes, has begun, and the French are again on the
Marne, and the south bank is again in English hands.
Château-Thierry has been taken, 20,000 prisoners and
400 guns. People here may well look grave; the meaning of America is coming home to them at last. They
comprehend now that it means an increase of the French
reserves at the rate of 300,000 fresh, well-equipped men
per month, whilst Germany can bring up no fresh
reserves. General Foch, with his talent for waiting,
seems to be the great French General at last.

This success has been mainly won by the French and
American troops. In four days General Foch has completely transformed the situation in the West, and the
German blow at Paris has failed Here people ascribe
the bitter reverse to deserters having betrayed the
German plans, and to the "unshattered nerves of the
fresh Americans," whilst others speak lugubriously of a
newly invented artificial fog arising from the enemy's
lines, which completely hid the fatal attack of the tanks.

I was very glad to see that the English Press comments on the decent state in which the Germans left
Château-Thierry, comparing it advantageously with their
behaviour when they occupied Belgium.

We are expecting further severe attacks, and Germany
will be confronted by new tasks, but the bulk of the
people still have unlimited faith in Ludendorff and
Hindenburg, although they know that they are burning
their stores and blowing up their ammunition in their
retreat.

It is sadly tragical to look on and see the slow fate
of Germany overtaking her I, who have watched the
people struggling, and seen their unheard-of sacrifices

and stolid resignation, cannot but pity them from my heart. In spite of their odious officialdom, which makes the Prussians so disliked everywhere, the whole world must admire them for the plucky way they have held out, and even the enemy says how pathetic it is to see the poor, half-starved, half-clothed German soldiers going bravely forward to meet all those fresh well-fed Americans.

In the estimation of many, it is but the first move of those very Americans towards the conquest of Europe. She seems to have all the Allies in her hand already.

.   .   .   .   .

As was to be foreseen, the Czar has been murdered: a wretched end, and yet almost the only possible one for such a pitiful monarch, burdened from the cradle with the sinister heritage of merciless barbarous forefathers. "The sins of the fathers shall be visited on the children" is what forces itself on one's brain, thinking of his miserable death. What will become of his children? Russia is at present like an enormous arena chosen by fate for the scene of a million bloody tragedies, and we are the cold-blooded spectators looking on.

KRIEBLOWITZ, *August* 1918.—The cold dry weeks of June and the despondent outlook for the harvest gave place to rainy weeks in July, which came in time to repair the damage done, so that the promise of a good harvest cheered the hearts of the hungry watching people; and August has fulfilled these expectations, and the crops have proved to be abundant everywhere. Only the late corn and oats are suffering under the cold rainy weather of the last two weeks, and the precious cut corn is beginning to sprout, too damp to be brought in. In these lean years the eyes of all Germany follow anxiously the news of the harvest in the newspapers. The late potatoes are a success; one can hear the universal sigh of relief at these tidings.

Meatless weeks have been ordered, as too many

milk-cows are being slaughtered. If the war continues much longer there will be no live stock left at all.

. . . . .

Our house has been full of guests for the last six weeks, which has consequently brought us a lot of news.

I have already mentioned Madame Rizoff and her two children. She is now a penniless widow. We heard that her husband died of a heart-shock brought on by excitement at the German peace with Russia. He was a very clever man and foresaw what a fatal peace it was for Bulgaria, and how unwise (in her own interests) it had been of Germany to make such a peace. Rizoff had a high reputation as a politician, and too late, after the peace had been ratified, the Emperor consulted him and said, "If only you had given me your views and opinions before!" This is quite characteristic of Germany; she always recognizes her diplomatic and political mistakes a few days too late.

Baroness Sternburg was here too, and was daily receiving news from American friends to the effect that the American laws are being made so severe against German aliens that any one communicating with their relations in Germany will lose their money, and it is very uncertain if it will be refunded to them afterwards. What a panic there will be among the German and Austrian princes and dukes who have married American heiresses!

Herr von Jagow and his wife were also among our guests for some time, and my husband's old friend Count Richard Coudenhove, who had been a prisoner in Siberia for two years and had much that was interesting to relate about Russia and the Russians.

I will not name all our guests, but will give a few details of the more interesting things they told us.

The universal opinion is that the new State Secretary von Hintze, though personally a nice man, is not a clever one, and his appointment was a great surprise. His Majesty put him into office without consulting Hertling at all. Kuhlmann, they said, was so swollen with his own importance that, when summoned to headquarters after his famous speech, he imagined he was going to be congratulated on it, instead of which he was greeted by His Majesty in his impulsive way with the words, "I have appointed Hintze in your place."

People say that Kuhlmann made his fatal speech on the spur of the moment, without consulting Hertling at all. This is quite in accordance with his character, as he is always more inclined to act on the inspiration of the moment than to subject his actions to carefully-thought-out plans.

The whole political situation is so perilous at the moment, that every one feels something momentous must be going to take place. The constant changes in official circles denote weakness and uncertainty, and there is in reality no strong man at the wheel of the ship of Germany.

"A victorious army never rebels," people say, but an army in retreat is very liable to be seized by the spirit of mutiny, and certainly the mass of the population here would be ready to back any definite movement.

Capitalists and large landowners are beginning to talk in earnest of the possibility of their land being confiscated and their property divided up in the Bolshevik manner. The whole public spirit is so depressed and the universal suffering so great, that the people are threatening to take matters into their own hands. You can hear this intention expressed at every street corner. A shopgirl said it openly to my husband the other day: "We are going to stop the war now; those in command have failed entirely and have never kept their promises which they so often made" Another friend heard in the tram: "It is high time for the Emperor to abdicate to bring about peace, and the sooner this is made clear to him the better"

The soldiers are embittered at the way they are treated in comparison with the officers, and the country

is overrun with invalids with grievances. Wounded
men refuse to consent to operations which might heal
an injured limb, on the ground that they would then be
sent back to the front, and they have no intention of
going there.

Every one is now able to see through the official
telegrams which for so long hoodwinked the masses.
They know that the constant shortening of the front
spells "Retreat." They know, too, that troops are
again being transported back to Russia, where the great
combat between English and German influence is in full
force. The whole economic future of Germany depends
on her getting a firm footing in Russia, and having command of the vast unexploited treasures waiting for
Western capital to develop. This, they say, accounts
for the murders of Mirbach and General von Eichendorff.
The murders are systematic.

.   .   .   .   .   .

Ludendorff has publicly acknowledged the failure of
the great offensive; it seems the growing lack of ammunition is the ominous cause of the defeat. So many guns
have been left in the hands of the enemy, and there is
not enough iron left to make new ones.

There have been public protests against the misleading
statements made by Prince Heinrich as to the results
of the Marne battle, on the same day that Ludendorff
had admitted that their strategic plans had failed. He
naïvely seems to have thought that the opinion of some
unknown Turkish attaché, that the Marne battle was a
German victory, was of more importance than the confession of the great generals. It is so incredibly foolish
to try and hoodwink the people like this, when the truth
must ultimately leak out.

The Bavarians have a special complaint that the war
reports are always partial to the Prussians. They say
that as long as the losses of life and material are sustained
by the Crown Prince's army, no mention is ever made
of them; but as soon as Prince Rupprecht's army is

being beaten, every detail of the defeat is made public, and an open confession is made of the enemy having penetrated the German lines.

It seems impossible now for Ludendorff to force any decisive successful battle this year. Officers here say that his plan of separating the British army from the French was not impossible and would have been successful, if the heavy losses of the Allies had not been so speedily made up again. In a single month 355,000 men were thrown across, and every gun had been replaced.

It is apparently the unity of command which restored the Allied fortunes, and if the American troops go on coming over at the rate of 300,000 a month, the American army alone will soon be as big as the German.

Men home on leave have been giving me vivid descriptions of the last great fights, and one's brain grows weary of it all. No wonder that half the army have ruined nerves!

One young officer, just returned from the front, stated that 30,000 German prisoners were taken on one day, and that eight of his brother officers were killed at his side in one minute, he alone surviving.

They say that air-battles have been the most characteristic feature of the offensive, there being sometimes as many as forty planes engaged in the air, and that the swift advance of the Allied armies was mainly due to the systematic co-operation of aeroplanes and tanks. The Germans withdrew without destroying any land, so that no "no man's land" was created this time, that great numbers of artillery officers were taken prisoners, and every one speaks of the pluck of the British tank-crews with great admiration.

In their retreat the Germans destroyed their petroleum dumps to prevent them falling into the hands of the enemy, and my narrators described the effect of the burning stuff rising like great forests of flames in the darkness of the night; but in spite of their retreat

Ludendorff succeeded in getting his guns away from the English pursuers.

.   .   .   .   .

There are reports current here to the effect that King Ferdinand is going mad, and is subject to fits of melancholy and weeping. This, I presume, we may class with the rest of the reports of this nature, according to which all the remaining monarchs in Europe should have been long since dead or in a mad-house; although the responsibility of this war is enough to send any one into an asylum.

Ferdinand is probably frightened at the dimensions which the Czecho-Slovak uprising is taking on. It has come in most opportunely for England, and may mean the freeing of Russia from the Bolshevists and prove a serious check to Germany's plans.

.   .   .   .   .

I was intensely glad to see that twenty-nine British officers succeeded in escaping from that wretched camp at Holzminden; one is only surprised at their being able to dig out a tunnel of sixty yards long without being discovered. I wish more could escape in the same way.

BERLIN, *September* 1918.—We are again in Berlin, but only for a few days on our way to Munich, while Gebhard is attending the extra sitting of the Herrenhaus. The members have been called up to try and settle the Prussian Suffrage Reform Bill, which is always being shelved, thereby causing a great deal of bad blood.

This Bill is a typically characteristic instance of His Majesty's rash impulsive way of acting. He promised universal franchise to the people, and now the Herrenhaus has to try and help him out of the quandary by amending the Bill in such manner that what it gives with one hand will be snatched away by the other. At the same time it is almost certain that if the people do not gain their votes, this, combined with the retreat, will lead to a very desperate state of affairs sooner or later.

Berlin is indeed a gloomy place at present. The news from the front is more and more depressing, there is nothing to eat, and the methods employed to prevent the depression from gaining ground goad the people to fury. Hindenburg has forbidden any one, whatever his personal feelings may be, to speak of the present position as being anything else than hopeful! The grotesque irony of such a command, when the Allied troops are advancing hourly, would be amusing if it were not so tragically foolish.

Prince and Princess Taxis dined with us one night. They had returned quite unexpectedly to town. They had been staying with her mother, Princess Metternich, near Wiesbaden, but the danger of the aeroplane attacks had been so great that, after spending several nights in the cellar, they preferred a hurried retreat to such a perilous sojourn. The castle is on the direct route to Frankfort, and the flyers all passed over it. They described the terrifying but marvellous spectacle of such an attack, the planes skimming along like big birds, surrounded by smoke and exploding shells; the black night suddenly rendered lurid by the fire from the defence guns; the awful noise of shooting all over the town, and the crashing of falling bombs on the houses. On one day ten flyers were brought down and forty people were killed in Frankfort, besides many dangerously wounded.

I was glad to see a face the other evening which reminded me keenly of other times. We were dining at the Adlon with Prince Pless, Prince Hatzfeldt, Graf Magnis, and Herr von Jagow. We were waited upon by a very smart gentleman whom I thought I had seen before. He informed us that he had been head-waiter at the Carlton Hotel in London for seventeen years, and had at once recognized Gebhard and Prince Pless.

The tables were filled with different members of the Herrenhaus, and as all the numerous political grievances of the day were being eagerly discussed, it was interesting enough to listen to them. The articles by Dr. Davis, the Kaiser's American dentist, were the chief topic in the English papers. We all feel that it is not quite square to publish these little private sayings, uttered in confidence in an idle moment, and which take on such a different colouring when seen in the glare of the hostile searchlights of peoples at war. They are significant, however, of the mental calibre of Davis, whose *Memoirs* would have no interest but for this Royal gossip. The courtiers here are quite right for once—"If he *will* make a confidant of a dentist, what else can you expect?"

On my remarking to my neighbour at dinner that I imagined the *Memoirs* were very much exaggerated he laughed and said, "Oh, not in the least; the Emperor has often boasted of the home-truths he had been telling his dentist." I asked him what the Emperor must think of it now. "Oh," was the reply, "we take good care that he does not see the English papers while there are such things in them."

.   .   .   .   .

To-day Gebhard lunched with Graf Oppersdorff to meet the Russian revolutionary representative Joffe. It was very interesting, of course, although they had to avoid politics. Gebhard describes him as a clever, ordinary international Jew, who has been all over the world and speaks every language. He praised England tremendously, admiring especially the methods of English politics and colonization

How curious it is to note the immense power which a handful of Jews have suddenly gained in the country which until now was the seat of absolute despotism, and where for centuries the Jews have suffered such a martyrdom of cruel oppression. It almost looks sometimes as if our little continent were destined to be the bone for America and the Jews to pick.

We are on the way to Munich, where I hope to spend some weeks. I hear that the feeling between Prince

Rupprecht of Bavaria and the Crown Prince is so embittered that the Bavarian Prince has threatened to withdraw his whole army.

MUNICH, *September* 1918.—*A propos* of peace—I
have just heard a story which has really made me feel a
little more cheerful, as it is founded on fact. A man here,
a high official, has a friend who before the war held a
responsible position in a big bank in London. A few
weeks before it broke out, he was dismissed from the bank
on the grounds that there was going to be trouble with
Germany, and that he had better get back there as soon
as possible. At that time there were no public rumours
of war. He has been in Berlin ever since, and about a
fortnight ago he suddenly received a letter from the aforesaid bank, offering him a new post in it with a high
salary from the 1st of October 1918 onwards. He was
more than astonished and wrote back, saying there must
be some strange error, for the war was waging more than
ever, and he could neither quit Germany nor enter England, as far as he could see. Whereupon he received a
prompt answer saying that there was no mistake, and
repeating the offer of the post from the 1st of October.

It is very hard to write anything definite about the
present state of things here. I myself feel almost
frightened at the way things are closing in on all sides
on Germany. The Germans calm one another by
saying that the retreat is only impelled by strategical
motives, and that Hindenburg means to take up his
position on the Siegfried line behind the Scheldt Canal,
whilst the hostile forces are meant to spend the winter
in the devastated land outside.

I wonder what the real meaning is. Do Hindenburg
and Ludendorff at last realize the truth of Kühlmann's
words, "The war can never be settled by military
methods alone," and are they cunningly retreating in
time, that peace may be based on the fact that the German

army has quitted the enemies' land? Or do they fear the spirit of their own troops? Again and again I have heard rumours of German regiments refusing to attack when ordered to do so; in other words, that a spirit of mutiny is arising here and there amongst the exhausted soldiers.

MUNICH, *Sunday, September* 29, 1918.—To-day I noticed an especially scared look on the faces of those around me, and on my inquiring what had happened they told me that the Allied troops have made another combined offensive and have managed in places to break through the Hindenburg line; that news has come of Bulgaria's movement towards a separate peace; that Malinoff has already proposed a truce, and that all the Germans residing there have been given notice to leave the country, and that Czar Ferdinand is about to abdicate in favour of his son. In addition, the news of the Turks' defeat in Palestine has become a public fact. This means of course an end to Germany's dream of a colony in Asia Minor and a direct traffic route from the Baltic Sea to the Gulf of Persia, whilst the Bagdad railway line will remain a monument of things that were not to be.

And yet, with ruin staring at them on all sides, there are still people here who continue to protest that every-thing stands well, and that any one who spreads a report to the contrary will be punished with five years' imprisonment with hard labour.

Down here, in a quiet retreat in Munich, I expected to be quite out of touch with the feverish world of to-day, especially as at this time of the year there is no one as a rule in town; but I have been agreeably disappointed, and during my three weeks' stay here have met more friends and heard more news than during the whole last six months.

Amongst the many birds of passage who have passed through during the last ten days were two very interest-ing figures, no less personages than those young Princes of Parma, brothers of the Empress of Austria, who negotiated with Clemenceau some six months ago, and are said to have handed over the notorious "Peace-letter" written by the young Empress. Great excitement would prevail were their presence here known, as having served in the Red Cross Department of the Belgian army they are considered to be hostile. This casts a glamour of romance over their appearance, which is further heightened by reports of one of them being betrothed to the future bride of the Crown Prince of Bavaria. They were seen to enter the "Königshof," the hotel where my husband is staying, on a visit to the old Queen of Naples, who has lived there since the beginning of the war, and who is herself a romantic figure, reminding us of historical episodes of an almost forgotten past.

MUNICH, *October* 1918.—The crash has come at last, and although so long expected, it seems very sudden to most of those people who insisted on always looking at things through spectacles *couleur de rose*. The strangest thing to me is the panic which seems to have seized on those very men who, until now, have borne the responsibility of all the calamities of the last four years with such stoical optimism

Hertling, the good old polished man of learning as he is, has accepted the situation, and has made his exit with the quiet courtly bow of the last representative of the *ancien régime,* and a new era has set in.

Here is another of those strange paradoxes which the war has so often shown us: the heir-presumptive to a throne chosen as their leader by the men who are striving to abolish all thrones for ever. Enter Prince Max of Baden, who has in reality been quietly working together with Solf, ever since last autumn, to bring about just that event which seems to have fallen so unexpectedly from the skies. It remains to be seen how far this new man will acquit himself of the almost superhuman task of clearing this modern German Augean stable of the collected abominations of strife and warfare. Impossible as the task seems, the gesture with which he undertakes it has already won him the confidence and sympathy of more than half the people of Germany.

On the whole a great sigh of relief escapes from the lips of the tormented nation on this eventful Sunday in October 1918, when the new peace programme has met the eyes of the world.

"This means peace!" you can hear at every corner of the streets, where people stand hurriedly reading the unusual news. And "peace" smiles in the eyes of every little shopgirl in the baker's or grocer's shop as she hands you your loaf of coarse half-baked bread, or bag containing 100 grms. of lard.

For the wealthier classes and the militarists things bear a different aspect. They could very well support another year or so of the war materially, as they are not half-starved and overworked like the greater mass of the people. For them the metamorphosis from rosy dreams of world-power and expansion and increased wealth to the gloomy realities of an impoverished, humiliated Germany is all too overpowering.

I wonder what the feelings of a Ludendorff and a Hindenburg must now be? As the move can never have been made without their consent, they must indeed recognize the hopelessness of their position and the defeat of their plans. So many figures of colossal import are striding across the stage of Europe to-day that one can only find a parallel in the classical days of history. One would expect Shakespeare to arise again from his quiet resting-place in the little church at Stratford to pen the dramas of all these men, kings and princes, warriors and statesmen, who, filled to overflowing with some frenzy of patriotism or self-worship, have fought like fanatics, only to be toppled over and cast aside by the impulse of some divine law.

Ludendorff, the strong dictator, is said to have had an interview with the Kaiser a few days ago, during which he burst into tears, admitting that nothing more could be done by his army, and begging the Kaiser to dismiss Hertling and bring in a democratic government under the banner of the Socialists.

What must this step have cost a man like Ludendorff, who until now was the greatest opponent to Socialism, thus having to plead its cause?

For the ordinary looker-on this new peace movement is so surprisingly quick and sudden. Is the Kaiser in such fear of losing his throne that with one swoop he leaves his high place in the sun of the divine right of kings, and agrees to all these new demands which practically deprive him of the most precious jewel in his crown, and leave him an ordinary mortal like other people? There are many persons who admire him more for this one act than for any previous one during his reign. He, as well as King Ferdinand of Bulgaria, has probably made a virtue of necessity, and seeing the shades of Bolshevism approach every day nearer, has crowned the long years of his reign with an act of abnegation.

Naturally the Pan-Germans are still shouting and protesting in the old bombastic rhetoric for which they are so famous. The pillar-posts are covered with blood-curdling placards, depicting the towns on the Rhine devastated by bombs and fire, in case the military efforts of the army relapse, and an open-air demonstration has been made in front of the "Iron Hindenburg" in the Tiergarten without the police of the now democratic government interfering, a thing which would have been impossible under the iron rule of the military dictatorship.

In the meantime we are all in an agony of suspense to know what Wilson's answer will be. Will he prove himself great enough to bear the huge responsibility of the destiny of almost the whole world, which fate has placed in his hands? Will he recognize himself as the instrument of a divine will, or show himself to be but the puppet of party strifes and short-sightedness? These and many other questions people are pondering with anxious eyes.

BERLIN, *October* 17, 1918.—We returned to Berlin yesterday, and find things in a terrible state of depression and gloom, portentous of the break-down which we have been expecting for so long One hears the wildest rumours as to what is going on, and every moment some one keeps coming in with a fresh account of what is supposed to be taking place

Ludendorff has had a nervous break-down. The army is practically in a state of mutiny, and one whole division is said to have already surrendered. The soldiers, they say, are already turning on their officers and throwing hand-grenades at them, and a train full of officers returning from leave back to the front was stopped, and they were all forced to get out and return home. At the same time one hears of innumerable soldiers writing home indignant at the proposition of an armistice, and saying they will not hear of one on the terms proposed by the Entente.

The population of the Rhine Provinces are shuddering at the idea of the huge German army settling down to winter quarters in their land, as they say there is no more discipline left. I even heard of people in Frankfort being privately advised to leave, as it has been whispered the enemy might possibly be there in a fortnight.

In any case, exaggerated as these reports may be, the universal demoralization of the people is very great, and one has sometimes the impression of a flock of sheep who have lost their leader and are going about in a dazed sort of manner, looking about for a loophole of escape from the impending evil.

    .   .   .   .   .   .

Somebody told me of having seen King Ferdinand at Mannheim, when he was there doing his cure, and heard his farewell words, which had been: "Au revoir next year, when I shall be back again for the cure as a private gentleman, no more as a king. My friend William will also have abdicated by then; he and I have both outlived our time."

The Emperor—the poor Emperor! "How are the mighty fallen " The Caesar once so omnipotent, with his dream of riding down that magnificent Heer Strasse at the head of a conquering, victorious army, passing through the massed multitudes assembled to greet him, entering Brandenburger Tor, the smiling figure of Victory pointing the way down Unter den Linden! And now this shadow of a king, struggling with destiny to keep his throne but a few days, a few hours, longer.

I have felt bitter enough towards him at times in the past, thinking he could have done more to prevent the unnecessary suffering and cruel methods employed during the war: in particular, the violation of Belgium's neutrality; the sinking of the *Lusitania;* Miss Cavell's death; the ruthless submarine warfare; the use of poisonous gases; and the senseless air-raids over unfortified towns.

But now that his time has come, one pities him. A deplorable position for a great king to be the object of pity. Why has he let things go so far? Why has he not already abdicated, instead of waiting until he is forced to do so? Every child in the street is saying, "The Kaiser must go." He absolutely seems to cling to his shadow of a throne, and people say, curiously enough, it is the Kaiserin who is advising him and begging him not to go.

Last Sunday he was seen walking through the Tiergarten, a white-haired, broken man. At least he shows physical courage in doing this, as there are, I believe, men enough who would like to shoot him.

It is a pitiful sight to watch the death-throes of a great nation It reminds me of a great ship slowly sinking before one's eyes, and being swallowed up by storm-driven waves. I feel intensely for Germany and her brave long-suffering people, who have made such terrific sacrifices and gone through so much woe, only to see their idols shattered and to realize that their sufferings have all been caused by the blundering mistakes and overweening ambition of a class of "supermen."

What a bluff this whole last offensive has been! It really looks like a mad adventure on the part of Ludendorff, seen in the light of ulterior events. They ought to have accepted the American proposal of peace made last January. Prince Rupprecht as well as Hindenburg urged the Kaiser to do so, but it seems that the Crown Prince, and especially Ludendorff, begged for one last offensive. How right Hindenburg was when he said: "Let us threaten the offensive as much as you like, but let us avoid it at all costs."

It is said that the Emperor was absolutely in the dark as to the real strength of the American army, Ludendorff suppressing all information, so absolutely did he rely on his offensive. On hearing this I could not help exclaiming: "Well, however much Ludendorff wished to keep the Emperor in ignorance, surely the Emperor could have found it out for himself, as he sees the English papers." He probably is like the unbelieving audience to whom I remember reading the following extract from an English paper: "Last week 35,000 American troops landed daily, and the Americans are landing on an average 350,000 troops a month." The only remark I heard on it was: "Bluff! English newspapers always lie!"

At the same time the poor soldiers declare that it is not so much the overpowering number of the American troops which has turned the tide, as the fact that there is no more rubber left to make gas-masks, and that they cannot face the gas without them; and then the terrible English tanks. The poor fellows shudder at the very name of them. They say they were prepared for ten or twenty, but during the last few weeks they have been advancing in columns of hundreds. Even the German officers admit that this form of weapon is the first military invention which has proved too much for the genius of German militarism.

.   .   .   .   .   .

The news of the sinking of the *Leinster* has just reached me. What a deplorable deed, to say the least of it;

just at the eleventh hour, when Germany is trying to prove to the world that she desires peace simply from humane reasons. At that very moment she orders the sinking of the *Leinster,* and 450 English civilians are drowned, most of them women and children. Of course, Germany excuses herself with the old tale that it was a mistake, and that she has had no time to call in her submarines. At the moment when Germany's destiny is hanging on a hair, such an awful responsibility is left to the discretion of the lieutenant in charge, and he, as it happened, is a boy of 22 years of age, who by his error plunges hundreds of families in sorrow, and again summons up the burning indignation of all England.

BERLIN, *October* 23, 1918.—To-day there was a general feeling of suppressed excitement everywhere in Berlin. The Reichstag was opened, and every one was quivering with excitement to hear the new Reichskanzler's speech.

The new Note to America was made public, and then Wilson's answer to Austria fell like a bomb-shell. It means the entire break-up of that country and for people in any way connected with it. Personal friends of mine, the Larisches, came to see us. They say they feel as if the ground had been suddenly cut away from under their feet. Everything changes for them, as their father's estate will become Polish, and they are only one example out of thousands.

Austria will be reduced to quite a small kingdom, but as the young Kaiser very sensibly says, he much prefers being king over a small, happy country than being Emperor over a big, unhappy one. Perhaps Kaiser Wilhelm will come to look at things in the same way.

Meantime the aversion towards the Kaiser is increasing daily. Wilson's answer to the second German Note will probably decide his fate. As events go, it looks pretty clear that disturbances and riots, even civil war, are not to be evaded. From our windows last evening I could see rows of armed policemen lining the street, and on inquiring what they were doing there, was told that the people had threatened to attack the Admiralty as a demonstration against submarine warfare. The whole affair, however, ended calmly, and there were no riots. The Germans luckily do not know how to make an effective demonstration.

Mounted policemen patrol the streets near the Brandenburger Tor day and night, and one has an unpleasant feeling that our house will be one of the first to be raided, if anything serious does occur. It is very difficult to know what to do; in the country the castle would be attacked for food, and here the Bolshevist element will probably let themselves go at the big houses near the Tor, although some people say we are safer here than anywhere else in Berlin, as machine-guns are in readiness all round this part of the town. I cannot say that makes the vicinity more attractive on the whole. Many people have already hired cellars to retire to in case of emergency, and are hiding their silver and valuables.

BERLIN, *October* 24, 1918.—Last evening there was another demonstration going on under our windows, caused by the triumphal procession accompanying the notorious Socialist, Liebknecht, who has returned from prison, where he has been for the last two years. He was seated in a carriage with his wife, surrounded by flowers, and they drove slowly by the Reichstag and through some by-streets, landing finally at the Russian Embassy. There Liebknecht addressed his assembled friends in a speech tainted with Bolshevism.

The people are gradually awakening to a sense of their power, but all the same there are still invisible hands pulling the strings of justice, or rather injustice, and ready to nip any pacific movement in the bud. A large peace meeting was dispersed two days ago, the orator not being allowed to speak, on the plea that no permission for the meeting had been obtained, although the request had been sent in three times.

Whilst depicting the last agony of the country at large, one is apt to forget the sufferings of the individual, but what the war is not destroying in human life, the terrible grippe epidemic is carrying off.   One hears of whole families dying out in a few hours, and it is an extraordinary fact that most of the victims are young girls and women.   An uncanny idea, death thus restoring the balance between men and women for life.

.   .   .   .   .   .

There was an unusual hour of excitement and interest to-day in the Herrenhaus, which generally dozes over questions of moment.   My husband and eleven others, Prince Pless, Count Magnis, Counts Galen, Hochberg, etc., suddenly took a line of their own, stood up, and declared their intention of voting for the Universal Suffrage Bill. There is no doubt that it will soon be a *fait accompli.*

There is great groaning over the hardness of Wilson's second Note.   A man from The Hague tells me that Wilson would like to make moderate terms for Germany, but that England and France are blind with victory, and will not let him do as he likes.   They mean to punish Germany for her falseness and for her brutalities.   He added: "England seems quite to forget that for four years they have shut off Germany from the outer world, and have been cold-bloodedly starving her women and children the whole time."

There are different points of view—each nation's vision is only focussed on the brutalities of the other.

Another man, a German officer who has just returned from three years' imprisonment in England, declares that it was the sinking of the *Lusitania,* the death of Miss Cavell, and the Zeppelin raids that raised the English army.   Before the *Lusitania* there had been no enthusiasm in England about the war, but after that they were all like mad dogs let loose, and rose as one man to avenge the dastardly deed.

As for air raids, I am told I must not give my views on this subject, but I have good reasons for feeling bitter.

Last spring my mother had to go to a nursing home in London for an operation. The very night after the operation there was an air raid near her hospital, and the fright brought on a heart collapse so that her life was despaired of.

BERLIN, *October* 26, 1918.—Gebhard heard from the Duke of Schleswig-Holstein, whom he met in the Herrenhaus, that the Emperor does not mean to abdicate unless he is forced to. He was so terribly cut up by the bad news from the front, that he collapsed and retired to bed for three days; but as soon as he received the news of some local success he quite cheered up again, and became as sanguine and hopeful as ever. This change of mood is typical of the Kaiser and all his entourage; they are entirely swayed by the news which is dished up to them by Ludendorff, and seem incapable of forming an independent opinion of their own, otherwise things could never have come to such a pass. If the Kaiser had really investigated all the information of the last twelve months, and, above all, listened to the pessimists, he would not have been so surprised by the turn things have taken now.

Prince Münster, who was again here last night, told us he had been spending the day trying to see Prince Max, who is laid up with grippe. If things were not so tragic, I should be inclined to smile at some of the incidents which thrust themselves on one's vision at the most critical moments. Picture, for instance, Prince Max, a man on whose every word the whole world is waiting, lying in bed in a high state of fever, and his worried A.D.C. going in and out on tip-toe, anxiously trying to extract an answer on matters of burning importance.

Luckily, Prince Max seems to be at last the right man in the right place. People have confidence in him here, and in England they seem to be appreciating his policy. I see there was quite a laudatory article on him in the *Nation*. It is said that when he has once assured himself that a thing is right, no Ludendorff or any other power on earth can persuade him to act to the contrary.

Count Paul Münster, who was dining here last night, gave us a graphic account of his journey from Hanover. His train was packed with German civilians returning from Belgium. They were rather depressed at the manner of their exodus, for, having devoted themselves during the last four years to the work of helping the population, spending time and money on the reorganization of the ruined land, in return the inhabitants spat in their faces as they left.

One of them described the return of the King and Queen of the Belgians from their long exile; it must have been a moving scene from all accounts. They landed at Ostend, and were carried shoulder-high by English sailors, amidst dense throngs of people all bowing to the earth in reverent respect. Not a word was spoken, he said; only a murmur of welcome and relief passed through the massed populace, who could not speak for tears of emotion, and it might rank as one of the most impressive scenes in history.

BERLIN, *October* 25, 1918.—Nothing but Wilson's third Note is being discussed now, and as the translation is extremely unclear, every one interprets it according to his own sweet will. I have now seen the original English text, which has been published in some of the German papers, and we at once saw there was only one interpretation possible, which is that the Entente do not wish to negotiate until the Emperor abdicates, as they do not trust his word.

This reading seems to have struck other people in the same way, for a luncheon party was quickly arranged at Prince Eulenburg's house to-day, at which the Kaiser assisted, and where it was discussed whether he should abdicate at once or not. They seemed to have decided to break off negotiations and to stand by the monarchy, or at least leave the casting vote to Hindenburg.

I was just on the point of going to bed when a message came saying that Prince Munster wished urgently to see us. He told us that he had heard of the aforesaid resolution, and was brooding on it on his way here to ask us to give him some dinner, when he suddenly felt he must do something to prevent Germany making such a hopeless mistake. So, certain that Hindenburg would be dining at his usual quarters at that hour in the Generalstab, he had gone straight off there and asked if he could see the Field-Marshal. On being told that he was at dinner, he begged the astonished Ordonnance-officer to give his name to the Field-Marshal, and ask if he might have a few moments' conversation with him. A few minutes later Hindenburg came out into the hall, taking him by both hands and shaking them warmly, at the same time asking him, "What is it?" He asked Prince Münster to join him at supper, and in the dining-room a place was immediately made for him next to the Field-Marshal.

He then explained that he had heard of their intention of breaking off negotiations, in order to save the Kaiser, and entreated them to reconsider their decision, or in any case to take time and keep things going, not to commit a step which must inevitably imperil the Fatherland.

To these words Hindenburg only answered gloomily, "I stand or fall with my Kaiser."

Prince Münster did not let himself be discouraged, and continued his argument. He said that if the Field-Marshal as well as the Kaiser went, there would be no central figure for the people to look up to, and the country would be inevitably lost, that the nation must have some one in whom they could trust, some one who represented their ideals, or chaos and anarchy would infallibly ensue. To which the company present said, "Hear, hear!" He argued that if Hindenburg stayed on, they might still save the Kaiser, hear what the Allies had to say, and keep on with the negotiations. Should the conditions for an armistice be incompatible with the honour of the nation, then they would appeal to the country and make a last stand, the like of which had never been known.

Hindenburg was deeply moved, and hurried into his military motor to drive straight to Prince Max at the Foreign Office, to offer him his decision. They are now there settling the matter.

. . . . . .

One hears so many conflicting opinions about the Kaiser's abdication that it is difficult to arrive at any definite conclusion oneself, without perhaps doing injustice to a man who I believe, whatever others may say, only acts from a high sense of duty. On the one side it seems as if it would bring peace nearer if he went, as he, like all Hohenzollerns, has deprived the people (or at least wished to do so) of their own free will in the question of government, and has prevented their expanding or developing politically, fearing it might lessen his personal power. On the other hand, the Hohenzollerns rescued Prussia from a state of poverty and insignificance, and consolidated the German Empire into a power so great that it has taken the efforts of the whole civilized world to break it. But now the course of history is being changed, ancient forms of government must disappear under the stress of new ideas and new forces, and as some one said to me, "The German nation must be apparently disloyal, to save themselves from themselves." In other words, they must put their honour aside and make what may seem a "dishonourable peace," to save the country from inevitable effacement.

It seems to me, whatever way they decide, the end will be the same, so better now than later. If it came to an appeal to the country, half the men would not respond, as they ask why they should sacrifice themselves when the end is pre-ordained. It is known and owned by many military men that the guns are worn out, that the English and French ones shoot farther, and that a great deal of the ammunition does not fit, so that the artillery could not last more than a fortnight.

My personal feelings of dislike and bitterness towards the men who have perpetrated so many brutal deeds during these four years is counterbalanced somewhat by sorrow for the good and brave men of this land who have sacrificed so much for false ideals, and at the sight of a great country crumbling into ruins, destroyed by the culpable ambition of a few self-seeking men   My feelings are shared even more intensely by other English women married to Germans, who are all more or less pained at the downfall of a nation which has offered so much to the world, and whose fundamental feelings and attitude towards life in general are more in harmony with our own than those of any of the Latin races.

BERLIN, *October* 29, 1918.—Things seem to be hurrying towards a catastrophe, and the new Government, the heirs to all the enormous errors of the late one, are having a hard time of it to keep law and order. For the moment everything seems to be depending on the Kaiser's abdication. Public opinion says that as Ludendorff has gone he ought to go too, and the road to peace would be smoother. Like two drowning men, the one is dragged down by the other to destruction   It is said that on Ludendorff's proposing his demission to the Kaiser, the latter accepted it with the words, "In fact, it would render *my* position easier if you went," and nothing more.

The whole country is waiting breathlessly for the conditions of the proposed armistice, which the Entente are about to issue, and which every one surmises will be utterly impossible. Prince Munster has just come in from the Kriegsministerium and the Auswartige Amt, and reports that they too are prepared for the terms being unacceptable, and there is one party which hopes that the country will call up every available man to make a last desperate stand, after the old platt-deutsch motto: "Lever dod als Slav !"

I see that Balfour and Lloyd George have gone to Paris, and that Lord Grey and Henderson have joined

Lord Lansdowne in his "Peace Campaign." Things appear to be tending to an end at last The next few weeks will be harrowing to a degree, but the general opinion is that peace will be signed on or about New Year's Day.

The Emperor left for the Grosse Hauptquartier yesterday evening; there were reasons for believing that he was in danger here, so he has been sent away The barracks in Berlin were closed last Sunday. No soldier had leave; they were told off in small companies with loaded rifles to guard the castle and keep order in the streets. Rumours were abroad that the Russian Embassy is a nest of Bolshevism and is secretly spreading it all over Germany, and Liebknecht is beginning to-day the first of a course of eighty speeches in different towns, each of which will begin with the words: "Two years ago I went into prison a socialist. I have come out of it an anarchist. I will tell you the reason why."

    .   .   .   .   .   .

It appears that Hindenburg did send in his resignation a few days ago, but withdrew it after much persuasion, and Prince Münster, who dined here last night, confessed that he could not help feeling a little proud seeing that Hindenburg has followed his advice as to the delay. He told us that, among other things, Hindenburg has said to him · "You advise our postponing the breaking off of negotiations until we have seen the conditions of the armistice, but do we really need to wait before we see them? You know as well as I do what they will be like."

Prince Münster further showed us a copy of his letter to Hindenburg, setting forth reasons for his remaining in office. I give one of the chief paragraphs here: "The German people would not have understood if they had first been told that the present Government and the sudden peace offer of same, which must have seemed quite inexplicable to the uniniated, was made 'at the request' of the Oberste Heeresleitung (the military leaders). And now, if this same Oberste Heeresleitung, at the moment when Wilson declares himself willing to carry out the mediation for which *he has been asked,* had declined same without waiting to hear the conditions which the hostile military leaders will fix as introduction of eventual peace negotiations, then our people would have lost their faith in the man whom they made their ideal. Now they will recognize that they were right in doing so. Uphold them in this faith, Herr Feldmarschall, by dutifully and unselfishly remaining on in these *most bitter times!* This faith in *you* is the only thing that still remains to the uncertain Fatherland to fortify it Should you go too, then Bolshevism will descend upon us."

Ludendorff is regretted by few. His most ardent admirers are now his chief foes. They try to do him justice, calling him the "German Napoleon" with the keenest brain in the country, but, as they say, he and Hindenburg have brought the country to this pass, by deliberately deceiving the people and by underestimating the economic capabilities of their own land, as well as those of the enemy. He was a military despot, and at the same time a tool in the hands of a few great industrials who worked him for their own ambitious ends. He alone is responsible for the unexpected offer of peace put forth by the Foreign Office, which seemed to most people a sudden and untimely confession of weakness. He had at last realized how useless any further fighting was, and in a moment of panic telegraphed to the Foreign Office, hoping to put all the onus of the act at their door, but they in return have exposed him and his doings.

The more one thinks over the history of this war, and the terrible sufferings of the German nation, the more one is astonished at the way they have borne the yoke which has been laid on them. Seemingly not one single man (with the exception of Liebknecht and Harden, who were promptly punished for it) has ever dared to stand up publicly and protest against a system which was so palpably leading the country to destruction. It almost seems as if the whole nation had been hypnotized, and if any one gave the slightest signs of awaking from his phlegmatic trance, he was treated as a dangerous lunatic and put into a strait-jacket.

It seems to me that the loss of position and fortune, even of life itself, would have been worth the effort of saving the country. But so few men are possessed of moral courage, while they nearly all have physical courage, and would much more readily stop a bullet than try to stem the tide of popular opinion.

Professor Nicolai, whose open appeal to his countrymen in the *Times* I have just been reading, is one of the very few men who dared to seem disloyal to his country, purely from reasons of loyalty. For venturing to attack the German methods of warfare he was degraded from his rank as army surgeon and incorporated as a private combatant soldier, and only evaded certain death at some exposed position at the front by escaping to Denmark in an aeroplane.

BERLIN, *October* 31, 1918.—The news of Austria's separate peace has fallen like a bomb on poor Germany, who like a sinking ships sees herself being deserted, even by the rats, as some one bitterly remarked   Now Austria, which, for unpolitical people, was the spark that set the firebrand in flames and involved Germany in the conflagration, has betrayed her in a dastardly manner.

This morning my maid came into my room to tell me that Emperor Karl had fled from Vienna, taking eighteen vanloads of furniture with him and all the crown jewels. He is said to be seeking refuge in a castle in Hungary, which, judging from the chaos and revolutionary spirit surging there, seems rather extraordinary.

My husband's man of business rang him up just now (10.30) to say that, although it is not yet in the papers, Germany is already acquainted with and practically has accepted the terms of the coming armistice, and that in effect they mean capitulation. Some of the conditions seem to be as follows: Cologne is to be occupied by the English, Baden-Baden by the Swiss, Strassburg by the French, Metz by the Americans, Heligoland by the English, and so on.

The other conditions will soon become public property. I just note down these items as interesting me most.

The German banks have in a way ceased payment, as there has been a panic for the last week. There is a rush, and over five milliards have been drawn out by the people. In order to prevent a catastrophe no one may draw out more than 200 Mks. at once.

Every moment the telephone brings us fresh tidings of foreboding for Germany. Its shrill call seems ominous of coming evil. The Austrians, they say, are helpless to prevent the enemy marching through their country, and the French and Italian troops are already approaching Germany. The former they expect through Dresden and the latter through Bavaria, while the Serbians will come through Silesia.

The Austrian troops are already returning in disorderly bands, plundering the villages through which they pass for food, and a state of confusion reigns in the Austrian Embassy here, nobody knowing to whom they are responsible for anything.

Our friend Count Larisch has received a wire from his father in Austrian Silesia, advising him to come at once and help to arrange matters. On preparing to start they were told it was practically impossible to get there, as the whole railway service in Austria is disorganized. Another friend, Graf P——, an Hungarian in the Embassy, has also had a telegram from his father bringing the news that his sister's castle in Hungary has been burnt to the ground and nothing is known of the fate of his sister and her eight children.

.   .   .   .   .   .

In addition to the news of burning castles, destroyed crops, dismembered countries and the approaching enemy, friend Death is making havoc among the population at

home in the form of the grippe. There is hardly a family
that has been spared. From our housekeeper at Krieblowitz I hear that the whole village is stricken with it,
and the wretched people are lying about on the floors
of their cottages in woeful heaps, shivering with fever and
with no medicaments or any one to attend them. The
doctor from Canth is unable to come, as he is absolutely
overworked, having the whole district to look after,
his colleague being already dead of the grippe. I wired
at once to the Convent of the Grey Sisters at Breslau,
asking them to send a nurse, which they did immediately,
and I heard this morning that from the moment of her
arrival she only had three hours' sleep for the next
forty-eight hours, there were so many people to attend to.
Again I telegraphed to Breslau begging them to send
another sister to help, but they replied regretting that it
was impossible to do so, as the epidemic was so virulent
in Breslau there was not a single sister to be spared. I
then hurried away to "Wertheim's" (the Harrods of
Berlin) and bought up as many clothes and comforters
as I could without a "Bezugschein," to send to the poor
people, and bribed the saleswomen in the different
departments to sell me things by promising to send
them each a partridge for dinner. They told me that
hundreds of their staff were at the moment laid up with
the grippe, and that seventy of their girls had died last
week of it.

Herr B——, who has just arrived from Hamburg
and lunched with us to-day, says it is like the plague
there, 400 people dying in one day; and as they have
not coffins enough to put the corpses in, they have used
furniture vans to carry them to the cemetery, and on the
way there an accident happened to one of them; the
van fell over and the poor bodies fell out and were strewn
all over the road. How ghastly!

We are returning every day nearer to the barbarism
of the Middle Ages in every way. I am often astonished
that there are no religious fanatics nowadays to run

through the streets, dressed in sackcloth and ashes, and calling on the people to repent of their sins.

BERLIN, *October* 1918.—Last night Prince Münster, who dined with us, told us that he had been to the officers' prison camp in N—— to see Mr. F., a son of an English friend, and was shocked to find that his nerves and his health are utterly broken down, as he had been a prisoner ever since August 1914 He had been happy enough, he said, as long as other Englishmen had been with him; but, on their all being repatriated, he was left alone with only the companionship of French and Roumanians. This, together with the monotony of only being allowed to walk round one square garden for four years, had so told on his nerves that he felt he was going out of his mind.

Prince Münster, who is always very kind-hearted in such matters, telephoned to the Commandant of the Xth Army Corps, and obtained permission to have him removed to a rest-cure resort in the Harz Mountains, and, wonderful to relate, was so eloquent that he gained permission to carry him off then and there to his own place in Derneburg for three nights

One can imagine the joy of Mr. F. at once more finding himself in the midst of the comfort and luxury of English home-life with an English hostess at the head of it. Princess Münster was at home, and, needless to say, took care that he should enjoy those two days. Prince Münster then wrote to Prince Max of Baden, reporting the whole case, and Prince Max, who was ill with the grippe, telephoned to him, giving him a free hand to act as he liked in the matter. He came at once to us to tell us the good news and to get our help in making the arrangements for his immediate return to England. Prince Münster brought him to lunch with us on his way to Aachen. You can imagine what an interest it was to us to see and talk once more with an English officer, and to speed him on his way, and what pleasure it gave Princess

Münster and myself when we heard that he had safely arrived in England.

Probably Mr. F., who has been shut up all these four years in a German military camp, will never realize to the full what Prince Munster has done for him.   Only my husband and myself know how much credit he deserves for this great act of kindness, and what a feat he has performed in overcoming all the difficulties in the way. He has simply spent the last four days going backwards and forwards between the Kriegsministerium and the Auswartige Amt, meeting at every step with fresh difficulty and being continually referred to somebody else. But Mr. F. told me that he did understand, and would always feel an undying gratitude towards Prince Münster.

Curiously enough, Prince Münster tells me that the man from whom he received the kindest aid in the matter of repatriating Mr. F. is General Hänisch, the Commander of the Xth Army Corps, the very man whose name is held in abhorrence in England and other countries, as the arch-Hun in torturing and worrying the prisoners.

BERLIN, *All Saints' Day, November* 1918.—November has set in with its usual cheerless atmosphere of dull grey impenetrable mist.

I have just returned from early Mass and still feel some of the peace one can only gain to-day from communion with the dead.   They alone know peace in these days of fierce strife and hatred when every man's hand is directed at his brother's throat.   Sometimes, indeed, something like a thrill of envy seizes on me, when I hear that he or she, people I have known well, have fallen asleep, all the horrors of existence over—"Ueberwunden," as the Germans say.   Ah! who knows what we all have still "zu uberwinden!"   Years perhaps still of malice and hate before the sun again sets over a world full of charity and goodwill.

Hardly had we left the quiet holy atmosphere of the church, when Graf Westfalen told me the news of Graf

Tisza's murder.   He had been shot walking with a lady in the street, and she had been wounded too, it seems.

Baroness Sternburg came in to see me in a great state of perturbation.   On her way she had met Frau von Schwabach, the wife of one of the great bankers here, who had confided to her that she had all her most valuable jewels in her muff, and was carrying them to the bank, as a revolution was expected within the next three days She added that they were sending all their most valuable pictures into a place of safety, and had themselves decided on dispersing, each to some different place, as it will not be safe to stay on in their big luxurious house in the Tiergarten.

Baroness Sternburg had just been to the bank to try and get some money, but they had refused to change her cheque.   The bank manager, however, had given her £50 from his own money, saying he had known her for years and was so sorry for her in her lonely position here.

Countess Radolin and her sister, Baroness Bissing, came in to lunch.   They were nearly heart-broken at the break-up of Germany.   They are so essentially Prussian, and such fervent royalists, that they could not speak of the expected abdication of the Emperor without tears in their eyes.   They are, of course, absolutely military in their ideas, and blame the Foreign Office for all the mistakes that have been made.   I suggested that perhaps Ludendorff ought to have a great share of the blame too, but they would not hear of it; and I wondered to myself whether they realized, what we were perfectly cognizant of, that Baron Bissing had intensely resented Ludendorff's interference in the government of Belgium, and had entirely disapproved of Ludendorff's ordering the deportation of Belgian workmen into Germany.   In fact he had even sent in his resignation because of it, but had been prevailed to stay on, and died shortly afterwards.   He let it be thoroughly well known, however, that Ludendorff was interfering too much in many departments of administration about which he knew nothing at all.

7.30 P M.—This afternoon May Larisch came in, full
of fresh news as to what is going on in Austria. She also
blames Ludendorff, on the ground that Count Czernin
had personally begged him several times during the course
of the last eighteen months to make peace, as Austria
could not hold out any longer, but that the "Dictator"
would listen to no one. She told me, too, that Prince
Max Furstenberg has arrived this morning from Vienna
and reports that all is quiet there, and that the Emperor
has returned temporarily, but his family and household
are still in Hungary.

The Austrian Ambassador, Prince Hohenlohe, and his
wife have gone to Vienna to receive orders, as all com-
munications by telegram and telephone have been cut off
for the last few days.

Our nephew, L. C. S., came in to tea and stayed to
dinner. He is working at the Press Bureau of the General
Staff, and says he sees many interesting telegrams that
are never published at all, and that the war telegrams
in the papers are very different from the original ones
received. He says that Erzberger is now their chief, and
all telegrams and correspondence have to be submitted
to him, and that Ludendorff's successor is Erzberger's
and Scheidemann's friend, and, although a General, he
has never been to the front at all, but has been working
in one of the Wirtschaftsämter here in Berlin throughout
the whole war. He has been chosen for this responsible
position in order to please the people, with whom he is
very popular, as he never forbade their holding socialistic
meetings or making demonstrations.

He further told me of a meeting he had witnessed a
few days before between Hindenburg and Tirpitz. Tirpitz
had asked for an interview with the Field-Marshal, but
having been shown into the room, Hindenburg received
him very coldly and immediately showed him out again,
saying that his time was so taken up he could not give
him an interview. This demonstrates clearly enough
how much the Field-Marshal and the military authorities

blame Tirpitz and the U-boat war for the climax of
to-day.

BERLIN, *Sunday, November* 3, 1918.—The universal
opinion is that things are coming to a head this week,
and the movement will probably begin to-morrow.   No
one seems to be quite clear whether it will be the long-
whispered Revolution (with a capital R), or whether the
masses of the people are going to revolt and turn on their
tormentors, as they now regard the ruling classes.

We have been warned to keep our outside blinds
down all day, and to make ourselves as little observable
as possible.   I begin to feel that our house is in an
unenviably prominent spot, and that any one inclined
to wreak their feelings of revenge on Brandenburger Tor
would probably include us as well.

They say it is to be a choice between Scheidemann
and the Emperor.   One of them must give way, and the
people are going to settle which of them it will be.

The Russian Embassy is the centre of much suspicious
observation.   There has been a remarkable number of
Russian couriers arriving for some time past with boxes
and baggage of all kinds, which are never examined, of
course.   These couriers are never seen to return.   There
are reports that the Embassy itself is full of ammunition
and weapons, and we suspect it is a hotbed of Bolshevism
and anarchy.   They ought to have been sent away before.
Liebknecht is seen to be constantly going in and out of
the Embassy, and publicly proclaims his anarchistic views.

It is expected that the conditions of the Armistice will
be made known to-morrow and will be accepted by Germany on Wednesday, and then we may look out for riots

We continue hearing distressing reports of the wild
disorder prevailing in Austria and Hungary.   Nearly all
our own personal friends are grievously affected by it
A friend just arrived from Vienna told us that near Horn,
Count Hoyos's estate, thousands of Italian prisoners have

been liberated by the Czechs, and are now at large ravaging and plundering all the castles in that district.

I hear that the Entente does not by any means intend leaving Austria at the mercy of Germany, which is brimming over with wrath at the way Austria has stolen a march and concluded peace alone. The Germans forget that Austria made an earnest entreaty to Prussia last year to make peace, and on her refusal entered into private negotiations with America with the present results. And now the almighty Wilson is going to protect the broken-down peoples from the anger of their former allies. In the meantime the land is like a seething cauldron of furious nations all more or less at war with one another, with the hapless young Kaiser trying in vain to still them.

We continue hearing such ceaseless abuse and criticism of Kaiser Wilhelm that I sometimes feel like blushing with shame at people who have always professed such loyalty to their sovereign, and now that the reins of government are slowly falling from his hands turn round and openly rend him. Just those who were amongst the most cringing of his satellites are the most ferocious in their attacks on him, and do not hesitate to denounce him publicly at luncheons and dinners. Many of them he has really made, and these are the worst.

The deplorable part of it is that, whilst condemning them, I have to ask myself whether these people may not be right; and if he really is false. People who know him best, and who try to do justice to his character, say little more than that he is a man of very able parts, possessing a wonderful memory and an unusual capacity for comprehending technical questions of engineering, architecture, etc.

·   ·   ·   ·   ·   ·

Yesterday I had tea with Frau Solf, and we had a long talk together. Poor woman, she was very sad, and on my congratulating her on her husband's position, she only answered: "It has come too late. A year ago there

might have been reason for congratulation, but now all
the mistakes have been made and he will have the thank-
less task of negotiating with England, knowing that he
cannot save the situation, as he might have done a year
ago." Further, she said, she was in constant anxiety for
his life and health, for besides working unceasingly night
and day, they had received all sorts of roundabout
threats that, when disturbances should occur, her husband
and the other ministers will be in great danger.

I have just been warned by a friend who shall be
nameless that the demonstrations are to begin to-morrow.
This made me very nervous, and I asked him if they
expected bloodshed of any kind. He said he hoped not,
as they had managed to get the Bolshevist Embassy
away in time, otherwise no one knows what might have
happened. They were hurried off last night with scant
ceremony, so that they may be across the frontier by
to-morrow. One of their numerous cases which I mentioned burst open conveniently in the luggage compartment, and a whole mass of papers came to light, full of
anarchist proclamations to the people, stirring them up
to bloodshed and plunder.

My friend said it was he who had given the order for
the Embassy to be removed, and the mission had to be
carried out as secretly as possible, so as to take the
conspirators by surprise and prevent them having any
opportunity of communicating with any one here The
commissaries of the police suddenly appeared at eleven
o'clock last night, ordered them to be ready to leave by six
o'clock this morning, and stayed on keeping a strict
watch over them, not leaving them until Joffe with his
personnel of seventy Russians were safely despatched in
the seven o'clock train this morning, without any one in
Berlin being aware of the fact.

I must confess I heaved a sigh of relief at this news.
Please God it will save bloodshed to-morrow, and at any
rate we have a body of some fifty policemen always in
readiness lodged in the stables at the back of our house.

My friend smiled. "I don't think you will have one of them here to-morrow, as they will probably all be busy fighting the rabble in the street," he said.

On my husband's return I of course recounted all these interesting facts, whereupon he at once sent for the head of the police, and without appearing to know anything of coming events, presented him with a box of excellent cigars, in return, as he said, for their looking after us so well all these days. The man told him that some of his men had just been called out to put down a demonstration in front of the Russian Embassy.

If any one had told me years ago that I should ever be within a few miles of a "revolution" breaking out, with the probability of blood being shed, I should have been paralysed with fear. And here we are face to face with one, and I even feel comparatively calm and thankful, because from information received, the revolutionary party have decided to pass by our house without plundering or demolishing it, as my husband has never taken any active part in politics and they have nothing against him.

BERLIN, *November* 8, 1918.—To-day is the fourth anniversary of my brother Wilfred's death, who fell at the battle of Ypres. We went to early Mass this morning to commemorate it, and on returning from church we were greeted with the news that the Socialists had given the Kaiser an ultimatum for abdication until one o'clock to-day. From that moment we have been in a ceaseless state of unrest and anxiety. We are completely cut off from the outer world, as all train services are suspended in and out of Berlin. Even the telephone has been cut off between Berlin and other places, and no telegrams can be sent off. This morning we tried to telephone to Krieblowitz, to hear whether our Jäger who is bringing us our food supply had started or not, but were unable to do so.

As we are practically at an end of our provisions

Gebhard went out in search of food, and managed to bring in quite a quantity of things—ducks, a turkey, vegetables, etc.—a proof that there are still some things to be had by paying a high price for them.

I had been advised not to leave the house, but between twelve and one o'clock eventually went out to get a little fresh air. The Wilhelm Strasse was lined with armed policemen, and all the different ministerial offices were closed very early and the employees sent away, as every one had been warned that raids from the mob were to be feared. Thousands of loafers were standing about Brandenburger Tor, others of a rather rough-looking appearance were marching towards the castle. Early in the morning I had been already awakened by the sound of loud singing in the street, and on looking out of the window I saw hundreds of young sailor lads marching by, carrying parcels and looking very pleased with themselves. No one seems quite to know who they are, or what they are doing here. Some say they have mutinied, seized the trains by force, and come to Berlin for protection, having killed or imprisoned eighty of their officers beforehand. Others are said to be expected from Kiel, and the Stettiner station is being armed, artillery being posted there to prevent the trains being seized.

Prince Wedel, whom we met in the street, shook his head and repeated what many others are saying, that it was a mistake of the Kaiser not to have come to Berlin and faced the people. He presumes he is anticipating the wish of the Socialists to hand him over their ultimatum personally.

BERLIN, *Evening, November* 8, 1918.—Baroness Roeder and her husband, who only arrived from Stuttgart yesterday, came in to see us. They have been spending the summer in Switzerland and were exceedingly surprised to find what a state Germany is in, and especially the pandemonium existing in Berlin. He, poor man, is looking quite crushed and broken-hearted. For him life is practically over. He was Master of Ceremonies, and for more than fifty years a faithful courtier to the Emperor; and now at one stroke the whole structure of existence dissolves before his eyes and melts away as if it had never been, leaving him stranded. There will be probably no pension forthcoming, and so the future is a perfect blank to them. In addition to this they have just had the terrible news of their son-in-law's death at the eleventh hour. Only a few weeks ago he had come into his father's estate and fortune, and now everything goes to his little son, a child of five years old.

The particulars of this officer's death, as he related them, are very harrowing to hear. He was colonel of one of the crack Wurttemberg regiments, and a great favourite and very popular with every one. The officers under him were the flower of Württemberg. They were, strange to say, in reserve and seemingly out of all danger, with no idea of an attack, when suddenly they found the enemy upon them. They had broken through three lines of trenches without the Germans firing a shot. The surprised regiment did its best to stave off the attack, but within an hour, from 750 men there were only 100 survivors to relate how things had happened.

.   .   .   .   .   .

I wonder what the result of the meeting of the delegates for an armistice to-day will be? General von Winterfeldt and Erzberger went off two days ago. What a humiliating errand, and what a curious meeting for General von Winterfeldt and Marshal Foch, who some short years ago were intimate friends, as Winterfeldt lived for many years in Paris. Every one expects that France will take her fill of revenge and make terms as hard as she can. Poor Germany is not in a position to resist any humiliation; she is completely exhausted.

.   .   .   .   .   .

Amongst other news of the day, some one told me that when the Russian Embassy was searched yesterday they found a list of the houses of rich people that they intended raiding. Thank God, our name was not amongst them, but we can never know when we may be unconsciously offending the powers that are to be, or when we may come into their black-list.

.   .   .   .   .   .

My husband, who has just come in from Unter den Linden, reports that he saw van-loads of armed soldiers being driven towards the Schloss. He was told that the Kaiser was expected to return, and that the Socialists intend seizing the train and taking him prisoner, but do not intend to murder him. Prince Heinrich has escaped under dramatic circumstances from Kiel. They say he has gone to Denmark with Tirpitz, as they are both on the list for court-martial and punishment, owing to the submarine warfare and the deceptions practised by them on the nation regarding it. The Marine-Amt here is filled with soldiers, as a raid had been planned.

The first intimation that people here got of the so-called "strike" in Kiel and Hamburg was when the Kriegsministerium here rang up the Marine-Amt in Kiel, asking for particulars from the Admiralty. They were answered by the words, "Hier die Genossen," and they vouchsafed the further information that some eighty officers were shut up safely and that everything was in the hands of the Genossenschaft. One can imagine the astonished faces of the chiefs here!

.   .   .   .   .   .

Thank goodness, our Jäger has just arrived from Krieblowitz with fresh food, or we should be badly off indeed. He says he took nearly two days to get here, as no trains were running, and goodness knows when he would have arrived if at Sommerfeld an order had not suddenly come that no soldiers were to be allowed to come to Berlin for fear of them joining the rioters So they were all turned out of the train and a few civilians were allowed to take their places instead.

BERLIN, *Morning, November* 9, 1918.—It is beautiful sunny weather, and from my window I can see the people standing about in groups talking and gesticulating excitedly. Some of our servants went out to ask them if they were going to make a riot, but they answered: "No, they were not going to make a disturbance, but as the Government could not put an end to the war, they meant to show them how to do it."

Numbers of sailors and soldiers are driving by in motor-cars; they all seem to have nothing much to do. We are expecting the armistice conditions every hour; they have already been handed over by Marshal Foch, and, as we hear, are to be answered in seventy-two hours. The courier has just radio'd from the front that he cannot get through the German lines, as the fire is still continuing. They have radio'd back, informing him that the firing has been caused by an ammunition depot exploding accidentally. So now he will be hurrying towards us to bring the important news.

We have been told that the German Commission arrived very late for the meeting with Foch. They were delayed by the awful state of the roads, which were nothing but large pit-holes caused by shells, so that a sequence of punctures had been the result. I hope the conditions will be of a nature to quiet the growing agitation of the people, and give them some tangible prospect of better things, otherwise I fear we shall have our house-tops falling over our heads, and perhaps burying us in the debris.

BERLIN, *Evening, November 9*, 1918.—What a long time ago it seems since I wrote these last ominous words! And here we are right in the midst of the tumult of a great revolution. After all our expectations, it has in reality fallen on us like a bomb—the Kaiser's abdication and the revolution.

Outside there is a seething mass of people constantly coming and going. Sinister-looking red flags are waving where so short a time ago the black, white, and red were hanging, and the dynasty of the Hohenzollerns has come to a tragic end. Things had in reality grown quieter this morning, as we had heard that the decision had been postponed to Monday, and we had thought we still had one or two days of waiting before the dice fell.

I did not go out, but from my window could see the strange-looking loafers hanging about the street; young men, their hands in their pockets, with the hanging bent shoulders of those who all too young have had to bear a burden too heavy for them. They stood about quietly enough, with youthful, serious eyes, as if gazing into a future that was to be kinder and better. The faces of one or two struck me especially; one does not see them often hereabouts, and their look of patient strength had something pathetic in it. Nothing much happened, however, until after luncheon. Gebhard and I were sitting quietly reading our papers, when at about two o'clock a perfect avalanche of humanity began to stream by our windows, walking quietly enough, many of them carrying red flags. I noticed the pale gold of young girls' uncovered heads, as they passed by with only a shawl over their shoulders. It seemed so feminine and incongruous, under the folds of those gruesome red banners flying over them. One can never imagine these pale northern women helping to build up barricades and screaming and raging for blood.

Whilst my thoughts were running in this strain, our butler Karl came in to announce that the Kaiser had abdicated. Tears came into both our eyes as we grasped the momentousness of the hour, and although we have both often criticized him, we could not help pitying the fallen king in this hour of bitter trial. Just because fate placed him in such an exalted position, the fall is all the greater, the humiliation harder to bear; and any one living in Prussia, and knowing how the Prussians regard the Hohenzollerns as the founders of all their prosperity and good fortune as a nation, will understand how many loyal hearts will be cut to the quick at this undoing of their king. But it was no time to mourn for the individual, and our attention was soon fixed on what

was passing outside our windows. There, evidently no
one sorrowed at the loss of an emperor. There could
hardly have been a greater air of rejoicing had Germany
gained a great victory. More and more people came
hurrying by, thousands of them densely packed together
—men, women, soldiers, sailors, and strangely enough, a
never-ceasing fringe of children playing on the edges of
this dangerous maelstrom, and enjoying it seemingly
very much, as if it had been some public fête-day.
Although the processions of revolutionists were at first
orderly enough, one could easily perceive a change in
the temper of the people as time passed by. The patient,
phlegmatic expression which covers so much innate
strength in the Germans gradually changed to a more
emotional mood; eyes began to flash, faces became
flushed, and one had the feeling that it needed but a tiny
spark to kindle the glowing ashes into a flame.

In between the dense masses of the marching throng,
great military motor-lorries, packed with soldiers and
sailors waving red flags and cheering and shouting vehe-
mently, forced their way, the occupants apparently trying
to stir up the strikers to violence. A characteristic
feature of the mob was the motors packed with youths
in field-grey uniform or in civil clothes, carrying loaded
rifles adorned with a tiny red flag, constantly springing
off their seats and forcing the soldiers and officers to tear
off their insignia, or doing it for them if they refused.
They were mostly boys of from 16 to 18 years of age,
who looked as if they were enjoying their sudden power
immensely, and sat grinning on the steps of the grey
motors like schoolboys out on an escapade. This, however, did not prevent their occasioning a good deal of
harm in the course of the day, for of course some officers
refused to obey them, which led to bloodshed and even
death; for these youths did not stop short at violence,
and, I believe, any bloodshed that occurred was almost
entirely due to the unrestrained freedom suddenly placed
in their hands.

I think about 200 of these big lorries must have passed by our windows in two hours, and every moment the feeling of so many elementary forces being suddenly let loose grew more alarming. We, of course, had all our iron blinds pulled down and the doors of the house locked, and only kept one window open to be able to see what was going on.

Every moment groups of people collected in front of our window, gesticulating and shouting frantically; and to our private dismay, in one waggon-load passing by we distinguished French and Russian prisoners amongst the Germans, all waving the red flag, their faces glowing with delight at the unwonted freedom. We were not a little alarmed, for we knew that if the Germans begin fraternizing with the prisoners and liberating them, we may at any moment have a dangerous rabble of some two million Russians let loose on us, who in their underfed condition would stop short at nothing. The strangest and most disagreeable feeling of all was that nobody knew definitely what was happening and what was the meaning of it all. Every one seemed to be steering for Unter den Linden and Pariser Platz, and as the afternoon wore on we heard that an attack was being made on the royal castle. The great Brandenburger Tor was soon covered with climbers who succeeded in hoisting the red flag on it, and in front of the Adlon Hotel machine-guns were placed, and the mob went in forcing the officers there to tear off their badges. The revolutionists robbed the soldiers of their arms, and strutted about with them to the constant danger of the passers-by.

At tea-time Baron and Baroness Roeder came in and stayed on to dinner, as it was almost impossible for them to get back. Dr. Mainzer came too, to offer us the shelter of his Klinik, which lies in a garden-house in an unfrequented street. If there is danger, we shall go and take refuge there. Count Soden, from the Bavarian Legation, dropped in as well, and broke down into tears when we attempted to condole with him on the abdication of his king, Ludwig of Bavaria

Up till now we had only occasionally heard a stray shot or two, but during our early dinner at 7.30 news kept on coming in that things were growing more and more serious, and that a fierce battle was raging in front of the Schloss.

It is said that the mob are bent on ransacking the castle, and have already carried off silver and plate. They have looted the royal horses, carriages, and motor-cars, and are busy using them, as we have already heard the hoot which was until now the signal for the Kaiser's appearance on the scene. Of course, we cannot yet judge how many of the rumours spreading like wildfire may be true, for every one has some different story to tell.   They say that the waterworks which supply Charlottenburg have been blown up and half the suburbs are without water.

My husband has just escorted the Roeders back to their *pension,* with the help of our young footman Emil, but before they departed some one telephoned down to say that it was not advisable for us to spend the night in our apartment on the ground-floor, so I have written a note to our tenant Excellenz von Derenthall who lives on the top floor, asking whether we may sleep there for the night. She replied instantly that we should be most welcome.

On bidding Baroness Roeder good-night, she jokingly said she should die of fright if she heard even one gun-shot anywhere in her neighbourhood.   I quite agreed with her, but we very soon realized we were to hear many more than one.   On making arrangements for the night with the servants, we have just heard two shots in front of our windows in the Tiergarten.   Some scared women, who tried to get into safety behind our big doors, say that two women have been wounded in the Tiergarten from rifles going off accidentally in the hands of un-practised civilians.

Gebhard, who has just returned from accompanying the Roeders home, tells me they made friends on the way with a young revolutionary soldier, who escorted them as a guard. He says he spoke so quietly and sensibly about the situation, saying they did not wish any bloodshed at all, but that they had been goaded on by all the suffering and misery of the last four years spent in the trenches, and now the people meant to put a stop to it. God grant that it may go off as he says, and give us a peaceful night!

I have arranged for all the servants to sleep at the back of the house, in case of danger, and we are now going up to our new sleeping quarters with the kind old Derenthalls.

BERLIN, *Sunday Morning, November* 10, 1918.—More dead than alive, I will try and write down the events and impressions of last night, which I shall never forget. After we had all separated for the night, I lay awake, very tired. We were constantly disturbed by the sound of stray rifle-shots, and the feeling of uncertainty as to what was going on out there in the darkness of the huge city made sleep impossible. After thus passing interminable hours, as it seemed, suddenly about two o'clock the stillness was broken by the noise of a regular fusillade of machine-guns and rifles being fired off—as it seemed—over our very heads. Trembling with fear, I rushed into the dining-room accompanied by my husband, where we found Frau von Derenthall and her two little maidservants already assembled

There we sat crouched together in the darkness, for we dared not turn on a light, listening to the fierce fighting going on all around us from the Brandenburger Tor away over to the Reichstag, our rooms being filled with the fumes and smoke of the guns. Occasionally we crept out on to the balcony to try and see what was going on, but could only see small groups of soldiers all armed, with red flags in their hands, standing round the Tor. At the end of an hour the firing died away, and Frau von Derenthall suggested we should have a cup of coffee; and the two maids set to work and made us some. We could not help laughing as we sat there shivering in our dressing-gowns. Frau von Derenthall told us that all last year she had been wishing to ask us to dinner, but had not been able to get anything choice enough for "the smart Blüchers" for their first meal in her house, and had kept on postponing it until the right occasion should offer itself; "and this," she said with a smile, "is our first smart meal, sitting huddled together in the dark, sipping weak corn-coffee to keep up our spirits." Dear old Excellenz von Derenthall slept peacefully through all the tumult, being 84 years of age and stone deaf.

At about five o'clock we returned to our apartment, where we found that our servants had spent the night in very much the same way as ourselves. During the whole morning people were telephoning from every part of Berlin to know how we had spent the night. It was like being in the midst of a beehive alarmed by some hostile force All Berlin seemed to be humming and buzzing around us.

Baron and Baroness Gevers (the Dutch Minister) rang us up and begged us to come round to them and spend the day, though they regretted not being able to repeat their invitation of yesterday to sleep there, for there was such a panic amongst all the Dutch in Berlin they were all telephoning and asking for protection, and people kept arriving every minute. They mentioned that they had tried to get Baron and Baroness Roeder to come to them, but it was impossible to get through Unter den Linden. It was barred off for the people, and firing was going on in the Wilhelm Strasse, the Dorotheen- und Freidrich Strasse. I begged the Baroness not to worry about us, for if things became too hot we intended going to Dr. Mainzer's Klinik, far away from the zone of danger in the Winterfeld Strasse Then Prince and Princess Taxis rang us up. She told us it was quiet round their way, as the publishing office of *Vorwärts,* the great

Socialist paper, was just opposite their house, and so the revolutionists respected their quarter.

The early part of the morning was fairly quiet. We sat in our rooms, the iron blinds down and just one light burning, feeling comparatively easy in our minds. Some of the servants had gone out on a tour of exploration, and we ourselves heard nothing but a stray rifle-shot now and then, which however no longer disturbed my equilibrium, for as long as one heard no machine-guns one had got to the stage of considering it quiet.

At twelve o'clock Dr. Mainzer came to inquire how we were, and asked if I would like to come to his Klinik in the afternoon and spend the night there. I said that if things were going to be as bad as they were last night, I should. He and Gebhard were assuring me that all would probably be quiet now, and Dr. Mainzer was describing how peaceful and orderly the crowds were round the Reichstag and in the Tiergarten, when suddenly, as if in mockery at his words, a great burst of machine-gun firing cut short his sentence. We all rushed to the windows, and looking through the cracks in the blinds, we saw people hurrying in crowds from apparently every direction at once. We all ran out into the back court-yard, where we found Prince Henckel, his brother, Count Krafft, Prince Wedel, and all their households collected. They locked and barred all the entrances, as there was danger of the mob storming them in their rush for shelter from the firing.

The house was surrounded by dense masses of people, and, as the house-porter told us, there was going to be a fight between Brandenburger Tor and the Reichstag, presumably the Red Guard against loyal officers and soldiers. The whole street, he said, would soon be closed, and so, if we wanted to get away, we had only three minutes to do so. We therefore decided to go, and creeping out through the back entrance and crossing the back-yard, we managed to get into the street some distance off by going through a little public-house. The crowds in the street were so densely packed that we could hardly get through. Every one was frantic with excitement; one man had been killed and some wounded quite near our house. From every crossing we saw waggons full of soldiers and sailors coming, all armed with rifles and hand-grenades, and flying the red flag, whilst every soldier we met already wore the red cockade on his cap, which looked like a patch of blood over his forehead. It was not a morning for timid people.

We managed to force our way through the throng, crawling along in the shelter of the wall for fear of a stray bullet, until at Potsdamer Platz we found an empty droshky, and after some cogitation as to the advisability of taking it, and being abused by the mob as aristocrats, I feigned a sudden faintness, and Dr. Mainzer shouted out for some one to drive a sick woman to a Klinik. The driver consented and the crowd did not object, so we hurried in and drove here to this quiet house, which seems like a haven of rest after all the tumult and agitation of the last hours.

In the afternoon we were continually rung up by different people telling us news of what was going on. There are already so many contradictory reports rife that I shall wait and see before believing them. Every one's imagination is running away with them, and anxiety and uncertainty are at the bottom of many rumours of violence and bloodshed. On the whole I have the feeling that the mood of the people at large is rather like that of a goaded, tired wild beast, ready to spring and kill if exasperated any more, and yet just as ready to be quieted and tamed if food be given it.

Princess Taxis rang us up to say that the new Socialist Chancellor, Ebert, the successor of Prince Max of Baden, has already threatened to resign as he cannot hold the people. I hope this news will be soon contradicted, as Ebert, although a Socialist, is an orderly and well-meaning man enough, and if he is really forced to make way for Liebknecht it would be terrible, for the latter makes no secret of his anarchist intentions. He would let the rabble loose at once to fire and plunder our houses.

Early in the afternoon my maid and Karl telephoned to say that shooting had commenced in the neighbourhood, and later on she told us that a regular pitched battle was being fought just in front of our house, that some one had placed two machine-guns on the roof which were firing down on the crowd, who were returning the fire from below. Karl Langer, our faithful butler and friend, had run up to the top of the house and torn down the old flag to try and stop the firing. Prince Henckel and his brother, Count Krafft, were, she said, taking an active part in the defence. We were all loud in praise of her courage at being able to stand and telephone at such a critical moment. Later on the wires were cut off for the time being.

At the moment when things seemed to be looking their worst, Princess Taxis telephoned that the Entente had sent a radio-message from Paris, saying that they would make no peace with Bolshevists. Thank God! That was good news indeed, and sent our spirits up with a run. It came, too, just at the right moment, and meant the momentary reinstatement of Ebert as Kanzler, and renders Liebknecht's anarchical plans extremely distasteful to the majority of people. People are inclined to look upon the enemy for the moment as friends and rescuers in the hour of need.

Towards evening my brave maid Lisa and the Jäger arrived with clothes for us for the night. They had forced their way through the dangers of the excited mob, and gave us a vivid description of the "Blucher Palais" battle. I was rather amused to hear that our stalwart defenders, the twenty policemen whom we had so much counted on to guard us, had been forced to seek shelter and protection in our house, where—pale and trembling —they remained hidden a whole day and night, being fed by us, until plain clothes had been brought for them and they could thus escape in disguise. They were staunch and true men to the Kaiser, and had been very much cut up at his fall, and at the surprising turn that things have taken.

I must confess that I myself feel shocked and surprised at the universal rejoicing manifested at the abdication of the Kaiser. They could not be more jubilant if they had won the war. *Vox populi, vox dei!* He may deserve his fate, but it seems very hard and cruel to throw stones at him at such a moment, when he must be enduring untold anguish and sorrow.

Amongst the aristocracy the grief at the breakdown of their country, more than at the personal fall of the Kaiser, is quite heart-rending to see. I have seen some of our friends, strong men, sit down and sob at the news, whilst others seemed to shrink to half their size and were struck dumb with pain. There are men and women who have played an inconspicuous part enough at ordinary times, often pushed aside as people of no importance, who are now the most faithful to their monarch. But history takes no heed of the tears of the individual, and they only fall to join and swell the broad stream shed by mankind within the last four years, and which, as we hope, is carrying us forward to some brighter goal.

BERLIN, *Monday, November* 11, 1918.—Things seem to have calmed down a bit, and one only hears a little desultory shooting now and again. We feel that it is growing safe once more, and this morning Gebhard went off to our apartment, to spend the day there putting things in order again. Frau Mainzer and I determined to go out together to see what the world looked like after the deluge of the last two days, and whether there were any signs of the waters abating or not. I paid several visits, and we all congratulated one another at still being alive, but we are none of us very certain as to what the hour may bring forth. Our general impression is that the people are much too weak and starved to be really bloodthirsty unless goaded on by fanatics like Liebknecht and Rosa Luxemburg, and one cannot help admiring the disciplined and orderly way in which a revolution of such dimensions has been organized, with until now the least possible loss of life. Truly, a great storm is passing over the land, and princes are falling from their thrones like ripe fruit from a tree, but every one seems to be acting under the impulse of a divine law which is leading the German nation to a new phase of development.

I stayed to lunch with Countess Larisch, where I found Count Westphalen's little daughter, a child of 13 years, who is quite the heroine of the moment at present. She and her father, who came in later, gave us a description of the battle at the Schloss on Saturday   Count Westphalen is Master of the Horse, and as he told us, he was sitting quietly reading in one of the rooms at the Schloss, when suddenly there was a great knocking at the door.   On opening it, he saw the mob standing outside, demanding two of the royal motors to take up some injured people.   Of course, he guessed that this was only a fabrication, but agreed to give them two, which, he said, were always kept in readiness for all emergencies, and saying he would give the order for them to be brought out, he went away, closing the door behind him   He stayed away, however, longer than they approved of, and they began hammering and battering at the door, and on the servant saying he could not let them in without further orders, they smashed a side-window and climbed in, and proceeded to riot and shout through the whole castle.   One man in particular was extremely insolent in his manner to Count Westphalen, airing his views in a hectoring violent tone, and he it was who, running up to a room at the top of the castle, began firing from one of the upper windows   This, of course, was meant to stir up the mob below, and in fact caused the whole battle that ensued.   This method was employed systematically at all places where fighting took place, and the report was then spread that it was caused by loyal officers firing down into the people.   As has been later discovered, there is not a word of truth in such statements. At the moment when the mob broke into the castle there were no officers there, and the fight was only caused by Liebknecht's agents trying to incite the mob to bloodshed.

Count Westphalen went on to tell us that the rabble had poured into the royal stables, ransacked everything there, seized on several motors and horses (some of which have been returned), and began exploring the castle, carrying off any provisions they could find, and keeping him a prisoner locked up in a room until four o'clock the next morning. In spite of his remonstrances and entreaties to be at least informed as to the fate of his little daughter, he was not allowed to communicate with any one, and spent the long hours of the night in the greatest state of suspense as to what had become of her. The poor child herself went on with the story, and told us that on hearing a noise in the passage she had gone out to see what it was, and suddenly saw a strange mob of people pouring in. Her governess, with whom she had been left in charge, immediately lost her head and rushed away into the crowd outside, leaving her charge at the mercy of the rabble, and was not heard of until the morning, when she was told some home-truths by her employer.

The poor little girl had remained trembling in the hall, whilst the mob rushed past her. With the help of a faithful old man-servant she then left the house on foot, and together they made their way through the crowd and walked in the dark for about an hour, until they came to the Larisches' house at about eight o'clock in the evening, the poor child quite alarmed and worn out with all the excitement

Countess Larisch told me further that she herself had been an eye-witness when the soldiers had seized on the machine-guns in the Admiralty and had thrown them into the canal. There had been thousands of people looking on. It had been a sad and alarming sight, and the general feeling amongst those surrounding her had

been one of pity that so much good material should be
wasted in that way. Especially the loss of the leather
touched people to the quick. "How many pairs of boots
they could have made for us," was the general remark.

Evening.—This afternoon our nephew Ludwig Karl
Strachwitz rang me up from the General Staff. He said
he was still at his old occupation, but in plain clothes,
and there were several sailors and soldiers about him,
apparently entrusted with the task of managing everything; but as they themselves admitted they understood
nothing at all of what was to be done, they begged him
to continue in authority and go on with the work. It is
the same everywhere, in all the rooms at the Foreign
Office there is a sailor or soldier superintending the work,
and they say even Ex. Solf has one at his side. It seems
that they are all respectful enough in business hours, but
out of them there is no saluting, and they attempt to
treat their superiors as equals, needless to say not very
successfully, as old customs and habits cannot be changed
in one day.

Berlin, *Tuesday, November* 12, 1918.—As we heard
that everything was again quiet round Brandenburger
Tor, we arranged to return home, and quitted our
secluded haven of refuge, with heartfelt feelings of gratitude to the Mainzer family for all the kindness and
hospitality they showed to us as refugees. How strange
it seems to find everything so quiet and peaceful here,
after all the noise and excitement of Sunday, when there
was almost ceaseless fire over and around the house nearly
the whole day.

The few people I have already spoken to were depressed
and horrified at the terms of the armistice, especially that
the blockade is not to be raised, which means for so many
people a gradual death from exhaustion. As one Englishwoman said to me, the idea of continuing to exist and
work on the minimum of food still possible under the

circumstances was so dreadful, that she thought it would be the most sensible thing to go with her child and try to get shot in one of the numerous street-fights; whilst another lady whose husband is at the front, and from whom she has heard nothing for a long time, is contemplating turning on the gas on herself and her two small children, and putting an end to the horrors of living A diet of heavy vegetables, cooked without fat of any kind, with dry bread and potatoes, is not in the long-run consistent with the nerve-power necessary under the circumstances.

.   .   .   .   .   .

We hear Hindenburg has placed his services at the disposal of the new Government, so as to help organize the demonstration. What a grand old fellow he is, always doing his best for his country, and never thrusting himself into people's notice. He must be suffering agonies of humiliation and regret at the turn things are taking, and at the terrible blow to Germany's prestige; and yet he will never think of laying down his arms as long as his country needs him. He is indeed a genuine patriot.

So many of the other great men of the past are now wandering like hunted wild beasts, roofless and homeless in other countries, all power torn from their hands, unable to help themselves or other people. The Empress has placed herself and all the other women of the royal family under the protection of the Red Guards at Potsdam.

There is still a good deal of desultory shooting going on, and several soldiers have been wounded or shot in the suburbs whilst guarding the different stores. The same system is used everywhere to stir up the people to bloodshed. Machine-guns are placed on the roof of a house opposite to some assembly hall, and when the people gather for a political meeting, they are shot at by the hidden gunners on the roof, and the soldiers immediately return the shots.

From a young soldier who has just entered on his military service and was called up to help guard the royal castle at the beginning of the riots I heard a dramatic account of what took place. He told me how they had been hidden in the cellars some days before the demonstration began, and knew little of what was going on outside, so that the shock and surprise were great when suddenly the doors were burst open, and a revolutionist, a member of Parliament, entered and told them that the German Empire had ceased and a Republic had taken its place. With tears in his eyes, he said, he had taken off his badges and thrown them where the others lay in a heap on the flagstones, and then they were free to return to their barracks. With a thrill of indignation he saw how the mob rushed into the castle, and a few minutes later the Prussian flag was hauled down and the long red revolutionary standard waved over the place where the Hohenzollerns have housed for so many centuries   Out of the great gateway a rider dashed on horseback, waving likewise a red flag, and at the same moment one of the windows opened on to a balcony in front of the castle, and on the same spot where four and a half years ago the Kaiser made his great appeal to the enthusiastic people, Liebknecht appeared, shouting to the masses that they were now freed of the bondages of the past, and that a new era of liberty was opening out before them.   History repeats, or rather mimics herself in a somewhat tasteless way at times.   Still the episode is not without interest to the impartial looker-on.

The young soldiers themselves had a hard fight to get through the mob, who in some way seemed to make them responsible for the misdoings of the royal house they had been guarding, and ill-treated them accordingly, buffeting them and spitting on them, and even throwing some of them into the Spree.

BERLIN, *November* 13, 1918.—It is late, but I cannot sleep; my nerves are still vibrating with the excitement of the last few days, and brain and heart are filled to overflowing at the thought of the momentous things which are happening in the world. We dined at the L.'s, where, although we were a very cosmopolitan party, we were all more or less affected at the terrible outlook for Germany. A late moon was still shining brightly as we made our way home on foot The streets are very quiet now, and the few passers-by hurry along, almost afraid of one another, and avoid the shadows, for no one knows who or what may be lurking there. Before every important public building sentries are posted, and in front of the Brandenburger Tor, with its grotesque blue-black shadow of the galloping horses and the car of victory, I can see them pacing up and down.

An atmosphere of exhaustion rather than of peace pervades the places where so much tumult and confusion raged but a short time ago. A rising wind is beginning to moan sadly through the Tiergarten, tossing the bare branches of the trees dejectedly, and bringing in its train great masses of dark clouds, which to my excited imagination look like armies in mournful retreat, moving as if in rhythm to the funeral dirge of the melancholy autumn wind.

.   .   .   .   .   .

I never felt so deeply for the German people as I do now, when I see them bravely and persistently trying to redress the wrongs of the war, for which they were in truth never responsible. The greater part of them were men fighting blindly to guard an ideal, the "Heimat," some patch of mother earth, a small cottage half hidden in its sheltering fruit trees, ploughed fields rising on the slope of a hill up to the dark forest of pines, maybe, or a wide stretch of flat country where the golden corn-fields sway and wave in the wind as far as the eye can reach.

This everything, that meant "home" to them, they were told was in danger, and this they went out to save. I feel that in the past I have sometimes misjudged this people, torn by the conflicting feelings of love and admiration for my own native land, and indignation at the brutal methods of warfare employed here, and the mental suffering and agony I endured myself in the first years especially. But now I feel that a spirit of justice and good feeling is the only power that can ever heal the hideous gaping wounds of the nations, and it was in this frame of mind that I began talking to an old friend of ours this evening, Graf K——, a man who has seen much of the world and is a German of the best type. Of course, he is feeling very embittered now, but 1 will try and remember what he said and write it down as a "defence" of the German people.

There were three or four of us talking, and each had some criticism to make of the Germans as compared with other nationalities. 1 had made the remark that German women are as a rule more highly educated than English, but were wanting in a sense of humour and romance, and somewhat dull with all their learning, when Graf K—— intervened:

"I've been listening to your discussion, and with due deference to all your opinions, I must confess that, like most foreigners, you are utterly superficial in your judgment of us. Well, you've thrown down the gauntlet, and I'll pick it up.

"Does any one of you really know the German people? Berlin, for example, can hardly even be called a German town, so little does it represent Germany. And yet you come here, you English especially, consort with your own countrymen, read your own books, speak your own language, and maltreat ours just enough for every day's most common needs, and then think you know us. With the exception of music, what do you know of our art, our literature, which is the expression of our soul? Why, I know English women who have been living here for nearly twenty years, and never even read a German paper, much less a book, and can hardly phrase a single sentence of our language correctly. And yet they return to England to boast of their intimate and exhaustive knowledge of the German psyche. You condemn us for our want of humour; but it is you who don't know enough of our language to understand the rich stock of humour of our race. You know nothing of Jean Paul, of Reuter, the platt-deutsch humorist, or of Raabe, who is in his way the German Dickens.

"As for our wanting in romance, why, we are mostly born and bred in it, steeped in it from the cradle to the grave. It was our school of romantic poets who awoke an echo in all Europe, not least in England, and inspired some of the greatest musicians of the world. Certainly, our people have not the craving for the *sensational* that you English have, but I think that may be regarded as almost in our favour on the whole.

"For the rest, you understand us just as little as we do you. We are *au fond* a nation of peasants, tillers of the soil in the larger sense of the word, and therefore more intimately in touch with mother earth than you English, and we have the faults and virtues of the toilers of the fields. In the same way as your little country, the England proper of to-day, presents the appearance of a landscape tamed down to pleasure grounds or a well-kept park, so the centuries of undisturbed culture and the long era of prosperous industry and commerce have done their best to eliminate all traces of primitive man in you. You are the product of an artificial culture; we are much more the product of Nature. It is only in Scotland or the West of Ireland that you can find anything approaching the untouched virginity of our vast sandy plains, where the wind can rush at its own free will, whirling the snowstorms from the east, or of the grim twilight of our great pine woods, the birthplace of half the legends and fairy-lore of Europe, or the solemn beauty of our lofty snow-topped mountains, where man can be so utterly alone with God.

"You often call us brutal, but I take it we are strong and simple. It is from Nature that we have borrowed our rugged strength of character, and just as she is not always merciful but wild and callous and cruel, we at times too have grown hard in our struggle with her.

"The genius of our race is derived from the soil we have lived on. We are philosophers and artists, talents born in intercourse with Nature, but we are bad diplomats and politicians, qualities born of intercourse with mankind. We possess the shrewdness of the peasant, and not the cunning of the man of the world; and just as our bodies are more expressive of strength and dogged will, and look better in our own national costumes than in the dainty creations of Parisian ateliers, so our souls have not been trained to express our thoughts and feelings with those finer reservations that *you* call tact, and *we* a lack of straightforwardness. But given we are brutal and aggressive under circumstances, we are at the same time big and heroic, and our ideal men and women are the Siegfrieds and Brunhilds of the *Nibelungenlied,* figures that represent the primeval passions of mankind.

"We are often called narrow-minded, pedantic, and petty. People forget we have always been forced to turn our gaze inwards and concentrate our attention on ourselves and our mental development. We could not expand like the English, who have gained their broad-minded generosity, which we admire so much, chiefly from the fact that their inward gaze was set on far-off goals in other continents.

"Above all, we are fighters. Without any natural boundaries on the east or the west, there were always greedy neighbours anxious to invade us. But as we threw off the yoke of the Romans, the Huns, the French and ever again the French, we shall no doubt fight our way to a place in the sun again, despite the hordes collected to prevent us."

"You wish," said I, "to imply that we English are not inspired by Nature in our actions or manner of life?"

"I think," was his answer, "that the English of to-day are more the result of the civilization of towns than otherwise. For the rest, I have not attempted to analyse their mentality more closely. I chiefly wished to point out the chief source of those fundamental qualities which

characterize the German people, and which are so seldom
recognized by the casual observer who writes those
volumes of superficial trash for the benefit of credulous
readers. I believe if the nations understood one another
better there really might be no more wars."

This is about the substance of what Graf K—— said
this evening I suppose there is a good deal of truth
in it, and that we English are too inclined to expect the
same qualities in other nations which we are accustomed
to in ourselves, forgetting that climate and geographical
position are so important in the forming of a national
character.

BERLIN, *November* 14, 1918.—I shall perhaps write
little more now in my diary. The war is practically over,
and so to all intents is the social revolution. Every one
seems to be astonished at the quiet, unenthusiastic way
in which the latter has gone off. I even heard one man
deplore its orderliness from a poetic point of view. He
said there was nothing inspiring in it for the poet or
painter, no great passions let loose. It was simply a
matter-of-fact, well-organized strike based on purely
materialistic grounds.

I was myself astonished at the calm phlegm of the
crowd, which just stood out of range and watched the
shooting as if they were at a race-meeting. At the same
time, the state of things here is not encouraging, and
acquaintances are telling us to get away from Berlin as
soon as possible. Two camps have been formed amongst
the Socialists, the Ebert moderate party and the Liebknecht faction, and fierce fighting is expected soon
amongst the soldiers and sailors in the streets. Moreover,
there is a universal dread of plunder in the private houses.

Many people who still cling to the old régime are
fleeing across the frontiers to neutral countries; and
to-day, on bidding farewell to an official who is flying
for his life, I asked him if he thought the people were to
blame for all the misery that has come upon Germany.

He answered in the negative, saying they were only suffering from the long series of political errors committed since the Bismarck era. From the time of his dismissal one fatal mistake after the other has been made, and it is a wonder that the nation has borne with the perpetrators so long. The Kaiser's longing for a fleet to vie with the English, backed up by Tirpitz, whom Kuhlmann calls the "father of lies," is responsible for the great split between England and Germany, and war was the inevitable result.

We have determined to leave Berlin in a few days, to go and look after our home at Krieblowitz, as things are said to be none too quiet in the neighbourhood of Breslau.

KRIEBLOWITZ, *November* 16, 1918.—After an interesting but crowded journey, we are glad to find ourselves in the peace and quiet of the country again. The whole episode of the revolution seems like a fantastic dream.

Our train was crammed full of soldiers and sailors returning home from the front, and even though we went to the starting-place, the Charlottenburg Station, we found it already overfilled. The men swarmed in through the windows, climbing over the roof of the carriage to do so, and got in in every possible way they could think of, entry through the doors being quite impossible. Gebhard and all the rest of the household had to sit on their luggage in the corridors all the way to Breslau, whilst I managed to get a seat in a third-class carriage together with fourteen soldiers and sailors. They were rough working-men, but were kindness and consideration itself to me. They looked after my comfort in every way, and insisted on keeping all the doors and windows closed for fear of my catching cold. The atmosphere was indescribable, but I did not want to hurt their feelings by suggesting that a fresh air treatment suited me best.

I was interested in listening to their conversation, which I overheard by feigning to be asleep.

One sailor, who had come straight from the riots at Kiel, told ghastly stories of the bloodshed there, and of the men's grievances against the officers, and against the Kaiser and the Crown Prince. They all jeered at the Crown Prince playing the hero by sticking to his army. "A bit late it was," they said, "his becoming brave now." They also criticized the Kaiser's flight to Holland, saying that although he and his son both deserved to be shot, they would not have injured them if they had trusted the people and remained to face the crisis.

I could not help smiling when they began comparing notes as to who had learnt most English during the four years they had spent opposite to the British at the front, and from their conversation with the prisoners. Each of them produced a few words, and one man, after describing his friendship for an English soldier who had been a prisoner for three years, said that last Sunday, when the prisoner was set free, he went about the streets shouting, "Kamerad kaput," being the only words he had learnt all these years, and meaning to convey the fact "My friend, you are beaten."

They were all very cheerful, those soldier- and sailor-companions of mine, and often emphasized that they had gained what they had been fighting for, "Freiheit und Gleichheit," and that the German army had not been driven out of France and Belgium, but had been withdrawn after the armistice had been declared.

It was a great comfort to hear these men accepting the situation in this spirit, and one of the chief things that have struck me since the revolution is the universal relief that the iron clutch of militarism has been loosened for ever, and that there is so little feeling of rancour or bitterness towards the enemy. Even Excellenz Solf owned to my husband that it would be a great relief to him if the Entente should send troops as soon as possible to help to keep peace.

Quiet and order are only a question of food, and every one is admiring the clever way Dr. Solf has worded his negotiation to Wilson, making it appear as if food were guaranteed should quiet and orderliness prevail here.

KRIEBLOWITZ, *December* 1918.—Slowly the year is drawing to its close, and gradually, very gradually, I am beginning to comprehend that the war with its orgy of death and slaughter has come to an end. It is especially hard to realize, because the difficulties of every-day life are almost greater now than they were before—or seem so. The whole economic organization of Germany has crumbled away before our eyes, and no new system has as yet been formed in its place. The revolution, in fact, came too suddenly, even for the Socialists themselves, and what ought to have evolved from a natural course of events was prematurely hurled at us by the unexpected insurrection of the sailors in Kiel and Hamburg. Therefore the Socialists have not had time to develop a really strong Government, or to test the practical working of theories in a country which is still at heart for the greater part monarchical in its sympathies.

I believe myself that the German people in reality need something for their imagination—a figure-head that represents in some way the phantastic, the unusual, the ideal. There is no poetry in the figure of a short stout President, with a bald head, a top-hat, and a black coat. All the old fairy tales begin in the same way: "Es war einmal ein Konig!" and the Olympic figure with the clanking sword, the golden crown, and the purple mantle will be sadly failing in the history of the future; and all romance will be banished from those beautiful stately old castles on their rocky summits, which we find all over the country, when they have been turned into some state-edifice to meet the painfully prosaic needs of to-day.

. . . . . .

It was the long period of inactivity which led to the Kiel mutiny. The men had no outlet for their energies but to brood over grievances and grumble about their officers, and when, after the defection of Austria and

Bulgaria, these officers wished to make a last desperate attack on the British Fleet, the men refused to put to sea

This brooding spirit of revolt amongst the sailors has been classically expressed in a play called *The Sea Fight*, by Rich. Goering, one of the most talented of the school of young German poets now coming so much to the fore. But in the drama, a great battle comes at the critical moment, as the "befreeing" deed which leads the men's virile energy into another direction than that of active mutiny.

Germany's chief danger at the moment is her lack of a central strong Government to negotiate with the Entente, and to take the lead in the land. Instead of one there is a whole series of governments, and no end to the bickerings and jealousies between the different states, which are all aiming at reducing the power of Berlin. At the moment the proletariat are in possession of power, which they are using to enrich themselves as speedily as possible at the cost of the nation. I hear, if things go on as they are, the State will be bankrupt in a fortnight.

In Berlin the soldiers and workmen are disturbing all the existing law and order, dismissing the local boards without creating any new ones to take their place. Armed deserters and rowdies force the authorities to resign office at the point of their bayonets. Public and private food supplies are plundered and confiscated by bands of individuals, who terrorize over the unarmed civilians. Strikes are weakening and endangering the little life that is left in the land, and the enormous and disproportionate wages being lavished on the working people bid fair to paralyse all industry and trade. There are millions of people out of work, and yet everything is at stagnation point.

The nation at large is economically demoralized and corrupted by the organizations of militarism. The high wages paid for the most elementary work connected with the war has so ruined the labouring classes morally, that no one will work for any but an abnormal price, whilst domestic servants and charwomen are hardly to be had at all in the towns.

Another problem is what is to become of all the active officers who are being dismissed, and who in civil life have learnt nothing at all? Germany, with no power to expand, and morally blockaded by the rest of the world for years to come, offers but a disconsolate future for young men, however enterprising they may be. The French ideal, "l'esclavage allemand," seems the only possible solution, if the Entente insist on the conditions they are proposing.

Little miseries which seemed but pin-pricks a short time ago are gradually gaining in intensity, until they feel almost like poisonous darts. For years people have been struggling along, supporting as best they could the absence of everything conducive to a decent existence, but now it is almost impossible to bear it any longer. The ancient boots and shoes defy any more mending, the stockings consist of a series of variegated patches, dresses and mantles have been turned and dyed year after year, and most people's underwear has no recognizable resemblance to the dainty garments of pre-war times. They are of a nameless hue, and look as if they had been fished out of some forgotten patch-bag. As there is no soap, our linen issues from the wash-tub greyer and more hopelessly torn than we ever dared imagine, and certainly the German woman of to-day is the worst clad in all Europe.

It is a sorry outlook for Christmas, and not even the children will be able to indulge in any of the little luxuries which the "Weihnachtsmann" usually left at their door.

. . . . . .

I have had a letter from Berlin describing the festive entry of the returning troops. "It was not the triumphant procession we dreamt of formerly, but it is unique and striking in its way. Every one had done their best to give a brave appearance to their houses; flags were flying, carpets hanging from every balcony, house-doors were wreathed with green garlands, with the homely

'Herzlich willkommen' beaming a welcome in red letters
on a white ground. The men wore green laurel wreaths
over their steel helmets, each rifle bore its little spray of
flowers, the machine-guns were garlanded with green
branches, and children waving gaily-coloured flags sat by
the side of them, and many of the soldiers had a child or
a sweetheart riding pillion in front of him on his flower-
wreathed horse.

"A feeling of confidence, of fresh hope in the future,
seems to have returned with the troops, who responded
to the ovations with the buoyant seriousness of men who,
after seeing death so near, are not afraid of life. The
streets are so crowded and overflowing with men that I
am beginning to wonder how long it will be before these
reserves of latent energy will break forth and find a
channel for themselves if not speedily used to some good
purpose.

"A new feature in Berlin is the number of beggars one
now sees everywhere. All the blind, the halt, and the
lame of Prussia seem to have collected here and are reaping a golden harvest. Daily the traffic is stopped by the
demonstrations and counter-demonstrations which are
the order of the day. Even the children are beginning
them, and the opposing parties often meet and pass one
another in the same streets, whilst the soldiers set out to
keep order on their own responsibility. The results are
street-frays like the one on the evening of December 6,
when fourteen innocent men and women were killed. To-
day none of us can tell how soon we may be sleeping at
the side of the little pale 17-year-old milliner's girl, who
was shot on her way home, in the green shady groves of
the burial ground where the victims of the March Revolution of 1848 are buried.

"Liebknecht and Rosa Luxemburg are the people of
the hour—archangels or archdevils, as the case may be.
They have caught the imagination of the people, and are
powers we must certainly reckon with. Every day nearly
some new 'Extrablatt' appears: 'A thousands marks on

Liebknecht's head!' 'Liebknecht outlawed!' 'A hundred thousand marks for Liebknecht's corpse!' This is, of course, oil to the flames of his popularity, and is raising a fanatical dreamer to the Olympian heights of heroism. He is, at the same time, the bogy for frightening children to bed and the fearless hero with the halo of martyrdom already shining round his pale face We are all very unclear as to what exactly he wants, and perhaps the commander of a regiment here is acting in the most sensible manner by inviting him to come and address his men publicly."

. . . . . .

And now the great feast of Peace is at the door, and already the Christ-Child is beckoning from the lowly cradle in Bethlehem. Like the great star, the vision of universal love and charity hovers before our longing gaze, unattainable, unreachable as ever to those wanderers from the East.

Men's hearts are still filled with the lust of hate, ambition, and revenge. There are no eyes to see the angel hosts, no ears to hear their rapturous call in the silent star-filled Christ-night: "Peace on earth—good will among men!"

May the New Year bring us better things!

KRIEBLOWITZ, *January* 1919.—I am delighted to hear that all Germans agree in their praise of the English manner of behaviour in the occupied towns on the Rhine, whilst there are many complaints of the regulations and restrictions, and the disagreeable conduct of the French and Belgians. Every one praises the kind and dignified manner of the English towards the inhabitants. Many, I believe, wish in their inmost hearts that these troops would come marching down Unter den Linden, and believe that it would put an end to all the present turmoil. Possibly they might have done it if the Germans in their retreat had not destroyed the bridges and the transport. It would have made all the difference in the world to the future peace of Europe.

Hatred of the enemy seems now to have disappeared.

Indeed many people are inclined to look upon them as their saviours and protectors, and in their fear of the reign of terror which may be coming I believe would be glad if the Entente would send an army to Berlin.

By the way, the three English officers who have been sent on the Red Cross Commission to Berlin are making a great stir with their smart appearance; every one is admiring them immensely.

.   .   .   .   .   .

It is, after all, the royalties who are perhaps most to be pitied now. Often without ready money, no roof to their heads, and no food-cards, they are dispersed all over Germany, afraid of making themselves known for fear of the mob, and not accustomed to look after themselves in any way.

The fate of the Hohenzollerns can be read daily in the papers, but that of the Saxon royal family is the one which fills us with the greatest sympathy. The Crown Prince is at present living in two small rooms in Breslau. He has no money, and as he is living under an assumed name he cannot enter himself on the bread-commission, and has therefore no cards for provisions. A friend of ours, a lady, takes him his dinner in a basket under her arm every day. We are now going to supply him from here, but no one may know it, or we should be blamed for feeding princes whilst the poor are starving. The King of Saxony possesses a beautiful castle in the midst of a forest in Silesia, called Sybillenort. He has taken refuge there now, but as it was always kept as a show-place, and only used for two or three weeks' hunting occasionally, it is not fitted up with any ordinary comforts. There is no electric light, no heating, nothing for the winter, so that he is obliged to leave it now, and is looking out for a small place in the mountains. We have offered him Krieblowitz for the time being.

They will have no money until things are more settled, for the Saxon Government has sequestered their private property. On leaving Dresden, the royal family took some food with them, but the mob took it away from them at the station.

.   .   .   .   .

Officers returning from the front tell terrible tales of the mutinous condition of the soldiers. They seem to be filled with the one idea of revenging themselves for the misery of the last four years on their helpless superiors Their behaviour is often grossly brutal One can see the freed slave does not know how to use his freedom. Our nephews Strachwitz has just returned, after taking ten days to travel from Belgium here. Norbert, who was badly wounded, was twice turned out of the train because he was an officer, and on his attempting to enter a train again was shot at by German soldiers. At last, one kind-hearted man picked him up and pitched him into a cattle-truck. He travelled in this manner for five days, without his wounds being dressed, and living on mere bread and water. Dominik had to defend himself against 30 soldiers, and just had time to get into a train before they bayoneted him.

These are but two of countless stories. Some nurses returning home with a train full of wounded men said it had taken them ten days to get back from St. Quentin, as the engine-driver stopped the train every few hours, and came and collected clothes, shoes, etc., from them before going on farther, and in the end charged so much a mile, and had to be begged and entreated before proceeding at all.

All the high officers have disappeared from the face of the earth, as bands of soldiers are going from one house to the other to arrest them. Thus in Berlin, a warning was sent to the family of General von Beseler, saying that he had better disappear as danger was brewing; and hardly had he got away when a detachment of soldiers armed with rifles and a machine-gun suddenly appeared at his house and demanded him to be handed out to them. They only left the place on being assured that he was still in Warsaw.

Brandenburg is said to be a hell on earth. An officer told me that he could only get a plate with a few mushrooms for dinner at the price of Mk. 25, whilst his servant was given a big dish of meat and potatoes and vegetables; and the soldiers often attack and beat an unpopular officer. I have heard of some old Generals who have committed suicide at the present state of things.

.   .   .   .   .   .

As regards the Empress, one hears much praise of the way she worked throughout the war to try and heal the wounds caused by it until the last moment almost, when she was struck down by the sight of the awful doom awaiting her country and her own house. But one wonders how she could have continued so blind to the real state of affairs. She had not an idea that the abdication of her husband could really come about, and as she forbade a single word of politics to be discussed at meals, she had no means of "feeling the pulse of the people," or getting to know their views or their grievances. For instance, three weeks before the revolution, she was visiting a hospital in Brandenburg, and stopped and spoke to a poor wounded soldier who was frightfully mutilated, having lost both legs and an arm, and she said to him how sorry she was to see him thus, and had he any wish she could gratify to help him   The soldier said: "Do you want to know what my greatest wish in the world now is, and will you do your best to gratify it? It is that you will send one of your six sons out and that he shall get mutilated in the same way as I am. Then the soldiers would know you are genuine in your offers."

And at the Blindenheim, on another occasion, she went round distributing roses to the blind men. One man handed them back to her and said: "I don't want your roses; give me back my eyes!"

KRIEBLOWITZ, *January* 1919.—We are bidding farewell to Krieblowitz, for I wonder how long! I feel a pang at leaving the place and the people; one becomes

so attached to those one has lived among during times of
suffering and suspense, and these people have endeared
themselves to me by their patient, silent acceptance of
the inevitable.

I feel a pang also at taking my husband away from
them; they look upon him so much as their father to
come to in all troubles and difficulties, and he has endeared
himself to them lately by the way he has tried to find
employment for the many youths returning from the
front. He has had timber cut down and ponds filled up;
in fact he instantly put on a hundred or more men, provided them with food, and gave them high wages. This
saved the situation, and there has been no real plundering or discontent in our district.

    .   .   .   .   .   .

I have at last been able to receive a letter from my
mother, hoping to see me again at some not too indefinite
period; and we are putting every wheel in motion to
try and fulfil her desire.

I almost feel as if we shall never again be allowed to
find an abiding place where we can settle down and be at
rest. Four and a half years ago, in that memorable
August of 1914, we had to hurry away, leave our London
house, and pack up at a moment's notice and flee, because
we were Germans. Now, once more, we have to flee
from Krieblowitz, as there is danger of an invasion of
the Poles, who are said to be on the march into Upper
Silesia, and the miners are threatening to plunder the
big houses in the neighbourhood should their rations
run out.

At the same time we must either let or lend our apartment in Berlin, as all empty ones are to be occupied
either by soldiers or homeless people; and, worse still,
should Liebknecht get the upper hand, they will certainly
begin their régime by plundering the big private houses.
It is a pleasant look-out in any case, and so we think it
better to shoulder our baggage and wander once more.

We hope to be in Berlin on January 8, and intend

asking Sir R. Ewart to dine with us. I think that the moment we have an English General sitting at the same table, and see the English officers strolling down Unter den Linden, we shall really begin to feel that England is not so very far away after all!

I hope, too, to see some of my best friends once more before leaving Berlin indefinitely, and shall be especially glad to see, among others, for the last time probably, Madame Polo, the Spanish Ambassadress, and then Count and Countess Larisch, Count and Countess Moltke, Madame Rizoff, and Baronin Essen, the wife of the Swedish Minister, who was the kindest hostess possible when we took refuge in her house after being driven out of our own for the second time by machine-guns on the third day of the revolution

There are five ladies, all of them Austrian by birth, who, even at times when the fever of international hatred was at its highest point, never behaved otherwise than tactfully and kindly towards me. These are Countess M. Larisch, Countess M Tattenbach, and the three ladies known as the Kinsky sisters, Countess Henckel, Countess Clary, and Princess Lowenstein. Never by word or sign did they say anything to hurt my English feelings, and when I was in sorrow and their world was rejoicing, they would leave their family circle and come and spend a few minutes with me, condoling and sympathizing with me in my grief, anxiety, or suspense. These are things one likes now to remember.

KRIEBLOWITZ, *January* 15, 1919.—We actually had a visit here from some of the English officers now in Berlin, an event worthy of special record. Among them was a Lieutenant M——, who had been sent to help in repatriating the English prisoners He told us of the indescribable state of things in Berlin They had been obliged to transfer their quarters from the Adlon Hotel, which was anything but safe, to the Esplanade, which is not in quite such an exposed position. General Ewart and his staff had been obliged to do all their work in their rooms, as they could no longer go to the Embassy in the Wilhelm Strasse.   Owing to the waiters' strike they had to take all their meals in their rooms.   He gave me a graphic description of the scenes in the streets during the Spartacus "Putsch."   There were machine-guns at every corner, and more than once the people in the street threatened to shoot him, and one day smashed the window of the taxi he was in with a hand-grenade   He witnessed himself no less than three murders in the streets. One woman, a superior middle-class person, was deliberately torn limb from limb before his eyes, because when the mob shouted out "Vote for X——," she said, "No, don't."   The lack of food, the high prices, the universal demoralization amongst the German people is the best soil possible for the spread of Bolshevism, which is like a poisonous fungus born of diseased matter.   Germany is now like a man sick unto death, mortification is setting in, and other nations coming in touch with her will be infected in the same way.   The people have not only been disillusioned in their old ideals and seen the fall of all their own gods, but they see too that the ancient code of Might over Right is just as potent in the enemy now as it was before amongst their own leaders.

In the prevailing disorder, Spartacus reigns supreme, and as the Government have not as yet gained the upper hand over the "freed slaves," the streets are often stained with blood, and even corpses may be seen lying on the pavement where some struggle has taken place.   Our house is in the most dangerous position of all, and is at present filled with Government troops, who use it as a stronghold from which to shoot at the rebels. The method in this madness is the wish of the Spartacus group to prevent the National Assembly being constituted and to introduce the Commune, or dictatorship of the proletariat. Rosa Luxemburg and Liebknecht are still at large, although a high price has been set on their heads and there are men enough willing to shoot them.   People are growing so accustomed to the nightly shooting that I have heard friends saying they cannot sleep if it ceases for a night! When there is no fighting going on in the streets, there are always crowds of agitated people swayed here and there by the excitement of the moment.

Political agents scream and shout to the listening crowds, and woe to him who dare oppose the popular opinion of the moment. He may be lynched on the spot, or at best be scuffled off into some neighbouring house and saved by the skin of his teeth.

Motor-cars dash through the streets, their inmates scattering thousands of white leaflets, "vote for this or that man," whilst clouds of them come flying down from the blue sky where, high above the noise and discord of the streets, a flyer is skimming like some great white bird. Berlin, the cleanest and most orderly of European towns, is now the most disorderly, and a perfect bedlam into the bargain. It is all very tragical, but as I have said before, food will mend everything. A few days ago the man-servant of the Saxon royal family came down to Krieblowitz to cater for food for some of its members, who are now settled in their house in Breslau. He told us that, owing to their having no connections with the tradespeople in Breslau, they would have absolutely starved if we had not been able to help them out with food. We were very glad to be able to send them some things—a goose, fifty eggs, vegetables, butter and milk, etc. The letter of gratitude which we received from the family itself was most pathetic. It is almost inconceivable that in a few short weeks such people should be reduced to such a condition as they are. The man-servant, who is one of the good old-fashioned retainers of royal households, such as one reads of in story-books, told us of the royal family's flight from Dresden on the day of the revolution. The day before they had the intimation that an attempt on their lives was being planned. They, however, took no further notice of it, until on the following day a certain Herr von N——

came with a list of people who were to be murdered next. day, and their names were amongst them. Within a few moments the family had made up their minds to fly, and preparations were commenced in all haste. They determined not all to flee together, but to depart separately and by different doors. Thus the King, Prince Joachim Georg and his wife, the Crown Prince, his brother and sisters all went different ways, and the account we heard was that of the flight of Prince Joachim Georg and his wife. For five days they wandered about on foot, taking refuge and hiding in different friends' houses. They had to cross ploughed fields, scramble over hedges and ditches, until at last, after spending a day with our cousins, Count and Countess Schall, they were smuggled into a train at a small village station, and thus reached Breslau quite incognito. The man-servant himself told us how, dressed in Red Cross uniform and accompanied by two Russian prisoners as guards, he had escaped with the royal jewels, worth two millions of money, hidden under his coat. All these facts sound so romantic that I sometimes feel as if I had been transferred into an exciting and thrilling novel à la Walter Scott, where fugitive royalties, faithful followers, fair ladies in distress, hidden treasuries, and the bloody realities of the revolution form a varied and moving spectacle against the sombre background of the Silesian landscape, with the vast secretive forests and their lovely hunting-lodges in which more than one crownless prince is lying low for the time being.

KRIEBLOWITZ, *January 23*, 1919 —In the midst of a rush of legal and financial business which we have to complete before departing for Holland, we were forced to drive over to Breslau last Monday. On arriving there we found an invitation awaiting us from no less personages than Prince and Princess Georg of Saxony, just the people who have been so much in my mind lately. They wrote asking us to come to tea on the following day, which we did. Besides the Princess (who is a Bourbon) and her husband, the brother of the King of Saxony, the Crown Prince was there too and entirely won my heart by his simple friendly manner.

Our hosts overwhelmed us with thanks for the little we had been able to do for them in the way of food, and then told us about their experiences on the day of the revolution. They must have been awful. Later on Baron von Busche and Baron Metzsch gave us some more details. Baron Metzsch is gentleman-in-waiting to Princess Mathilda of Saxony, who, as his advice on the first hint of danger, left for her not very distant country seat of Pilnitz; the other royalties, who did not take the situation very seriously, following her in the course of the evening. Next morning, however, they had a rude awakening to the brutal reality of the hour, when a motor-car bearing a red flag drove up to the castle, and a man got out who on being shown in to Baron Metzsch gave him a paper on which a warning was written that the King, his brother, and other members of the royal family were to be shot next morning; but if they consented to come away in the motor-car, they would be taken to a place of safety. Baron Metzsch was obliged to go and break the news to the royalties and force upon them the necessity of deciding at once what they were going to do. The King resolved to leave the castle at once, but protested against leaving it under the protection of the red flag, as there was no precedent of a Saxon king ever having done such a thing before. He spoke and acted with great dignity, and within a quarter of an hour they had left the place on foot. Princess Johann Georg, who is very delicate and a little lame, and used to nothing but the greatest comfort and luxury, had to climb up a steep hill and scramble over rough fields and hedges until she finally found shelter, having nothing with her but a small handbag containing a toothbrush and a pocket-handkerchief. Baron Metzsch himself spent the greater part of the night wheeling away the crown jewels and other valuables in a wheelbarrow to a hiding-place which is at present known only to himself and a trusted servant. I could write pages on all they told us of their different experiences, but must refrain for obvious reasons. On the day following the tea-party with the Saxon royalties we invited Count and Countess Henckel and their daughters. We were just sitting down to tea when who should walk in with my husband but the Crown Prince, followed in a few minutes by his aunt and uncle, Prince and Princess Johann Georg. We were all very much surprised, but after having presented the Henckel family, we were soon at our ease, chatting together in a most friendly manner, and enjoying the informality of the whole proceeding. Although we did manage to laugh at times, I cannot say that we were gay, and I think on the whole our conversation would have melted the heart of the most inveterate of the "Soldaten Räte."

True, the scene was not without novelty, and if it had not been so tragic for some of us, it might have formed an excellent study for a comedy. There we were, three royalties in exile and some eight members of the best-known Silesian families sitting round a tea-table to which every one contributed some little bit. One of us produced a packet of sugar from his pocket, another one proudly brought forth bread and butter, whilst we offered a bottle of fresh milk and some home·made cakes, each of us being as proud of our offering as if it had been some costly jewels. We all smiled when some one wondered if the "Soldaten Rat" would grudge us our delicacies if they saw them. Then we started talking about our individual prospects and wondering how soon we should all be utterly ruined. The royalties were, I think, in the most doleful position, as they had absolutely nothing but what small allowances the "Soldaten Rat" doled out to them.

Count Henckel prophesied that if the strikes in the mining districts continued much longer, or if the Poles entered Upper Silesia, in six weeks he would be a ruined man, whilst my husband finished by saying that if the Entente insisted on the requisition of all the agricultural implements, he too would be pretty close to ruin, and so on, and so on.

We have almost completed our preparations for a long departure from here, and in a few days shall be on our way to Holland, whence I hope at no too distant date to get over to England. The thought of it makes me feel quite solemn, when I think of all that has happened since I last saw the dim shores fading in the distance. At this eleventh hour I cannot refrain from writing down some of my doubts as to the policy of the Entente towards Germany. I have listened to the voices of every class of people here, and I sometimes fear that England has missed the right moment for restoring touch with the German people, and laying the foundation for a lasting peace in Europe. After the revolution, in the great wave of reaction against the war which set in here, the Entente could have done anything with the German people had they made the slightest overture towards a reconciliation. People were ready here to make reparation for the wrong done by their leaders. But now they say that Wilson has broken his word, and an undying hatred will be smouldering in the heart of every German. Over and over again I hear the same refrain, "We shall hate our conquerors with a hatred that will only cease when the day of our revenge comes again."

BERLIN, *February* 1919.—A friend came in to spend the evening with us yesterday, and had come straight from Amerongen, where he had spent two hours with the Emperor.

First he was taken up to see the Empress, who was suffering from a bad cold. She sat there working, and was ready to talk quietly about ordinary subjects. He said he could notice a sort of home-sickness for her children and grandchildren, and a craving for home life more than anything else. Neither she nor the Emperor, he was told, would even mention the Crown Prince, but always change the subject at once when his name crops up.

After having remained talking with the Empress for about fifteen minutes he was taken down to the gallery in which the Emperor takes his exercise daily, and there he walked with him for two hours. He told us the first sight of him was a great shock. The Emperor has grown a long white beard; he brushes his now quite white hair straight back, and his complexion is sallow and unhealthy; but he bore himself with great dignity and spoke quickly and with reserve.

He said that he had felt from the beginning of his reign that the military powers were too strong for him. He had tried from the moment he came to the throne to assert his own authority, but he was too young and perhaps too impulsive Later on he found that he was powerless in their hands, though he was always trying to break loose and work out his own ideas for his country

He said that he had enough English blood in his veins to know that the only thing was to go in with England, but he was always talked over by his military authorities and diplomats. Military authorities and diplomats of all countries are responsible for the war, not crowned heads. He will not own or realize that Germany did wrong in her invasion of Belgium He says he has proofs that if Germany had not done it England meant to; and that England had made a secret treaty with the Belgian King at the time Lord Haldane was in office, to the effect that they would be permitted to attack Germany through Belgium if necessary.

He would not blame any of his Generals by name. He says he knows what marvels they have done for him throughout the war in defending Germany against the whole world It is only where they began mixing themselves up with the political side that they made the blunders. The only man he blames personally by name is Prince Max of Baden, who, he says, deceived him from the moment he became Reichskanzler, by telling him all was going well, and all the time allowing the scheme for his abdication to be worked out behind his back. In fact his abdication was made public before he had actually signed it.

He complained most bitterly that he was deceived and lied to from the outset of his reign, and especially throughout the war. His ministers never told him the truth, his military authorities never let him know how things really were, and the naval authorities quoted and stated absolutely fabricated figures.

I did not give my opinion, but I cannot help thinking that if a man is an Emperor one of his chief aims should be to employ every person and every method by which he can arrive at the truth.

The Kaiser says he was treated as a nonentity by his General Staff; that they made a point of contradicting every order or command that he gave; that he was turned out of the room whenever the telephone rang at Headquarters, so as not to hear the commands and the real facts. He was never allowed to speak more than a few minutes alone with any one who was likely to give him the truth of what was going on. He was never told the true state of affairs at the front nor the strategy of his Generals.

He was hustled backwards or forwards from the Eastern to the Western Headquarters, so as to keep him "out of the way," when his Generals were especially occupied.

My informant also told me that the Kaiser deeply regretted the death of Miss Cavell and that the order for the execution had been given by a drunken General who was personally vindictive towards England. The Emperor gave an order then that no woman was to be executed without his sanction.

.   .   .   .   .   .

I suppose the late Kaiser must be one of the most wretched men in the world at present. One hears so many adverse criticisms of his conduct, and hardly ever a word of pity or compassion for his lot. Every one is full of wise sayings as to what he ought to have done at the critical moment, but he is universally condemned for running away from his country. Some people abuse him for not having abdicated a month before, making his grandson heir to the throne and Prince Frederick Karl of Hesse or Prince Max of Baden regent. Others condemn him for not placing himself at the head of his troops and taking his chance like the rest, as rumour said he had intended doing; or again, he ought to have returned to Berlin and addressed the nation from the same balcony as he had done at the declaration of war. People do not realize that it would require a man of almost superhuman mental strength to decide what was the right thing to do at such a moment and carry it out, for when the worst came the military leaders realized that there was not even a single battalion left whose loyalty could be depended on. Even had he wished to return to Potsdam or Berlin, he could not have got through, as disaffection was spreading like fire and all the bridges were in the hands of the retreating troops.

Who knows what mental agony he may have gone through before making his final decision—perhaps the only one he ever did make during the war; for from the moment the war broke out he had nothing more to say and knew only half the truth During all his reign he had suffered from the hallucination of grandeur, and had never had the moral pluck to insist on hearing the truth, but at last every artificial screen was torn aside, and in one awful moment he was forced to face it in all its implacable nakedness, and come to a decision alone.

Whatever the truth may be of the Emperor's personal responsibility for the war (and I am told that there are documentary proofs which he lives in dread of coming to light), every one in Germany is opposed to the idea of his being brought to trial before a public tribunal; but if the Entente insist on it, many people think that the most dignified attitude for him would be one of absolute silence, beyond the words, "Murder me if you will, but I shall not attempt to defend myself, as that would be putting the blame on other people, which I don't intend to do."

There are whispers that the blame should be laid at the door of thirty-eight men of all nationalities, whose names are known to a few. These men are recorded as having worked systematically together for years, until they brought the war to a head. The rest of the actors in the preparations were but puppets in their hands. Some day their names will become known.

Of all the other royalties, the Crown Princess is certainly the most popular in Germany at present, and not only there, but I hear also amongst the countries of the Entente. Many people say that if she plays the part cleverly she may yet live to see her boy the Emperor of Germany. She has nerve as well as tact, and it is said that she faced the situation at the time of danger and saved it more than once.

I have heard that a week or two ago a band of Bolshevist plunderers went to her palace in Potsdam and demanded admittance, saying they had come to search the place for hidden stores of food. She ordered them to be shown to her sitting-room, where she kept them waiting for a few minutes. After calmly entering and shaking hands with them, she asked if there was anything she could do for them, whereupon in a much humbler voice they said they had been sent to see if she was hoarding food. "Yes," she replied, "I have stored up some food; I won't pretend to deny it. I am the mother of many small children, and I could not sit down helplessly and see them starve without storing something for a rainy day, any more than you would care to see yours starve if you could help it. I am ready to share what I have with your wives and children, but I am not going to give up all I possess." Upon which the Bolshevists turned and left the room without another word. I do not know if the story as I have told it is apocryphal, but certainly the Princess did later on give up some of her stores of food.

IN THE TRAIN ON THE WAY TO HOLLAND, *February* 4, 1919.—After a few agitated days in Berlin, where every one is convulsed with rage, despair, hunger, and cold, we finally found ourselves seated in a train bound for the west, after having passed through all the formalities of revolutionary officialdom, which is rather more round-about in its methods than it ever was under the monarchy. We had a cold but otherwise comfortable journey, and with every mile that carried us away from poor tormented Germany I breathed more freely, whilst a vague dreamlike feeling of gladness crept over me, that after the nightmare of the last four years I was on my way to my native land. I gradually became conscious of what it meant to me, and that there behind me lay the land in which I had passed so many dreary years, and at the same time also a feeling of pity and of gratitude for the kindness and affection of many friends whom I had met with in the country I was leaving, in which I had witnessed so much suffering heroically borne. There was a heightened feeling of fate and destiny with me, as I once more turned to take a farewell look at it, and I felt as if I had passed from some huge tragedy, sombre and sad, as I cast off the shadows of the last years and gave myself up to the joy of picturing my return in, I hope, not too distant a future, to my country.

On the evening before our departure, General Sir Richard Ewart and his A.D.C. Lieut. Breen came to dine with us, and it was very interesting to hear the General's views and opinions of life in Berlin, and his experiences in East Africa, where, as he told us, he had been spending two years with my brother-in-law, Admiral Sir Edward Charlton, fighting against the German General, Lettow-Vorbeck, for whom he expressed much admiration, and who, he said, was down in the annals of the war as having "fought clean" and made a gallant defence against great odds. It was a strange coincidence that whilst waiting for our train one of the first people we saw at the station should have been Lettow-Vorbeck on his way back to Germany from Africa.

Sir Richard, who was busy repatriating prisoners of war, said that the men who had given him most trouble were those of the Casement Brigade, who were very unwilling to return to England, not knowing what fate might be awaiting them there, or whether they might not be tried for their part in the Casement episode. One of them, we heard to our great amusement, had been spending all his time last week shooting at the Bolshevists on the top of the Brandenburg Tor, which he seemed very much to prefer to returning home to the bosom of his family.

We were fortunate in our exodus compared with the experiences which befell many of our friends. Perhaps one of the most thrilling was the flight of the Duke and Duchess of Croy, who had already arrived in Holland two months before we started, having literally, at the outbreak of the revolution, to fly for their lives, as their estate lay in the midst of an industrial district where the inhabitants were far from friendly; and when murmured threats reached their ears, they stole out one evening with knapsacks on their backs and reached the frontier on foot, their country seat, fortunately, being only two hours from the Dutch frontier. Then they had to elude the German and Dutch sentries, and were at one moment nearly given away by the Dutchess's bulldog, which objected to being dragged under a barbed-wire fence. However, "all's well that ends well," and I hear that they and their children are now comfortably settled at The Hague, where we hope soon to join them.

Of two other friends who had thrilling experiences, I think it simpler to quote from letters. The first is one that I received this morning from my friend, Mrs. Albert, an American:

"We crossed the frontier yesterday, and I am going to tell you about our last few days in Berlin.

"On Sunday, January 5, the Spartacus had their first big procession, 50,000 strong. It took three hours to pass the Esplanade Hotel, where we were staying. We decided, if that was what we had up against us, that we had better get away as quickly as possible.

"I had my passport, but my mother had to get her American passport *viséd,* and we were obliged to go to the Polizei-Präsidium for the purpose. We started early the next day, driving past your palace to the Brandenburger Tor. The Tiergarten was full of Spartacus people, and masses of Government troops were coming up Unter den Linden to Wilhelmstrasse. Finally forcing our way through the dense crowds we managed to reach the Alexander Platz, only to find the Präsidium deserted and the great doors inside chained The sentry told us there was no one there, and that no one could go in Our hopes of getting the pass vanished, and we were on the point of turning away in despair, when a big motor flying red flags drove up. I turned at once and asked the man next to the driver, 'Have you any influence here? I only want an American lady's passport to be *viséd.'* He looked at me, and said in perfect English, 'Must it be to-day?' 'Yes, to-day.' 'Well, I can't guarantee it, but jump into the car and I will see what I can do.' At lightning speed we were whisked round the corner to the main entrance. The crowd fell back on all sides amid the waving of red flags and cheers, the doors were flung open, and we found ourselves in the deserted court.

"A sailor came up, and our unknown friend asked who was in. We heard the answer, 'Only Herr Eichorn.' This was the very man they were after, the Polizei-President Eichorn, a Spartacus of the deepest dye. 'Take us straight to him,' said our friend, and we followed up to the top floor through long deserted corridors, till we were admitted into a room full of armed sailors. The

THE HAGUE, FEBRUARY 1919   325

men were violently excited, and everything was in greatest confusion There were piles of rifles and machine-guns at every window.

"It did not take long for us to realize that we were in the most dangerous spot in Berlin. After an anxious delay, we were ushered into a vast room with a great desk in the centre. The room was in perfect calm and order, with no occupant save a huge sailor standing by the desk. He was a magnificent-looking fellow with fair hair and clear blue eyes, dressed in black leather from head to foot and wearing a belt full of pistols. He first looked at us sharply and then opened the next door, and Herr Eichorn came in. He was a thin, pale, insignificant-looking man, but he had a keen, intelligent look, was perfectly cool and composed, and asked very cordially what he could do for us. On hearing our request, he said, after a moment's reflection, 'My signature alone may not suffice; we must also have a Government seal.' While we were waiting for the seal, the roar of the mob outside seemed to grow louder every moment, and I heard our friend whisper to Herr Eichorn, 'I have a 50-h.p. car outside; you'd better come, as there is no time to lose.' But Herr Eichorn quietly answered, 'No, I stay.' They went into the next room, leaving us alone with the sailor, who told us he was the chief of the guard of thirty sailors, and that they had held the Präsidium for three nights! The men were pretty well exhausted, but they would have to hold out still as there was more trouble to come. He had a smart military cap on his head, and drawing himself up to his full height, said, 'The Kaiser gave me this as a souvenir. He used to wear it, and now I wear it. I was his bodyguard on the *Hohenzollern* for years, and now I guard Herr Eichorn, and I will guard him with my life and soul to the last.' Thrilled and moved almost to tears, I felt like joining the guard myself and fighting against anything.

"The messenger arrived with the seal, and Herr Eichorn soon returned to sign and seal the passport.

While he was doing so, a sailor rushed in shouting, 'They are coming!' Our friend again tried to persuade Eichorn to flee, but in vain. With a hurried 'Good-bye' we left him with his faïthful bodyguard. We had only got as far as the Kaiser's palace when we saw the masses of armed soldiers and civilians coming down the Linden. Their faces were stern and determined; we knew they were making for the Alexander Platz.

"Before leaving Berlin we received a telephone message from our unknown friend saying that there had been a terrible fight at the Prasidium that night; Eichorn had been rescued, but the sailor I had spoken to had lost his life."

Countess S—— relates her experiences as follows:—
"The civil war which has been raging in Berlin and Leipzig drove us to seek quiet in Munich, where we took a villa in the outskirts of the town. We hoped that the Nemesis which is pursuing so many of our kind would lose sight of us in our obscure retreat, but we soon found that we had only escaped from the frying-pan into the fire, and a few weeks after our arrival the revolution broke out worse than ever. Again we could not sleep for the noise of guns and hand-grenades, and the prospect of a regular pitched battle should the Government troops attack the town. Worse than all, we had been warned that my husband's name was on the 'black list' of aristocrats who were to be arrested and probably shot. I never knew a quiet moment after I heard this, and you may imagine what my feelings were like when one day a band of revolutionary soldiers actually appeared, demanding my husband and saying they were to search the house for hidden weapons. How fervently I thanked God that Egon was not at home, and I don't think I ever wished anything in my life before so intensely as that he might not appear until I had managed to assuage their wild curiosity and get them out of the house. It seems that some one had denounced us as storing hidden weapons, and also that there was a secret passage under

our house leading to one of the royal palaces. Well, I had a bad hour of it, until they had pried into every nook and corner, searching every crack in the wall, and lighting up every stone in the cellar before they were assured that I was not fooling them, and that the report was a cock-and-bull story. I managed, however, to get on the right side of them in the end, and they went away in a much less bloodthirsty mood than they came, and even assured me on bidding farewell that if all the 'g'spusi' (aristocrats) were like the countess (myself), the people would not have so much to say against them. I smiled to myself—I am not an Italian for nothing. However, I did not wish to have my amiability put too often to the test, and so again we packed our tents and fled to Berlin as soon as we could get away, and here we are once more homeless vagrants, staying with friends in the Grunewald and enjoying the pleasures of a country retreat."

February, 1919.

Now that the actual bloody part of the great European tragedy has reached its conclusion and the day of settlement has come, I shall discontinue keeping note of the events as they appeared to me during the last four and a half years and more of my sojourn in Germany. It was at best a sad work, this jotting down of disasters great and small, for there was hardly ever a ray of light to vary the long gloomy chapter of history, unless it was a sidelight cast now and then on some individual deed of self-sacrifice and heroism, otherwise passed over unnoticed in the greater events of the war.

I wonder if I have learnt anything since I wrote the hurried lines in my diary in those days of flight in 1914? Certainly I have tried to be just in my judgment on all men, and if my love for my native country may have rendered me partial in some ways, and made it easier for me to see things from its point of view, far be it from me to cast a stone at the misguided but battered people whose heroism and self-sacrifice have often verged on the superhuman, and always called forth my admiration.

Not only has the great conflict swept away kingdoms and empires, undone a whole code of civilization, and destroyed innumerable forces of ethical and aesthetic value in every country, but it has also loosened or torn asunder all those finer ties which bound the members of different countries in friendship and kindly intercourse with one another.

Instead of a courteous friendliness we were accustomed to meet from acquaintances and friends in former times, we English or Americans who happen to have alien husbands are subject to mistrust and suspicion everywhere. Instead of our position being alleviated by the end of actual hostilities, we shall be treated as pariahs and outsiders in every country.

From the very outbreak of the war our position was difficult, and the more conscientiously we tried to act up to our feeling of duty to both countries, the more keenly did we feel the slights and insults we often had to bear Destiny devolved upon us the task of trying to be impartial (as far as this was possible) to both countries, and of endeavoring to keep up some shred of courteous feeling between them.

It was not an easy moment for many of us, when, loving our country and our families with every fibre of our being, we followed our husbands abroad into their own land, urged by loyalty to them to try and be just in our opinions, at a moment when our relatives were falling at their hands, and all the evil spirits of hatred and resentment were let loose on the world.

True, our relations in England and America remained faithful, but very often their partisanship for us made them liable to petty persecutions themselves. Here, where we were subject to suspicion and mistrust at every step, and our simplest sayings were wilfully misconstrued, our husbands fought our battles loyally, and although they were patriotic in the best sense of the word, were regarded with doubt in both countries. Now, at this time of spurious peace, we are worse off than ever. We may not return to the home of our youth, even for the most fleeting visit to our parents who are dying to see us, because our husbands, no matter what their way of thinking may be, happen to be aliens; for the same reason our money and belongings are kept back from us. In Germany again we are looked upon doubtfully because our sympathies may be too international; in neutral countries we may not visit or associate with society for fear of compromising our friends; whilst in order not to compromise our husbands we may not be seen talking to English or American friends or relatives anywhere in public. Thus, everywhere we feel banished and in exile, and long for a time when a more charitable feeling shall prevail in the world. These complaints are of course not to be limited to the English wives of Germans, but may be applied to all women married to aliens. There is indeed no place under the sun for us, and absolutely no laws to protect us and our property. One lesson which I hope and believe all women in the same position as myself will have learnt is, that it is our imperative duty to try and restore friendship and confidence as far as possible between the inimical nations, and that we ought all to unite in this common task.

INDEX

THE END

CPSIA information can be obtained
at www.ICGtesting.com
Printed in the USA
LVHW082148010519
616348LV00008B/453/P

9 781376 157741